CW00642312

Inequality, Growth and 'Hot' Money

NEW DIRECTIONS IN POST-KEYNESIAN ECONOMICS

Series Editors: Louis-Philippe Rochon, *Laurentian University, Sudbury, Canada and* Sergio Rossi, *University of Fribourg, Switzerland*

Post-Keynesian economics is a school of thought inspired by the work of John Maynard Keynes, but also by Michal Kalecki, Joan Robinson, Nicholas Kaldor and other Cambridge economists, for whom money and effective demand are essential to explain economic activity. The aim of this series is to present original research work (single or co-authored volumes as well as edited books) that advances Post-Keynesian economics at both theoretical and policy-oriented levels.

Areas of research include, but are not limited to, monetary and financial economics, macro and microeconomics, international economics, development economics, economic policy, political economy, analyses of income distribution and financial crises, and the history of economic thought.

Titles in the series include:

Post Keynesian Theory and Policy
A Realistic Analysis of the Market Oriented Capitalist Economy
Paul Davidson

Inequality, Growth and 'Hot' Money

Pablo G. Bortz

University of San Martin, Argentina

NEW DIRECTIONS IN POST-KEYNESIAN ECONOMICS

 Edward Elgar
PUBLISHING

Cheltenham, UK • Northampton, MA, USA

© Pablo G. Bortz 2016

All rights reserved. No part of this publication may be reproduced, stored in a retrieval system or transmitted in any form or by any means, electronic, mechanical or photocopying, recording, or otherwise without the prior permission of the publisher.

Published by
Edward Elgar Publishing Limited
The Lypiatts
15 Lansdown Road
Cheltenham
Glos GL50 2JA
UK

Edward Elgar Publishing, Inc.
William Pratt House
9 Dewey Court
Northampton
Massachusetts 01060
USA

A catalogue record for this book
is available from the British Library

Library of Congress Control Number: 2015957869

This book is available electronically in the **Elgar**online
Economics subject collection
DOI 10.4337/9781784715014

ISBN 978 1 78471 500 7 (cased)
ISBN 978 1 78471 501 4 (eBook)

Typeset by Servis Filmsetting Ltd, Stockport, Cheshire
Printed and bound by CPI Group (UK) Ltd, Croydon, CR0 4YY

Contents

Tables

Foreword

The mainstream of the economics profession was caught unprepared and unaware when the Great Financial Crisis struck in 2008 and has been left clueless in the face of the subsequent secular stagnation until today. Mainstream economics is in an existential crisis – even if most economists are still in a state of denial. Willem Buiter was only more explicit than most when he wrote (in the *Financial Times*, 3 March 2009) that mainstream thinking 'tended to be motivated by the internal logic, intellectual sunk capital and esthetic puzzles of established research programmes rather than by a powerful desire to understand how the economy works – let alone how the economy works during times of stress and financial instability'. Luckily, a few determined economists, going against the powerful mainstream current, have never given up their desire to understand how the economy works – and continued building an 'economics for the real world'. This volume on *Inequality, Growth and 'Hot' Money*, written by Argentinean macroeconomist Pablo Bortz, must be counted as a new – and impressive – contribution to this vibrant school of real world economics, as it combines rigorous macroeconomic and econometric modelling and informed theoretical understanding to shed new light on economic growth, income distribution, foreign debt, financial stability and crisis. Its main source of inspiration is Michał Kalecki's (wage-led or profit-led) model of economic growth. This framework is skilfully applied to the Argentinean open economy (1950–2006), and the econometric findings reveal that Argentina is not a profit-led economy; hence, macro policies which help restore profitability (by wage share repression) must fail in bringing about economic growth. But this book offers much more: it develops the Kaleckian model in two further directions to make it even more relevant to the real world.

The first development embeds Kalecki's macro model in a comprehensive ('no-black-holes') two-country Stock-Flow Consistent (SFC) growth model in the best tradition of Wynne Godley and Marc Lavoie. Dynamic simulations using the complex SFC model bring out the overwhelming importance of financial flows and stocks in determining the exchange rate, the current account deficit and real economic growth. This explains why cutting wage costs to improve export price competitiveness may not improve the balance of payments, and why one must not blame the fiscal deficit for causing a current account deficit. EU policymakers dealing with Greece and Spain should take these important lessons to heart and stop insisting on 'internal devaluation' and 'fiscal austerity' as solutions to the Eurozone crisis!

The second extension is the introduction in the Kaleckian model of private foreign indebtedness (as an endogenous variable). Private capital flows to firms and households in the emerging and developing economies (EDEs) have surged in the 2000s and even more so after the crisis of 2008. These inflows, often very short term, have been fuelling domestic credit expansion and asset price inflation, raising financial fragilities and making these EDEs vulnerable to a sudden stop or reversal of these capital inflows. This is exactly the issue explored in Chapter 5, which not only presents an innovative Kaleckian model featuring private foreign debts (denominated in foreign currency), but also empirically applies it to South Korea and Mexico – two emblematic (but structurally different) EDEs which experienced large private foreign capital inflows, followed by a sudden stop and reversal. The analytical and econometric findings underscore the need for capital controls – and as this book uncovers, this is the exact view put forward by Keynes, who argued that '[i]n my view, the whole management of the domestic economy depends upon being free to have the appropriate rate of interest without reference to the rates prevailing elsewhere in the world. Capital control is a corollary of this' (CW, Vol. XXV, pp. 148–9).

Willem Buiter is certainly right in dumping mainstream economics (for being 'useless'), but the present volume shows him evidently wrong when he concludes that in its place, we have only 'an intellectual potpourri of factoids, partial theories, empirical regularities without firm theoretical foundations, hunches, intuitions and half-developed insights' (*Financial Times*, 3 March 2009, http://blogs.ft.com/maverecon/2009/03/the-unfortunate-uselessness-of-most-state-of-the-art-academic-monetary-economics/#axzz3yT0PEBbJ). Building on the work of Keynes and Kalecki, Pablo Bortz's book is testimony to the fact that we do have a theoretically consistent, viable and empirically grounded framework for macro and monetary policymaking. There is an alternative: do read this book.

Servaas Storm
Delft University of Technology, the Netherlands

Preface

The writing of this book at the suggestion of Servaas Storm and the prompt response of Louis-Philippe Rochon coincided with many changes in my life. I changed my country of residence three times; changed jobs three times; moved back and forth; almost lost my work due to my computer crashing; spoke Dutch, Spanish, English and French at different times; and progressed with the book.

Looking back, even though it was a short span of time, it was very profitable for me as an economist and for the material that I included in the book. Important articles and books appeared in between; the global economy changed in ways remarkably germane to the argument of this book (notably, the fall in commodity prices and the reversal of financial flows in emerging countries); and I got the chance to refine and develop the message, economic implications and policy aspects of the theoretical contributions included here. Alan Sturmer gave a first round of criticisms on the initial draft of the manuscript.

The main influence in the process has undoubtedly been Servaas Storm. With his relentless encouragement, he motivated me to finish the book even amidst several changes and developments that happened in between. He provided comments, suggestions and criticisms on several chapters, and inspired me to strengthen and remove many of the weaknesses in my ideas. Without him, this book would not have seen the light of day.

I profited from discussions and debates with many people, some of which I met at the different workplaces that I had in 2014 and 2015. Notably, the people at the Centre for International Economy and UNCTAD's Division of Globalization and Development Strategies were subjected to endless talks around the topics tackled here. I want to thank in particular Gabriel Michelena (who patiently read previous versions of Chapter 4), Alex Izurieta, Alfredo Calcagno, Joerg Mayer (who read Chapter 5) and Edgardo Torija-Zane, who wonderfully played devil's advocate in questioning my ideas and forcing my to clarify, contextualize and revise my arguments. I would also like to take the opportunity to thank Sebastian Gechert, Thomas Theobald and Sebastián Valdecantos.

Other sources of encouragement in this tough process have been Demián Dalle, Adriana Diaz Arias, Alfred Kleinknecht, Gustavo Murga,

Alexa Obando, Manuela Robba and Marianela Sarabia. The editors at Edward Elgar Publishing corrected a good number of mistakes and typos. But most of all, I want to thank my family, without whom none of this would have been possible.

Buenos Aires
September 2015

1.　Introduction

1.1　AFTER A STATE OF COMPLACENCY

The 2008 crisis shook the state of complacency that predominated in the mainstream of the economics profession, epitomized in the description of the 1990s and 2000s as decades of the 'Great Moderation' (Stock and Watson 2002; Bernanke 2004), or in the eulogy of Milton Friedman at his 90th anniversary, again by Bernanke (2002). Statements from around this period by Robert Lucas, Jr. (2003) reflect his optimistic assessment of the state of macroeconomic thinking at the time, saying that 'macroeconomics in this original sense has succeeded: Its central problem of depression prevention has been solved, for all practical purposes, and has in fact been solved for many decades' (Lucas 2003, p. 1). A few years later statements like these were ridiculed, as the crisis exposed the widespread ignorance in the mainstream regarding the trends and developments that led to the Great Recession, because the prevailing and most popular models made no room for the effects of finance on economic growth, not to speak of income inequality, a non-issue for the conventional discourse in academic economics (with some notable exceptions).

In the years that have passed, there has been growing awareness about some ignored processes that have come to the front of the debate, in part due to new popular books (notably, Piketty 2014) or due to renowned economists making their cases (as will be discussed below, regarding Summers). The recovery out of the 2008 crisis, slow by historical standards, has cast doubts on the growth prospects of developed economies, while at the time of writing this book a geographical reconfiguration in the pattern of growth is taking place in developing economies. The sluggish growth rates observed in advanced countries, and the fact that even the satisfactory growth rates of the United States observed in the 1990s and mid-2000s have been characterized by unsustainable bubbles (Palley 2012), have fed a debate about the possibilities for higher sustained growth and fears about a possible 'secular stagnation', an idea which made headlines in the 1930s and which was revived by Lawrence Summers (Summers 2014a, 2014b; Backhouse and Boianovsky 2015). Sluggishness or outright stagnation had previously been observed, amid wild fluctuations, in many developing

1

countries during the 1980s and 1990s, with some notable and perceptible exceptions in East Asian countries, which were able to maintain high rates of growth during a substantial period of time.

One other major development refers to the growing disparities in income appropriation between different classes and portions of society in the last 30 to 40 years, mainly in advanced countries but also in emerging economies. Larger shares of income accrued to a minority of the population, dubbed 'the one percent' (Galbraith 2012; Piketty 2014). When we look at the 'functional' income distribution, that is, a typology that classifies earnings into those derived from wages and those derived from profits, we also observe that the labour share of income has been on a downward path since the late 1970s and early 1980s. Some graphs will be presented below, but with politicians making a campaign flag of these inequalities in many countries, and with the coverage given even in the mainstream media, the reader is surely aware of the tectonic split in the pattern of income distribution which has operated since the 1970s in most of the capitalist economies, which have become so established that these can be safely called a stylized fact.

With more recognition in the mainstream literature we can highlight the ever larger amounts of capital flows across the globe, growing at a faster rate than international trade. Restrictions on financial movements between countries have been progressively lifted since the early 1970s, mirroring the financial deregulation operated at the domestic level in most advanced countries and in several developing economies. In fact, there was a huge 'traditional' argument on the benefits of these policies as soon as they started to be adopted, as set forth in McKinnon (1973) and Fry (1980), among others. Just as financial (and banking) market deregulation would help in the development of those markets, increasing savings and canalizing them into more profitable and efficient investment, so would capital account openness enable access to foreign savings, supplying the necessary funding to develop domestic financial markets and compensate the existent lack of savings (and resources), alleviating at the same time the restriction of economic expansion due to low foreign reserves and deficits in the balance of payments, or at least the recurrent shortage of foreign exchange. And financial flows did increase, both to developed and emerging countries, but in a volatile fashion that the traditional argument could not explain. In addition, they did not necessarily flow where they were supposed to, and their volatility did not prevent balance of payments crises by disciplining borrowers and lenders; quite to the contrary, at times these were provoked or exacerbated by sudden movements of foreign capital.

Three developments happened concurrently: slower rates of growth, increased income inequality, and greater financial flows coupled with financial crises. Is there a connection between them? Can these processes be accommodated into a comprehensive theoretical framework? Is there empirical value in pursuing this approach? What is the contribution we could make?

The relation between income distribution and growth is at the very foundation of Political Economy (and later, economics) as a discipline. However, with some exceptions the interaction between distribution and growth was excluded by the mainstream as a topic of discussion up until the crisis, revisited only by the heterodox fringe of academic economists, which comprises a rather wide variety of schools of thought. Within the heterodox literature, the Kaleckian approach stands out, as it represents (in our opinion) the most systematic attempt to tackle this interaction between inequality and growth (Rowthorn 1989 [1981]; Lavoie 1992, 1995b; Blecker 2002). Developed and enlarged precisely in the period to which we are referring, starting in the early 1980s, the Kaleckian approach, which will be revisited in the next chapters, has been providing insights into the multiple channels through which different patterns of income distribution may affect economic performance, even in a contradictory manner.

However, there is a gap in the (Kaleckian) literature, which refers to the absence of consideration given to 'hot money': financial flows of different duration between countries that affect not debts and credits but penetrate and distort the productive structure, investment decisions and income distribution in non-neutral ways. The objective of this book is to make a contribution in filling this gap, both at the theoretical and the applied level, showing and discussing examples and theoretical analyses, and performing our own empirical approximations with an analysis of different economies. The focus of the book will be on developing countries, because their rather limited financial markets tend to amplify the effects of financial inflows and outflows, even though the implications can be extended to some developed economies, as in the case of some European countries, for instance.

By way of introduction this chapter will present evidence on the three stylized facts that we have just mentioned. Thus we will first briefly summarize growth trends in different regions of the world, bringing out what in the view of this author is a notorious slowdown in world growth rates in comparison to the first three decades of the post-war period. Following this, we review evidence of recent distributional change. This book is not a thesis on the explanations of income inequality; however, some arguments regarding its development will be summarized. A politically charged topic has politically charged implications, and explanations are not neutral in terms of the implications for different groups of the population. Finally, we will revisit major trends in global capital flows, to give the reader an impression of the gigantic change in magnitudes that has happened in the post-Bretton Woods period. At the risk of repetition, the main thesis of this book is that the contemporaneous coincidence of these three big changes has not been a coincidence, to make a redundant point.

1.2   FEAR OF STAGNATION?

In 2014 Lawrence Summers, former US Secretary of the Treasury, gave a provocative speech in which he revived a 1930s' discussion around the likely stagnation of the US economy and its causes (Summers 2014a). Summers manifested that the US economy proved to be unable to maintain persistently high rates of growth without being propelled by financial bubbles, that is, it was unable to grow while maintaining financial stability. Similar things could be said about other developed countries such as Japan, or the members of the Eurozone. The piece sparked a heated debate, though Summers was not the first to notice such slowdown. Heterodox authors had already pointed to the substantial change in the macroeconomic regime operated in the previous four decades, noticeable not only in GDP growth but also in other indicators such as gross fixed investment, productivity and unemployment levels (Stockhammer 2004; Carter 2007; Barba and Pivetti 2012; Storm and Naastepad 2012). Table 1.1 presents the rate of change of GDP for selected countries and geographical regions, drawing on the World Development Indicators Database from the World Bank.

There are of course some divergences between and within regions and countries, with some East Asian countries performing better than others and than other developing countries, but overall we can confidently con-

Table 1.1   Real GDP average growth rates

	1966–69 (%)	1970–79 (%)	1980–89 (%)	1990–99 (%)	2000–09 (%)	2010–14 (%)
High income	5.56	3.81	2.97	2.46	1.88	1.88
Middle income	5.67	6.00	3.77	4.03	5.94	5.86
Subsaharan Africa	3.78	4.06	1.75	1.87	5.10	4.42
Latin America and Caribbean	6.37	6.96	2.52	2.70	2.95	3.60
Developing East Asia and Pacific	5.13	7.25	7.71	8.18	8.86	7.95
World	5.57	4.04	3.07	2.68	2.61	2.80

Source: World Development Indicators Database, World Bank.

clude that the world economy has gone through a period of successive and more frequent crises (Arestis 2006) which, among other negative impacts, has diminished the rhythm of economic activity. However, this performance is not unexpected in the context of the big distributive shift that happened in the same period in many countries, according to the framework to be presented in the following chapters. It is time to describe this shift.

1.3 THE WAGE SHARE AND OTHER MEASURES

Figures 1.1a–d present the evolution of the adjusted labour wage share for several developed and some developing countries. In the first 12 countries presented, the series represent the evolution of the adjusted wage share of income, with data taken from the Annual Macro-Economic (AMECO) database of the European Commission. In the case of South Korea, the graph shows the evolution of the ratio of compensation of employees to GDP, both registered in won at current prices. The data are from the Bank of Korea. Finally, for Mexico, we use the Labour Income Share of the Total Economy for the wage share, drawn from the OECD database.

Most of the countries presented in Figures 1.1a–d are developed ones, and a significant change in income distribution is discernible in many of them (though not all) starting around the late 1970s to early 1980s. That change is found in countries with 'strong' labour market institutions (such as France and Germany) as well as in those 'less-regulated' labour markets (such as the USA and Ireland), but not in the UK, where there is no clear trend in the context of important fluctuations. Around that time, a decreasing trend is observable for the wage share. Those findings are corroborated by Jayadev (2005, pp. 26–27), Bank for International Settlements (BIS) (2006), International Monetary Fund (IMF) (2007), OECD (2007), Rodriguez and Jayadev (2010) and Storm and Naastepad (2012, pp. 116–122).

This result holds not only for major developed countries. The European Commission (2007, p. 243) reports that since the mid-1990s, the labour income share has been on a decreasing trend for most new European Union member countries (Bulgaria, Estonia, Latvia, Poland and Slovenia, with weaker or increasing trends in the Czech Republic, Cyprus, Malta, Romania and Slovakia). Goldberg and Pavcnik (2007, p. 54) affirm that 'the evolution of various measures of inequality suggests that most of the developing countries experienced an increase in inequality during the past two decades'. The International Labour Organization (ILO) (2011, p. 56) states that 'since the early 1990s, the wage share . . . declined in nearly three-quarters of the 69 countries with available information. The decline

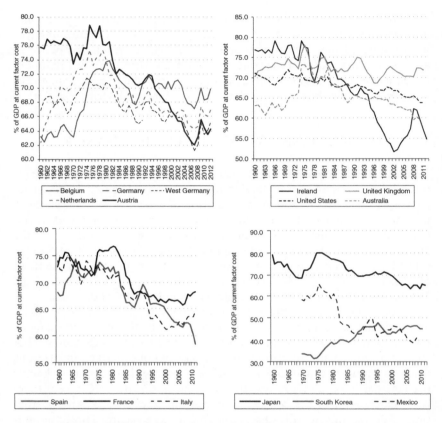

Source: AMECO database for Australia, Austria, Belgium, France, West Germany/
Germany, Ireland, Italy, Japan, the Netherlands, Spain, United Kingdom and United States;
OECD database for Mexico; own calculations based on data from the Bank of Korea for
South Korea.

Figure 1.1a–d   Adjusted wage share as % of GDP

is generally more pronounced in emerging and developing countries than
in advanced ones.' Stockhammer (2013, Figure 2) shows similar trends
starting from an early period (roughly, early 1980s) for a number of developing countries, according to data availability.

These features also hold for different indicators of income inequality.
Hein (2011, pp. 8–9; 2015) notes a worsening of the Gini coefficient
before taxes for the US, Japan, the UK, Germany, Italy and other developed countries, and similar results hold for the Gini coefficient after tax.
Regarding the top income shares, the seminal work of Atkinson, Piketty

and Saez (2011) shows a clear increase in the share of income accruing to the top 1 per cent, a trend starting in the early 1980s, in the US, UK, Canada, Ireland, Australia and New Zealand (all English-speaking countries); China, India and Argentina. The trend in continental Europe is more nuanced, as well as in Japan. OECD (2008) also finds similar patterns. Half of Piketty's book (2014) is dedicated to analysing movements in inequality, as is the recent contribution of Atkinson (2015).

What arguments have been presented to explain these developments? Stockhammer (2009, 2013) carries through a thorough review of the literature, but we can present a sketch of the theories at stake, following his presentation. The explanations can be classified into four groups, with some degree of overlap, and which are not necessarily mutually exclusive. Since in neoclassical economics income shares are determined by marginal productivity (Hicks (1966) is the classic on the topic), this approach says that skill-biased technological change represented by the development of information and communication technology (ICT) is the main driver of the increasing disparities in personal distribution, as well as in functional distribution, since it is a labour-saving technical development. Among supporters of this argument, one can mention Bentolila and Saint-Paul (2003), Jaumotte and Tytell (2007), IMF (2007), European Commission (2007) and Rajan (2010, pp. 24–26 and the references quoted therein).

Two other key factors are globalization and bargaining power. On globalization, interpreted as increased trade openness and capital mobility, the above-mentioned work by Goldberg and Pavcnik (2007) provides substantial empirical support, though they caution that 'the particular mechanisms through which globalization affected inequality are country, time and case specific; [. . .] the effects of trade liberalisation need to be examined in conjunction with other concurrent policy reforms' (p. 78). Their results are in line with those of Wood (1997), IMF (2007) and ILO (2011), though in the latter case results are not so robust for Latin American countries when one takes into consideration labour market deregulation.

Globalization itself has diminished the bargaining power of labour, and coupled with labour market deregulation has affected negatively the labour income share. Globalization is not the only factor affecting bargaining strength, but the effect of labour market institutions is complex to measure. In general, a robust finding in most studies is that greater wage bargaining (not at a firm level but rather at a sectoral or higher level) increases the wage share (Checchi and García-Peñalosa 2005). The ILO (2011) finds a similar impact of union density, though European Commission (2007) and IMF (2007) do not get those results. The impact of labour market deregulation on income inequality has been defended, rather surprisingly, by the former Chairman of the Federal Reserve Board, Alan Greenspan, in his testimony before the US Congress, in 1997, though he also stressed the impact of technical change on the bargaining position of workers and their 'job insecurity'. To quote at length:

> A typical restraint on compensation increases has been evident for a few years now and appears to be mainly the consequence of greater worker insecurity, possibly owing to the rapid evolution of technologies in use in the workplace. Technological change almost surely has been an important impetus behind corporate restructuring and downsizing. Also, it contributes to the concern of workers that their job skills may become inadequate.

> Certainly, other factors have contributed to the softness in compensation growth in the past few years. The sharp deceleration in health care costs, of course, is cited frequently. Another is the heightened pressure on firms and their workers in industries that compete internationally. Domestic deregulation has had similar effects on the intensity of competitive forces in some industries. In any event, although I do not doubt that all of these factors are relevant, I would be surprised if they were nearly as important as job insecurity. (Greenspan 1997)

The fourth argument presented as an explanation of the declining wage share and the increase in personal income disparity is financial deregulation, financial openness and the overall process of 'financialization' of developed and developing economies. The arguments are summed up in Hein (2012, Chapter 2) and extended in Hein (2015), where the author sketches the theoretical channels through which the wage share might be affected by the financialization process, defined as 'the increasing role of financial motives, financial markets, financial actors and financial institutions in the operation of the domestic and international economies' (Epstein 2005, p. 3). A more detailed explanation of the concept, its bearing in the expansion of the financial sector and the process of debt accumulation by the private sector is provided in Palley (2008, 2013).

If the wage share of the financial sector is lower than in the non-financial sector, then a shift in the sectoral composition of the economy in favour of the former will tend to reduce the aggregate wage share. The increase in the size of the financial sector, along with its impact on real productivity, is treated in Cecchetti and Kharroubi (2012), who study the relation of different indicators of financial development (private credit growth, bank credit, financial sector share in total employment) to economic growth and productivity growth. They find that the relation is that of an inverted-U shape, which implies that too large a financial sector has negative consequences on the economic performance, in their view due to a competing force with the real sector for scarce resources (Cecchetti and Kharroubi 2012, p. 14). The value added by the finance and insurance industry as a share of the US GDP certainly rose from less than 4 per cent in 1960 to 8 per cent in 2011, according to data from the Bureau of Economic Analysis. Philippon (2012) reached similar results, and the same trend was found in the UK by Burgess (2011), at least since 1995.

In turn, Dünhaupt (2012) finds that the wage share of the finance industry is lower than in the non-financial sector, which coupled with the structural shifts recorded by Cecchetti and Kharroubi (2012) among others provides some support for that thesis in which responsibility is assigned to a larger preponderance of the financial sector in the economy. Stirati (2010b) also counts the development of the service sector (including finance) as a major factor in the change of income distribution in Italy and other European countries.

Another stylized channel through which financialization has affected the wage share, and income distribution in general, is through the substantial increase in top management salaries, and capital gains on financial asset holdings. Lazonick (2011, 2012) and Lazonick and O'Sullivan (2000) analyse the changes in the management of corporations and their increased appetite for stock buy-backs, and therefore share price increase as a significant source of income. Wolff and Zacharias (2009) affirm that returns from asset holdings and different types of wealth associated with rentiers' income play an important role in explaining the evolution of income inequality in the US. Epstein and Power (2003), Epstein and Jayadev (2005) and Hein and Schoder (2011) highlight the importance of interest payments as an increasing proportion of the profit share for OECD countries, lending more support to the importance of higher rentiers' income for earnings inequality. Other studies with results broadly in line with those presented above are ILO (2011) and Orhangazi (2008), in the latter case dealing with the US economy.

A recent study by Dabla-Norris et al. (2015) gives support to almost all the explanations listed above. Finally, Jayadev (2005, Chapter 2) finds a significant negative impact of capital account liberalization on the wage share for over a hundred countries, using panel data from the United Nations National Accounts Statistics Database. These results match those from Stockhammer (2009), who also finds a negative effect of financial globalization on income distribution, and the findings by Furceri, Jaumotte and Loungani (2015), a paper we will discuss in Chapter 5. But now we turn to see some characteristics of this 'financial globalization'.

1.4   INTERNATIONAL CAPITAL FLOWS

Following the breakdown of the Bretton Woods international payments
system, there has been an upsurge in financial movements across the globe.
The restrictive policies regarding the financial system that came up from
the post-war agreements slowly but steadily eroded, and what Keynes
called a new orthodoxy was replaced by its opposite, namely the belief
in and the pursuit of liberalized financial markets (Helleiner 1994). The
literature on the evolution of capital and financial flows since the 1970s
is almost infinite, and so are the perspectives from which the subject is
approached.

When we look at global financial flows, two important characteristics
are evident to the naked eye: the increase in financial flows and their volatility, particularly when focusing on emerging markets. In Chapter 5 we
will show in greater detail more disaggregated features.

Taking data from the IMF Balance-of-Payments Database, Figure 1.2

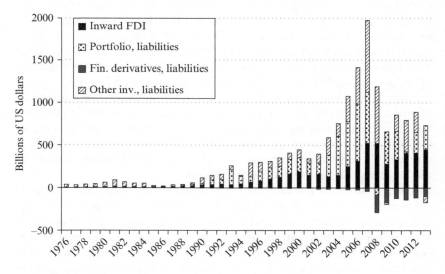

Note: Selected countries include: Argentina, Brazil, Bulgaria, Chile, Czech Republic,
Greece, Hungary, India, Indonesia, Ireland, Israel, Malaysia, Mexico, Poland, Portugal,
Russia, South Africa, South Korea, Spain, Thailand and Turkey. Data for all these countries
are available only from 1994. From 2005 they follow the criteria of the Balance of Payments
Methodology 6.

Source: Author calculations based on UNCTAD database and Balance-of-Payments
Database, IMF.

Figure 1.2   Change in foreign liabilities in selected countries 1976–2013

shows the increase in foreign liabilities of selected countries, that is, foreign inflows/outflows, for the period 1976–2013. We include among the countries some emerging economies such as Argentina, Brazil, India, South Africa and Turkey; former Soviet or communist countries such as Bulgaria, the Czech Republic, Poland and Russia; and high-income countries such as Israel, South Korea and Spain, among others. The components of liabilities, as reported by the IMF, are portfolio flows, direct investment, financial derivatives and other investment liabilities. We will explain the main driver of 'other' liabilities in a moment, but first we present the overall picture.

Several conclusions can be extracted from Figure 1.2. First of all, private financial flows to emerging economies have increased substantially, particularly in the last two decades. In second place, even though net direct investment seems to constitute the bulk of foreign flows, the other two components (portfolio and other private flows) have the most volatile behaviour, with fluctuations widening with the lapse of time. Thirdly, it must be remembered that these are foreign inflows. Possible outflows by residents, which can be acute in episodes of crisis, are not measured. And finally, when we examine what those 'other' liabilities are, we see that they are strongly correlated with periods of expansion and contraction of international bank lending, particularly related to US banking exposures. Since the decade of the 1980s in which US banks were in difficulties due to the Latin American debt crisis, the expansion of US (and other developed countries') banks has been a major driver of the international liquidity, with the crisis episodes clearly reflected in the data (Chandrasekhar 2008, pp. 9–11). The recent divergence between the claims of US banks on the rest of the world and the decline in other private flows is likely to be a reflection of the Eurozone crisis and the retraction of foreign lending by and to European banks.

Figure 1.2 has already given some indications regarding the widening in the fluctuations of capital movements. One explanation is that current account deficits and surpluses have reached magnitudes unseen in previous decades, both in nominal terms and in real terms, and in proportion to economic activity. Another feature that can appear in the data is that private flows did not necessarily flow to countries that need the funds to equilibrate their foreign balance, but also to countries that do not require in principle foreign savings, since they are becoming net creditors (as implied by a positive current account). That is clear in Asian countries but also in many Latin American and Middle East countries during certain periods.

The opposite side of this explosion of financial flows is an explosion of foreign debt. External debt peaked at different times in different regions, since the opening of the capital account and the internal

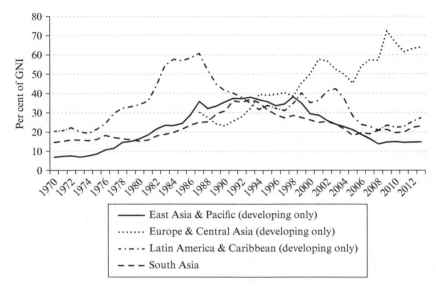

Source: World Development Indicators Database, World Bank.

Figure 1.3 External debt as percentage of gross national income

financial deregulation process did not occur at the same time everywhere, but the timing and the changes leave no place for doubt. Figure 1.3 shows the evolution of external debt as a percentage of gross national income (GNI).

In the 2000s, external debt fell as a share of GNI in the regions presented above, except for developing Europe and Central Asia. However, the debt build-up during the 1990s coincides with the integration into world financial markets, and that can also be seen in the East Asian countries and Latin America as well. The 1980s were a decade of economic stagnation for Latin America, and the increased foreign borrowing of the late 1970s (jumping from 22 per cent of GNI in 1975 to 36 per cent in 1981) was a major cause of such breakdown, and it was the ensuing long-lasting recession that kept the debt constraint at such high levels. In the East Asian case, something similar occurred during the 1990s, but the channels of transmission were different, something that will be analysed in greater detail in Chapter 5. The current account surpluses of the 2000s helped to ease the burden of foreign debt. But the number of balance of payments crises in the last 30 years is too high to be ignored. Mexico in 1982 and 1994; Argentina in 1980–1982, 1995 and 1998–2001; Brazil in 1994 and

1998; Chile in 1981–1988; South Korea, Thailand and Indonesia among others in 1997; Russia in 1998; Turkey in 2001; and the list continues.

1.5 ORDER AND AIM

The book studies the interaction between economic growth, income distribution and (private short) financial flows in an integrated analysis within a Kaleckian framework, which draws inspiration from the work of Michal Kalecki, a Polish economist contemporaneous to Keynes.[1] Lavoie (2014, Chapter 2) sets out the main differences between the Kaleckian approach (and generally post-Keynesian economics, of which Kaleckianism is a branch) and the mainstream or orthodox economics. Even though this book does not aspire to be a treatise on epistemology, it is important for our purposes to highlight some significant differences between the Kaleckian approach and mainstream economics. In particular, Kaleckian economics rejects the optimizing approach to agents' modelling, due to procedural capabilities, uncertainty about the future and multiplicity of objectives, all concerns for a realistic understanding of the economy (Lavoie 2014, p. 12). Secondly, as will be explained in Chapter 3, Kaleckianism adopts an institutional classification within a holistic approach, in which interactions between agents can generate results totally distinct from the original aims of the individuals, so called 'paradoxes'. A typical paradox is the 'paradox of thrift', in which individual attempts to increase savings will reduce income if the objective is pursued by everybody at the same time, frustrating the original intent. Kaleckian economists (as will be explained and developed in the next chapter) emphasize another paradox, the so-called 'paradox of costs': attempts to increase profits by reducing wages may cause abrupt drops in aggregate demand, reducing overall profitability.

The fact that the outcome of the interaction between income distribution and growth is ambiguous and can go in several directions is the core insight and major innovation of the Kaleckian approach. It also provides the justification for our attempt to use it as the ship in which we set out to navigate the study of the impact of financial flows on economic expansion and the sharing of such effects among the different sectors of the society. In order to put that in context, then, Chapter 2 will review how different schools of thought dealt with this interaction of economic growth and income distribution, one of the earliest and most defining fields of political economy as a discipline.

Chapter 3 will go deeper into the contributions of the Kaleckian approach to growth and distribution. The chapter will not only try to show the theoretical underpinnings of that framework, plus some discussions it elicited, but also how it gave place to numerous empirical studies to assess the relationship between income distribution and growth. We will also present our own empirical analysis, using two different econometric modelling approaches to the topic based on Argentinean data (1950–2006).

Chapter 4 is a first step into analysing in detail the interaction of global finance with growth and income distribution. In that chapter, we develop a Stock-Flow Consistent model, in which 'everything comes from somewhere and goes somewhere else'. We can also call it a 'follow-the-money' model, for that very same reason. It is a model in which we depict two countries that trade goods and financial assets between them. The defining feature of the model is a structural (core–periphery) asymmetry between these two countries. In particular, the government and the firms of one country can borrow not only in their own currency but also in the other country's currency, something very common in emerging economies, whereas the other country can always borrow in its own currency. The asymmetry is that the first country holds foreign debt denominated in the currency of the other country, while the second country holds debt in its own currency. We must note here that the stock-flow modelling methodology is not introduced as a *deus ex machina* into the analysis. A review is conducted in Chapter 4 presenting its characteristics, origins, developments and pertinence for the aim of this book.

With this model in hand, we perform several simulations which give us insight into the interactions and interdependence of distribution, savings and financial constraints of developing countries when faced with external debt accumulation in a foreign currency, as well as a more generally valid picture of fiscal performance, domestic savings, current account imbalances and financial flows.

The simulations made in Chapter 4 allow us to draw important conclusions to include in the model presented in Chapter 5, an authentic one-country Kaleckian model that incorporates foreign private debt, which has been markedly on the rise since the turn of the century, as shown by a more thorough revision of global financial flows presented in that chapter. After analysing how well this model can explain developments of certain countries and analysing its usefulness for empirical purposes, we review the challenges and policy options for emerging economies that are immersed in the ebb and flow of 'hot money', speculative capital that travels from one destination to another in a non-neutral way. Novel ways to protect one's economy from the dangers that these flows pose will be presented. The last chapter will present some final thoughts on the general philosophy and most important ideas that the book tries to convey.

NOTE

1. Well known biographies of Kalecki are Feiwel (1975), López G. and Assous (2012) and Toporowski (2013), among others.

2. Growth and distribution: the last 300 years

2.1 INTRODUCTION

The discipline of economics has been writing for centuries about the relation between income distribution and growth. Differences in incomes, wealth, social status and economic power were evident to past observers, and they did not refrain from offering explanations and suggestions about how these features might impact on the economic well-being and development of states and nations. The topic continued to be revisited as economics consolidated as a discipline, though the way to approach the issue changed as new paradigms appeared, each with their 'vision' and methodologies. In this chapter we will review how alternative schools of thought have framed and theorized the ways in which particular patterns in income distribution might affect and interact with economic performance in terms of capital accumulation and economic growth. When one adopts a social class stratification or functional income distribution perspective, one must consider both the source of income, its economic nature: profits, wages, rents; and the use of that income by agents: saving, or spending, and in what form of expenditure, consumption or investment.

This survey of different schools or paradigms, analysed through this source/use framing, will help us to place the message this book has to offer in the context of what other theories have previously said on the topic. However, in order to prevent this book from evolving into a thick textbook dealing exclusively with the history of economic thought, we have chosen to select 'representative' writings or authors within each line, hoping to convey the main points and conclusions of each school in a not-that-large space.

2.2 THE CLASSICALS

Choosing the work of the classical economists as our point of departure, it seemed natural for them to analyse the impact of changes in income distribution on economic growth through a stratification of society in terms of income classes, concerned about what we would call today the functional income distribution. Studying the laws that regulate the sharing of income among different classes was said to be the principal problem for political economists, in one of the earliest definitions of the newly developed discipline (Ricardo 1951 [1821], p. 5). It would have to wait until Keynes for that definition of the purpose of economic science to include a study of the level of income. Even so, classical economists were far from unanimous on the specific mechanisms, conclusions and views, with wider differences than can still be found today in the economic discourse and academics. Given the wide range of interpretations derived from the work of Adam Smith, it should not come as a surprise that we can find in his writings arguments that defend and uphold opposing positions.[1]

In the history of economic thought, the most echoed argument was that which posits that an income distribution in favour of the interests of the capitalist class is a necessary condition for the process of capital accumulation and growth. This idea, that we will name 'supply led', can be identified in familiar expressions such as 'saving is another form of spending'; it is already present in Adam Smith and its most elaborated form, within the classical doctrine, is the work of David Ricardo, whose Principles of Political Economy and Taxation first appeared in 1817. Given his theory of rent and the labour theory of value, Ricardo affirmed that as accumulation progressed, products that make up the consumption basket of workers tended to increase in price, at the same time as the amount payable as rent to landlords by capitalists rose due to diminishing returns to scale in agriculture. Therefore capitalists' profits diminished, and so did the incentive to expand capital (investment) and production. The distributional conflict highlighted initially by Ricardo is a conflict between industrialists/the new capitalist class and landlords/the rentiers (Kaldor 1955). The story goes as follows: initially, when few workers were employed in the agricultural sector, either because land was not yet entirely brought under cultivation or because of its high productivity levels (reflected in a high level of output per worker), rent was low and most of the product went to profits and wages. As accumulation proceeded and more capital had to be employed, or less fertile lands had to be cultivated, diminishing returns to scale set in. Capitalists in the first-cultivated lands earned much more than capitalists who worked less fertile fields or who were farther away from the urban centre. Competition made profits fall to that lower level and the difference between the average and the marginal productivity (what the more recently cultivated or the farthest land produced per worker) was the landlord's share. Rents increased and profits decreased in the agricultural sector as more capital was employed. Free competition assured the equalization of profits across industry.

In this analysis, wages are taken as exogenously given at a certain level, commonly understood to be the subsistence level. This is assumed for simplicity, but the reader should be aware that that was not Ricardo's position. Stirati (2010a) reviews the different interpretations on the topic. One can say, though, that as accumulation proceeded, and because of decreasing returns in agriculture, more and more labour had to be employed in order to produce consumption goods for workers, even when the real wage remained constant. This provides a fuel for conflict between capital and labour. But it is not the only one.

Technical progress in the consumption good sector tended to increase output per worker, and increasing therefore the profit share. However, in the third edition of his Principles, published in 1821, Ricardo added a chapter called *On machinery*. In a case of intellectual honesty not so frequent in the academic community, he recanted his previously favourable opinion of the effects of technical progress upon the fate of workers. In the times of Ricardo, workers did not welcome new machinery with arms wide open, with several episodes of angry workers, now known as the Luddites, attacking and destroying modern factories. And Ricardo was sympathetic to their cause, according to the arguments developed in the aforementioned chapter. Technical progress may increase the share of profits, causing 'a diminution in the demand for labour, population will become redundant, and the situation of the labouring classes will be that of distress and poverty' (Ricardo 1951 [1821], pp. 389–390).

However, barring technical progress from the analysis for the moment, we have shown that as accumulation progressed, profits decreased, in Ricardo's theory, and that would put a brake on accumulation itself. Underlying this proposition was the so-called Say's Law, which is manifested by the fact that stagnation in production is not caused by stagnation in demand, but rather it is caused by stagnation in supply. The following quote is as clear as can be:

> M. Say has, however, most satisfactorily shown, that there is no amount of capital which may not be employed in a country, because demand is only limited by production. No man produces, but with a view to consume or sell, and he never sells, but with an intention to purchase some other commodity, which may be immediately useful to him, or which may contribute to future production. By producing, then, he necessarily becomes either the consumer of his own goods, or the purchaser and consumer of the goods of some other person. (Ricardo 1951 [1821], p. 290)

Implicitly in this argument is the assumption that capitalists and landlords spend all their incomes, either for consumption or for investment purposes. In that way saving decisions drive aggregate investment. The limit to growth in Ricardo's theory was set by supply. However, as we have mentioned, full capital employment did not mean full labour employment, at least in the last edition of his Principles.

Keynes said that the logical consistency of Ricardo's argument swept away any kind of opposition and 'conquered England as completely as the Holy Inquisition conquered Spain' (Keynes 1973 [1936], p. 33), and he counted Marx as one of the 'conquered'. Marx saw himself as a follower of Ricardo, highlighting, with different emphasis at different times, points of coincidence and departures. It is not surprising that Marx's writings led to widely different interpretations in stark contradiction with one another. There are those that attribute recurrent and systemic economic crises to the falling tendency of the rate of profits, which would play the same role as the theory of differential rent had played in Ricardo's theory in order to justify the fall in investment. What sets them apart was that Marx could not accept the pervasive influence of diminishing returns in capitalism, a system that increases productivity (and labour exploitation) in a relentless fashion. Given those assumptions, 'the rate of profit can fall with a rising surplus value per worker only if the capital invested per worker rises fast enough to offset the increase in the surplus value per worker' (Foley 2008, p. 124). This tendency holds not only in the long term: in the first volume of Das Kapital, a fall in profits causes accumulation to slow down, and a fall in wages gives it back its speed (Marx 1867, Chapter XXIII, Section 1). One can find very disparaging statements by Marx about those who pointed to low wages or stagnating income of wage earners as the causes of crises in capitalism:

> It is sheer tautology to say that crises are caused by the scarcity of effective consumption, or of effective consumers. The capitalist system does not know any other modes of consumption than effective ones, except that of sub forma pauperis or of the swindler. . . . [O]ne could only remark that crises are always prepared by precisely a period in which wages rise generally and the working-class actually gets a larger share of that part of the annual product which is intended for consumption. (Marx 1885, Chapter XX, Part I.4)

The conflict between labour and capital is plain to see in the whole of Marx's work. Industrial capital was also in conflict with financial capital, because Marx also viewed interest as a deduction of profits (for an opposing treatment, see Pivetti (1991)). And the quotations previously presented point towards a rejection, quite explicitly, of underconsumptionist theories of capitalist crises (the first quotation actually ends with the words: '[Ad notam for possible followers of the Rodbertian theory of crises.—F.E.]'). However, many Marxist economists interpreted Marx's analysis precisely in terms of underconsumption. Sweezy (1942), especially in Chapter 10, presents the case for the underconsumptionist version of the 'fundamental contradiction of capitalism', by making use of one of Marx's best inventions, the scheme of reproductions. In it, Marx classifies producers according to the purpose of their output (for consumption or investment purposes). The faster the development of productivity in relation to wage growth, the flimsier are the foundations of aggregate consumption, leading to a decrease in the investment outlays of capitalists in that sector. Famous underconsumptionist theorists such as Paul Sweezy and Rosa Luxembourg can find their case defended in quotes such as this one from Volume III:

> [T]he more productiveness develops, the more it finds itself at variance with the narrow basis on which the conditions of consumption rest. It is no contradiction at all on this self-contradictory basis that there should be an excess of capital simultaneously with a growing surplus of population. For while a combination of these two would, indeed, increase the mass of produced surplus-value, it would at the same time intensify the contradiction between the conditions under which this surplus-value is produced and those under which it is realised. (Marx 1894, Chapter XV, Section I)

We are of the opinion that, ultimately, Marx referred to the falling trend of the rate of profit as the fundamental force behind the stagnation (and dismissal) of capitalism. And to that extent, his theory remains within the boundaries of a supply-led accumulation framework, as much as this was the case for Ricardo. Bellamy Foster (2013) is of the opposing opinion, developing the argument presented by Marx in Value, Price and Profit (1865), in the line of Sweezy's work, which Bellamy Foster also relates to Kalecki, as we will show below. A different path is followed by Shaikh, in some works that will be mentioned later. An exhaustive review of the literature is clearly beyond the scope of this book; we have limited ourselves to show what the contour of the discussion is, and provide the reader with some references if he or she wants to go deeper into the matter. For our purposes, we can extract two conclusions:

- There are elements in Marx that point towards a study of capitalism in which demand is not taken as given, and in which it plays a key role for accumulation and growth, being influenced by the state and evolution of income distribution.
- However, Marx puts the weight of his argument on a mechanism that plays the same role as diminishing marginal returns to agriculture in Ricardo's theory, namely to justify the falling trend of the rate of profits as an argument for the stagnation of capitalism. This mechanism is in complete agreement with a supply-side story and with a Say's Law point of view about the role and importance of income distribution for economic growth.

2.3 NEOCLASSICALS, OLD AND NEW

Around 1870 a number of authors developed what came to be the origin of marginalist economics, defined by the generalization in the use of the marginal principle (which Ricardo had only applied to the determination of rent) to the other factors including a change of emphasis, approach and boundaries, as Dobb (1973) puts it:[2]

> As regards causal influences and determinants, emphasis shifted away from costs incurred in production, and hence rooted in circumstances and conditions in production; towards demand and to final consumption; placing the stress on the capacity of what emerged from the production line to contribute to the satisfaction of the desires, wants, needs of consumers. From this shift of emphasis derived a certain individualist or atomistic bias of modern economic thought – preoccupations with micro-analysis of individual market-behaviour and action and the rooting of economic generalisation on such micro-phenomena. [. . .]
>
> Secondly and consequentially, what one may call the boundaries of the subject, as well as its structure of causal links and dependencies, were altered significantly, to an extent that was little emphasised or commented upon at the time. The system of economic variables and their area of determination were virtually identified with the market, or with the set of interconnected markets that constitutes the sphere of exchange. (Dobb 1973, pp. 167–169)

Distribution should reflect technical conditions, blurring (or discarding) a social stratification analysis. Diminishing marginal returns are not solely agricultural but also industrial. Wages and interest are the return for the labour and capital used in production; there is no 'net surplus' for the entrepreneur. This version is not a caricature of early marginalist thinking: it is actually the clearest exposition of its time, in our view, presented by John Bates Clark (1899, especially Chapter 7). To sum up the technical and efficient character of distribution in this theory, a small quotation will do: 'A natural price is a competitive price. It can be realized only where competition goes on in ideal perfection – and that is nowhere. It is approximated, however, wherever prices are neither adjusted by a government nor vitiated by a monopoly' (Clark 1899, p. 77).

There is no denial of the fact that crises could arise, but their explanation relied either on technological shocks, or government interference (or banking policy, somehow treated in a different way from every other capitalist enterprise) and the solution consisted in avoiding the latter and adjusting returns to the former. Examples of technologically driven business cycles are Schumpeter's and Wicksell's (in spite of what Schumpeter said).[3] Examples of monetary-driven business cycle theories are Mises's, Hayek's and Hawtrey's. There is no denial that monetary matters did have a substantive role in the theories of the former group, but they placed more weight on real factors. Solutions to the crises? One need look no further than the economists with whom Keynes was arguing: Hayek, Robbins, Pigou. In each case, the policy advice was to lower the nominal (and real) wage so as to stimulate labour demand and employment. It was the fault of government and of trade unions that this did not happen.

Clark's formulation permeated into the canonical neoclassical formulation on economic growth, Solow's growth model. The following quotation is a perfect example:

> we are assuming that full employment is perpetually maintained. [. . .] The labour supply curve is a vertical line which shifts to the right in time as the labour force grows according to (4) [the constant exogenous growth rate of population]. Then the real wage rate adjusts so that all available labour is employed, and the marginal productivity equation determines the wage rate which will actually rule. (Solow 1956, pp. 67–68)

Policy recommendations drawn from the neoclassical approach seek to facilitate this real wage adjustment to what exogenous productivity is assumed to be. This explains the proposals aimed at a 'flexibilization' of the labour market, a reduction in benefits to workers (such as subsidies through the welfare state and less labour protection) and taxes to employers, decentralization in wage bargaining in order to limit union power, and so on. These policies look for an increase in labour supply, a decrease in the capacity of wages to rise, and a change in capital–labour relations within companies favouring labour mobility and firm reorganization so as to boost productivity from an organizational point of view. In this sense, even though labour productivity is clearly the independent variable and the real wage the endogenous one in Solow's analysis, policies based on it try to affect both in a clear and definite direction: distribution should be accommodated to what labour productivity determines, and real wage adjustment will take care of the level of employment.

As for savings, the work by Solow (joined on this point by the so-called 'new theory of endogenous growth', which began with the work of Paul Romer (1986)) posits a positive relation between savings and growth rates.[4]

There are, however, two lines of research along mainstream lines into the effects of income distribution on growth. There are some articles that focus on 'the effects on growth of political consequences generated by a determined income distribution' (Perotti 1992, p. 311). The channel by which a determined distributive pattern can negatively affect growth is clearly explained in the abstract of Alesina and Perotti (1996): 'Income inequality, by fuelling social discontent, increases sociopolitical instability. The latter, by creating uncertainty in the politico-economic environment, reduces investment. As a consequence, income inequality and investment are inversely related. Since investment is a primary engine of growth, this paper identifies a channel for an inverse relationship between income inequality and growth' (p. 1203). In Alesina and Rodrik (1994) a different channel is explored, in which a higher inequality of wealth and income distribution leads to higher rates of taxation on capital, which hinder economic growth (p. 465), and in support of that theory they present empirical results that show 'a statistically significant negative correlation between inequality in land distribution (measured around 1960) and economic growth over the subsequent two and a half decades. [They] obtain the same kind of results for income distribution as well: initial inequality in income is negatively correlated with subsequent growth' (p. 467). The reader should not take the word 'taxation' literally; it encompasses 'any kind of redistributive policy that transfers income to unskilled labour while reducing the incentive to accumulate' (p. 466). Rajan (2010) also links inequality with lower growth and financial instability, though in his study income inequality is due to technological change biased against unskilled labour. In face of falling income households turn to debt in order to keep their consumption levels, but that cannot go on forever. This is also fuelled by financial deregulation and government-sponsored lending, especially to low-income borrowers, according to the author (p. 9).

The second line of research involves the determinants of growth in human capital in the presence of credit market imperfections. This framework also assumes that growth is determined by the increase in knowledge, capabilities, and other diverse and intangible assets or virtues generically called 'human capital'. If income inequality restricts the acquisition of those assets, either by limiting skills acquisition or by generally restricting investment in human capital (for instance, with costly rates for education or difficult access to credit), then it can certainly have an effect in explaining the correlation between a more compact structural income distribution and sustained periods of growth, as reported in one of the seminal articles of this approach, that of Galor and Zeira (1993).

2.4 KEYNES AND EARLY POST-KEYNESIANS

We need to state first Keynes's theory of effective demand in order to see what role income distribution plays in it. One can find many elements of Keynes's theory in the Treatise on Money (we would claim that one can find all the elements there, the problem being that there is also a natural rate of interest in it), but obviously we will draw on his major work, The General Theory of Employment, Interest and Money (1973 [1936]). There are countless interpretations about what he said, what he tried to say, what he meant, what he did not mean, and so on. For our purposes, we think it is enough to reckon Keynes's presentation of his theory in Chapter 3 (especially between pages 27 and 31) of the General Theory. It is a closed economy with no government activity, initially.

In our words, the theory can be described like this: as income grows so does consumption, albeit in a smaller proportion, measured by the propensity to consume. The amount of employment (and income) depends on the amount that entrepreneurs expect to be consumed, and the amount they expect to be invested, both quantities making up the effective demand. On the supply side, for each volume of employment there is a corresponding diminishing marginal productivity, which gives an aggregate supply price.[5] For a greater volume of employment, the gap widens between the consumption demand (and the level of employment associated with it) and the supply price associated with that volume, a gap that should be covered by the investment rate if employment is to increase or even reach the full employment level. Now, there is no automatic mechanism that brings investment to that level.

> The insufficiency of effective demand will inhibit the process of production in spite of the fact that the marginal product of labour still exceeds in value the marginal disutility of employment [so that there are still unemployed people willing to work at the ruling real wage]. Moreover the richer the community, the wider will tend to be the gap between its actual and its potential production. (Keynes 1973 [1936], p. 31)

The rate of investment is governed by the interplay of the rate of interest and the expected return of investment. The former is determined in turn by the supply of money and the liquidity preference curve, which measures the rate of interest at which people are willing to dispose of money.[6] The liquidity preference curve is called the state of bearishness in the Treatise on Money (1973 [1930], CW V, pp. 128–131). The expected return is heavily dependent upon expectations about future revenues and the rate of discount. Chapter 12 presents the case for the role of expectations in a way that no author has matched again, and the reader should read it time after time.

What about distribution, then? On a practical matter, Keynes had some involvement in the most ambitious redistributive scheme elaborated in his time, the Beveridge Plan, though he was a staunch defender versus the attacks of the British Treasury.[7] On the theoretical side, one can make a negative argument and a positive argument about the role of income distribution and distributional variables in Keynes's analysis. The negative argument refers to what distribution does not do. Keeping in mind that in the General Theory the real wage is determined by the marginal productivity of labour, a fall in money wages does not necessarily stimulate production, and it might well have the opposing effect not only by diminishing consumption, but also by affecting negatively expected returns from investment.

Keynes was accused in his time of not making any positive argument regarding the importance of income distribution and its changes on output. He did not take lightly that accusation, and responded accordingly. He reminded his critics of the factors determining the propensity to consume for the community as a whole, in which he specifically included the distribution of income, on more than one occasion (Keynes 1973 [1939], CW XIV, pp. 271–272). And having identified the inequitable distribution of earnings as one of the chief evils of the capitalist society of his day, he goes a step further. He states that low propensities to consume (associated with inequitable distributive patterns) 'hold back' capital investment, refuting those who believe that:

> The growth of capital depends upon the strength of the motive towards individual saving and that for a large proportion of this growth we are dependent on the savings of the rich out of their superfluity. [Our argument] may considerably modify our attitude towards the second. For we have seen that, up to the point where full employment prevails, the growth of capital depends not at all on a low propensity to consume but is, on the contrary, held back by it. (Keynes 1973 [1936], CW VII, pp. 372–373)

Keynes's theory is associated with what has been called the 'paradox of thrift': a more frugal attitude towards consumption might have the opposite effect to that intended, by lowering what entrepreneurs expect to earn from demand and lowering the employment level and income. 'Aggregate saving is governed by aggregate investment' (p. 110). Keynes was very eloquent on this point: 'If there is no change in the liquidity position, the public can save ex ante and ex post and ex anything else until they are blue in the face, without alleviating the problem in the least – unless, indeed, the result of their efforts is to lower the scale of activity to what it was before' (Keynes 1973 [1937], CW XIV, p. 222). These quotes show the path that the post-Keynesian school has followed in its defence of the argument that demand plays a key role in economic growth, both in the short and in the long run. In the most familiar growth models of this line of thought, the works of Joan Robinson (1962, 1965 [1956]) and Nicholas Kaldor (1957), increments in the level of savings in the economy (the main concern of marginalist economics) lead to a lower growth rhythm due to the fall in demand.[8]

Robinson's and Kaldor's models presented another solution to the instability issue in Harrod's (1939) growth model, alternative to Solow's (which assumes, as we said, factor substitution). But to explain that, we must first explain Harrod's approach. A central piece of his analysis is the 'warranted' rate of growth, 'that rate of growth which, if it occurs, will leave all parties satisfied that they have produced neither more nor less than the right amount. Or, to state the matter otherwise, it will put them into a frame of mind which will cause them to give such orders as will maintain the same rate of growth' (Harrod 1939, p. 16). We need two equations, of which the first is the warranted rate, and the other is the actual rate:

$$G_w = \frac{s\Delta Y^*}{I^*} \qquad (2.1)$$

$$G = \frac{s\Delta Y}{I} \qquad (2.2)$$

I^* and ΔY^* stand for the investment required to produce the additional *desired* increment in output. Equation (2.2) is an ex post identity. If both equations are equal, we are in equilibrium. What if they are not? Suppose G is bigger than G_w: actual output exceeded what entrepreneurs desired, so that they drew on stocks or equipment. The system will be stimulated for further expansion, until we reach full employment; and will fall into a deep depression if the inequality is the opposite. An increase in the saving propensity will bring, *ceteris paribus*, the warranted (desired) rate above the actual one, because of the repercussion on actual growth (i.e. in ΔY), causing a drag in economic activity (we do have a paradox of thrift in Harrod's model). One can think of the saving propensity in (2.1) as an ex ante desire for saving, and the parameter in (2.2) as an ex post identity like we said, if that helps the understanding (pp. 21–23). 'Departure from the warranted line sets up an inducement to depart farther from it. The moving equilibrium of advance is thus a highly unstable one' (p. 23). And we have not spoken yet about the natural rate, which measures the rate of growth of the labour force and productivity, the highest possible rate of growth if we assume full employment. The system cannot advance permanently higher than this rate, so if the warranted rate is above that one, then the system has a chronic tendency towards depression. The warranted rate is determined by the interplay of the saving propensity and the desired incremental output/capital ratio. We saw that Solow's solution to the inherent instability of the model was to give to the latter the responsibility for the adjustment and equilibrium. The alternative developed by the Cambridge School is based on an analysis of distribution. They recognize the existence of different savings rates associated with different income categories (or social classes), and they hold for the long run the 'paradox of thrift'. Their distribution analysis is rooted in Kalecki's and Keynes's analysis of profits, though not that of the General Theory, but that of the Treatise. And the basic idea is that consumption by entrepreneurs *raises* profits. Without bothering with definitions, the relevant paragraph is the following:

> If entrepreneurs choose to spend a portion of their profits on consumption (and there is, of course, nothing to prevent them from doing this), the effect is to increase the profit on the sale of liquid consumption goods by an amount exactly equal to the amount of profits which have been thus expended. . . . Thus, however much of their profits entrepreneurs spend on consumption, the increment of wealth belonging to entrepreneurs remains the same as before. Thus profits, as a source of capital increment for entrepreneurs, are a widow's cruse which remains undepleted however much of them may be devoted to riotous living. When, on the other hand, entrepreneurs are making losses, and seek to recoup these losses by curtailing their normal expenditure on consumption, i.e. by saving more, the cruse becomes a Danaid jar which can never be filled up. (Keynes 1973 [1930], CW V, pp. 125–126)

This also follows from Kalecki's theory about the short-period determination of profits, in which investment is taken as given due to decisions made in the past. At any given point, higher investment implies a higher profit share (Kalecki 1971, pp. 78–79), and that is what Kaldor and Robinson tried to model, and which provides the adjustment mechanism that solves the inherent instability in Harrod's model. However, for this mechanism to hold, a certain assumption must be made about a limiting capacity in output, either by saying 'it is given' (such as the short-period case in Kalecki), by assuming full employment (as in Kaldor's 1955 paper) or by assuming a 'normal' level of capacity utilization (Robinson's case). Higher investment implies more workers in the investment sector, driving up the demand for consumer goods in a sector which already operates at 'normal' capacity, leading to higher prices and lower real wages, generating in turn the desired amount of profits and the necessary change in savings and the 'warranted' rate (Kaldor 1955, p. 97; Robinson 1962, p. 58; Asimakopulos 1991, p. 174). However, it must be stressed that Robinson devised a whole range of possible paths, different types of 'golden' and 'platinum' paths, but in many cases the real wage might end up being a limiting factor (even without scarcity of labour, such as in the galloping platinum age, in which a lot of investment is directed towards that sector in order to build up capacity and profits rise) when workers do not accept a fall in the real wage. That is the 'inflationary barrier'. As we said, in both Kaldor's and Robinson's models, a higher accumulation rate is linked with a lower real wage rate.

A caveat must be made. Kaldor (1961) and Kaldor and Mirrlees (1962) introduce a 'technical progress' function, the role of which is to increase the natural rate of growth, by affecting labour productivity (initially it affected output per man-hour of the workers operating newly installed equipment (Kaldor and Mirrlees 1962, p. 176)). Later on, Kaldor (1966) would label this function as 'Verdoorn's Law', about which more can be found in McCombie, Pugno and Soro (2002).

2.5 KALECKI

Since we will adopt in future chapters a Kaleckian framework, the time has come to make a description of his work. Coming from a very different theoretical background from Keynes (the latter was a product of Cambridge; Kalecki was an autodidact with experience analysing concentrated industries and with a reading of Marxian economists), Kalecki tackled matters with a different approach. Kalecki applied his theory directly into a study of the business cycle, with an emphasis on income distribution and downplaying the importance of monetary variables.[9] We have seen already that in his work, by assuming a closed economy with no government activity and no savings on behalf of workers, profits are determined by investment and capitalists' consumption, and that by investing more capitalists will end up earning more. The similarities with the multiplier story are evident: one can replace the word 'saving' in Keynes with the word 'profit' in Kalecki and the result is pretty much the same (Kregel 1989, p. 198). Furthermore, since Kalecki rejects any assumption about a long-run 'normal' level of economic activity (least of all, full employment), we do not require a fall in real wages (as in Robinson or Kaldor's theories) from the multiplier to take effect: that is, a given income distribution might easily accommodate a higher level of output (and capacity utilization).

The main (economic) limit that Kalecki identifies for investment, besides the extent of the market, is of a financial character. His business cycle models are within the prototype of the accelerator–multiplier interaction, in which due to incomplete reinvestment of profits, demand fails to keep up with an increased capacity and the slump follows suit. The restriction on investment comes from the fact that firms would not be able to borrow more than a multiple of their own capital without increasing the risk they face (and therefore increasing interest rates). Kalecki called his limit set by the gearing or the leverage ratio *the principle of increasing risk* (Kalecki 1971 [1937], pp. 105–106). Raising equity in the stock market would not be an attractive solution either since it would diminish the ownership of current shareholders. *Accumulated* profits, as they increase a firm's own capital and reduce borrowing risk, expand the financial capabilities and allow a higher level of investment, though in later Kaleckian literature there were discussions about exactly which measure of profits was relevant for investment decisions (a discussion we will review in the next chapter).

We said that a shift of wages to profits does not stimulate investment. We said that, at any given point in time, profits are determined by investment (and the budget deficit and trade surplus). But what about the *distribution* of profits and wages? Kalecki assumed a mark-up over unit variable cost theory of pricing for manufacturing products (agricultural prices were set to respond to supply and demand conditions), in the context of constant returns to scale and excess capacity. The mark-up reflects the 'degree of monopoly' in an industry, which can be affected by the concentration in that industry, by non-price competition, by overheads costs (not covered in variable costs) and trade unions (Kalecki 1971 [1943], pp. 50–51). The degree of monopoly not only influences the distribution of income between wages and profits but also affects the inner distribution of profits itself.

Another point that is important to mark is that, besides the economic limits to expansion, Kalecki recognized that there were *political* limitations to growth (and full employment), arising from the business sector resistant to a steady level of full employment (Kalecki 1971 [1943], pp. 50–51). On one side, automatic government spending in case of slumps and public investment expenditure removes a kind of 'veto' power of the business sector, usually labelled 'the investment atmosphere' or, nowadays, 'the confidence fairy'. Public nationalizations might indeed compete with the private sector. But the main objection is that a sustained level of full employment may bring about a more conflicted relationship with organized labour, in terms of distribution, in terms of production relations and in terms of the impact of inflation on the rentier class.

Summing up, Kalecki extended to the long run an implication of Keynes's analysis in the short run: lowering nominal and real wages will not necessarily stimulate growth. Kaldor and Robinson upheld the 'paradox of thrift', but they still associated a higher level of investment with a lower real wage. Kalecki, even though he strongly influenced these authors (as has been shown in their theory of profits determination), rejected the negative association between wages and investment, with a clear macroeconomic understanding of the 'circular flow' and interaction between income distribution and expenditure, just like Keynes. However different their approaches were, and in spite of other actual differences in some areas (such as interest rate determination, or expectation formation), the similarity in their conclusions justifies the inclusion of the Kaleckian stream within the post-Keynesian current of economic thought. Keeping in mind the conclusions we draw from Kalecki's vision and thought, it is time to go deeper into what Kaleckian theory really means and what it proposes.

NOTES

1. A recent and detailed analysis of the theory (or theories) of economic growth presented by Adam Smith is Aspromourgos (2009).
2. A good analysis of the break with previous 'classical' economics (mainly Ricardian) as perceived by the early marginalists themselves, such as Jevons, Walras, Pareto and Fisher, can be found in Mirowski (1984). In essence, the argument is that these economists wanted to apply concepts and analogies from classical mechanics into the discipline. The sole exception was Menger.
3. Some traces of a business cycle theory in Wicksell can be found in his Lectures, Vol. II, pp. 209–214. A lecture given by him in 1907 on the issue of crises was printed for the first time in English in 2001 (Wicksell 2001), with a short introduction by Hagemann (2001). A thorough analysis of Wicksell's writings on cycles and crises is Boianovsky (1995), and a review of theories of the business cycle in the German-language area before 1930 can be found in Hagemann (1999). As for Schumpeter, a reading of his Theory of Economic Development (1934) will suffice, if the reader wants to avoid going through the two volumes of his Business Cycles.
4. Dutt (2003) and Kurz and Salvadori (2003), among others, study how the so-called 'New Growth Theory' has (not) dealt with income distribution as a determinant of investment and growth, apart from its influences on the political field.
5. In 1939, Keynes recognized that the evidence did not support the hypothesis of diminishing marginal productivity (see CW VII, pp. 394–412).
6. In the Treatise on Money, and in articles after the publication of the General Theory, Keynes withdrew the assumption of a given money supply, or at least its role as data and not a variable.
7. On the relationship between Keynes, Beveridge and the welfare state, see Skidelsky (2003, pp. 708–724) and Marcuzzo (2010).
8. Inside the same line of literature one has to mention Pasinetti (1962), who studies 'the system of relationships required to reach full employment' (p. 267), without assuming it as given. Pasinetti introduces some changes and extends the model of Kaldor (1957).
9. For the reader interested in learning more about Kalecki, we recommend reading Sawyer (1985) and López G. and Assous (2012). Another good reading is the collection of essays in Sadowski and Szeworski (2004).

3. Growth and distribution: the Kaleckian perspective

3.1 BY WAY OF INTRODUCTION

Most of the theories mentioned in the previous chapter link a higher growth rate with a lower real wage rate. Keynes does not discuss specifically the growth rate in the General Theory, but he stresses that savings are not a prior requirement for investment to occur (his strongest statement in this sense was a review of a study by the League of Nations, called 'The process of capital formation', 1973 [1939], CW XIV, pp. 278–285). Kalecki associated savings with different social classes, and in that way he questioned the classical argument with its same social stratification. Post-Keynesians adopted the 'paradox of thrift' to analyse long-run growth, but retained the negative relation between investment and real wages. This was challenged by Kaleckian economists, starting in the early 1980s.

The main assumption that Kaleckian models questioned was the existence of a 'normal' rate of capacity utilization (hereafter CU) towards which the economy should tend in the long run. Instead, they assume that the CU is an endogenous variable determined by aggregate demand, that only by chance will it be in the long run at its 'normal' value. This allows the possibility that higher real wages increase the CU rate, which in turn may raise investment, growth and also the profit rate, due to an accelerator effect in the investment function.

In fact, in the original models (Dutt 1984; Rowthorn 1989 [1981]), higher real wages increase the CU rate, investment, growth and also the profit rate. This is the so-called paradox of costs. Starting from Bhaduri and Marglin (1990), the possibility of several growth and demand regimes has been acknowledged, according to the impact of higher real wages on demand, investment and the profit rate.

In this chapter we will explain the 'canonical' or basic Kaleckian model, the critiques it has received, the replies and subsequent discussions that it has generated, the extensions it has endured in the last 25 years, some connections with other types of post-Keynesian growth models, and the contribution of this book to the Kaleckian literature. Another review of Kaleckian models can be found in Lavoie (2014, Chapter 6). We beg the

Table 3.1   Paradox of costs and paradox of thrift

	Classicals, Marx, Marglin, Duménil, neoclassicals	Robinson, Kaldor	Kaleckians, modern Sraffians, Marxists (Bhaduri–Marglin)
Paradox of costs		No	Yes or indifferent
Paradox of thrift	No		Yes

Source: Lavoie (1996, p. 116).

reader to be patient and to go with us through this rather long journey. To start with, Table 3.1 outlines the relations between growth, savings (related to the paradox of thrift) and costs (related to the real wage) in the different schools that we have mentioned and that we will mention. We highlight these two 'paradoxes' because they relate, as mentioned above, to the use and source of income and its impact on GDP. The paradox of costs, as can be inferred from what we said above, postulates a positive relation between the real wage and investment, and the precise mechanisms we will explain now.

3.2   THE BASIC MODEL

Lavoie (1992, p. 297; 1995b, p. 790) traces the main results of the Kaleckian model (that we are about to show) back to a work in Italian by Del Monte, in the mid 1970s. The typical model, an extension of Asimakopulos's (1975), was developed independently by Rowthorn (1989 [1981]) and Dutt (1984). While the latter deals with issues related to the development of India, Rowthorn's article criticizes conclusions we mentioned from the Cambridge School, in particular the inverse relationship between real wage and accumulation rate, and this is the work we will follow, in the version presented by Lavoie (1995b). We choose this paper because it sets the framework to interpret, integrate and answer the critiques. In Lavoie (2014) the basic model has a different investment function, but our formulation puts in stark contrast the different responses this model has generated.

The assumptions of this basic or canonical model (that excludes any consideration of technical progress and thus productivity, taxation, foreign trade, etc.) are those of a closed economy without a public sector. Rowthorn includes direct taxes (on profits) but this is not relevant to our argument, and it is not present in the models that we will show and use.

Table 3.2 Notation

$L = L_v + L_f$	Employed labour force = variable work plus fixed work
$u = q/q_{fc}$	CU = output / full capacity output
$v = K/q_{fc}$	Capital / capacity coefficient
$y_v = q/L_v$	Labour productivity
$y_f = q_{fc}/L_f$	Fixed labour requirement (proportional to capacity)
$f = y_v/y_f$	Variable labour / fixed labour relation

Source: Author's elaboration.

Without state activity, GDP (prices times quantities) can be decomposed into the wage bill and profits, which leads to:

$$p = w(L/q) + rpK/q \tag{3.1}$$

with q equal to Gross Domestic Product (in constant prices), where w is the real wage rate, L represents employed labour, K is the capital stock and r is the profit rate. With fixed or overhead labour (administrative personnel, for instance) and variable labour (workers directly involved in the productive process), we introduce the definitions shown in Table 3.2.

With this, substituting in (3.1) and solving for the profit rate, we have:

$$r = \left(\frac{u}{v}\right)\left[1 - \left(\frac{w}{p}\right)(1 + f/u)/y_v\right] \tag{3.2}$$

The model has two curves in the (u, r) space. The distributional relations are exogenous, so that the real wage and the mark-up are given (Bhaduri and Marglin 1990, p. 376; Blecker 2002, p. 131). We will mention some extensions in which they are endogenized.

What type of pricing do we adopt? The simplest way is to assume a mark-up over variable costs, which in a vertically integrated sector reduces to:

$$p = (1 + \theta)w/y_v \tag{3.3}$$

Since the degree of monopoly or gross profit margin (or the profit share) is equal to $m = \theta/(1 + \theta)$, we can get the following equation representing our first curve, the profit–cost curve (PC):[1]

$$r = u(m/v) - (1 - m)f/v \tag{3.4}$$

That curve shows the quantity of profits created at a given rate of CU, derived from the pricing equation. It should not be confused with actual profits, since its realization depends on effective demand. The latter is captured by our second curve, the *ED* curve, standing for *effective demand*. This shows the relation between saving and investment. The first is represented by a reinterpretation of the Cambridge equation as a savings function, so that:

$$g^s = rs_p \qquad (3.5)$$

with s_p representing the proportion saved from profits (we assume that workers do not save, though the argument does not change much if they save less out of their income than capitalists).

The investment function is the source of most controversies. The one proposed originally by Rowthorn was:

$$g^i = \gamma + g_u u + g_r r \qquad (3.6)$$

Investment depends on the current CU rate, of the current profit rate, and on γ, a parameter with different interpretations. Since saving and investment must be identical, we equalize (3.5) and (3.6), we solve for r and we get the *ED* curve:

$$r = (g_u u + \gamma)/(s_p - g_r) \qquad (3.7)$$

The stability condition is that savings react more strongly than investment to changes in the profit rate, which means:[2]

$$s_p > g_r + g_u u/m$$

This condition is more stringent than that of Cambridge models, in which the savings propensity must be greater than the reaction of investment, that is, $s_p > g_r$. The reason is that the term $g_u u$ adds an accelerator effect, making the economy more unstable.

In this model the paradox of thrift holds. An increase in the savings rate shifts the *ED* curve downwards, generating a lower accumulation rate and a lower profit rate. However, the main novelty is the paradox of costs, as shown in Figure 3.1. The effect of a change in wages is captured, in the *PC* curve, through the derivative of r with respect to m, which is positive. An increase in the gross margin (and a decrease in the real wage) shifts the *PC* curve upwards, generating a lower capacity utilization rate, a lower profit rate and a lower accumulation rate. These conclusions are in contradiction with almost all the existing literature, except for the underconsumption

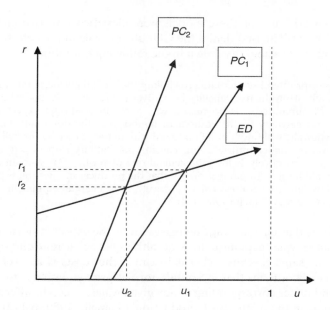

Source: Lavoie (1995b, p. 795).

Figure 3.1 Paradox of costs

theorists. This should surprise nobody, since Kalecki was strongly influenced by the writings of Rosa Luxemburg (1951 [1913]), who also inspired Sweezy together with Kalecki (Sweezy 1942; Baran and Sweezy 1966) and John Bellamy Foster (2013, for instance). And it did not take long for critiques to appear. Let us see what they were about.

3.3   FIRST ROUND OF CRITIQUES

There were two main waves of critiques of Kaleckian models, at the end of the 1980s and early 1990s, and between 2007 and 2010, and we will review them in a chronological order. The focuses of conflict were different: at first they referred to more conceptual issues, while later they dealt with the stability conditions of the models. Initially, critiques came from Marxists and Sraffians, from authors such as Duménil and Lévy (1999), Kurz (1990), Bhaduri and Marglin (1990) and Vianello (1989); later critics called themselves 'Harrodian', such as Shaikh (2007, 2009) and Skott (2010, 2012); and both times Marc Lavoie was on the defensive side, so to speak. Let us review both controversies separately.

The first critiques of these models were classified into two groups by Lavoie (1995b). The first denies the CU rate any role in the determination of investment decisions, as shown in the following quotation:

> A current profitability exceeding (or falling short of) the general rate of profits as a result of productive capacity being over (or respectively, under) utilized – it will be submitted – is no reason why a producer should expect that the productive capacity of the equipment (embodying the dominant method of production) he will find himself endowed with in the years to come will be similarly over (or under) utilized, thus causing profitability to persist in standing above (or respectively, below) the general rate of profits. For such an expectation would imply – to put it shortly – that the producer in question is planning to endow himself with less (or respectively, more) capital equipment than he expects to need. (Vianello 1989, p. 165)

The point is that current wage increases lower the expected normal profit rate, which is what capitalists look at, although the current rate of profit remains the same (because what is lost in higher costs is recovered with sales). Vianello affirms that in Sraffa's normal-price equations, 'the rate of profits and prices corresponding to any given wage . . . can be affected only by a change in the methods of production' (Vianello 1989, p. 172). At the end of the adjustment process, the CU rate will remain at the current level, with a lower profit rate. The investment function implied by this critique would be something as follows:

$$g^i = \gamma + g_r r_n \qquad (3.6a)$$

with r_n as the expected normal rate of profit. This means that the *ED* curve would be horizontal at the level of the normal profit rate r_n, as in Figure 3.2. A wage increase shifts PC_1 to the right-hand side, increasing in principle capacity utilization without touching the current profit rate. But firms expect a lower normal rate of profit, and they reduce their desired accumulation rate, lowering *ED*, up to the point where the new (and lower) normal rate of profits corresponds with a new (and lower) rate of aggregate demand, and a new (and lower) accumulation rate. Figure 3.2, taken from Lavoie (1995b, p. 796), will be useful to represent the changes. In this example, the actual rate of profits r_2 need not be equal to the new normal rate, and the same goes for the utilization rate.

Kurz (1990) and Bhaduri and Marglin (1990) also question the investment function, but from another point of view. To understand what they are saying, we have to decompose the profit rate like this:

$$r = \frac{P}{K} = \frac{P}{Y} \frac{Y}{Y_{fc}} \frac{Y_{fc}}{K} = \frac{mu}{v} \qquad (3.8)$$

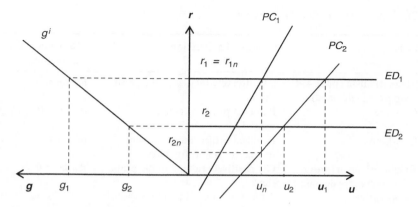

Source: Lavoie (1995b, p. 796).

Figure 3.2 Neo-Ricardian critique

The first term in the right-hand side of the equation, $\frac{P}{Y}$, represents the profit share of income; the second term represents the capacity utilization rate (Y_{fc} is the full capacity output or some normal level), and the last one is the inverse of the capital–full capacity output ratio. If we do this and insert (3.8) into (3.6), we obtain:

$$g^i = \gamma + g_u u + g_r \frac{mu}{v} \tag{3.6b}$$

We can now see that u appears twice in the investment function. 'The influence on the investment level of income distribution on one side and effective demand on the other is somewhat blurred' (Kurz 1990, p. 220). As Bhaduri and Marglin (1990) show, if we accept equation (3.6), even when the increase in u is exactly compensated by a fall in the profit margin, investment would still increase. This imposes unjustified restrictions to the behaviour of accumulation, in the sense that the relative importance of a variable (capacity utilization) is much greater than the other (profit rate), reverting its own effect.

What Kurz and Bhaduri and Marglin propose is simply to let the profit rate be the main determinant of investment, including both the positive effect of consumption and the negative effect of higher costs. This means that if we include capacity utilization as an argument in the investment function, we must also include the normal rate of profit or some other variable that reflects the rise in costs, such as the profit share of income (assuming no fixed labour), as chosen by Bhaduri and Marglin and Kurz:

Table 3.3   Conceptual summary

Concept	Coloquial expression	Mathematical expression
Stagnationism (wage-led aggregate demand)	**CU inversely related to the profit share**	$du/dm < 0$
Cooperative	Realized profit rate inversely related to the profit share	$dr/dm < 0$
Conflictive	Realized profit rate positively related to the profit share	$dr/dm > 0$
Exhilarationism (profit-led aggregate demand)	**CU positively related to the profit share**	$du/dm > 0$
Cooperative	Total real labour income positively related to the profit share	$d(WN/P)/dm > 0$
Conflictive	Total real labour income negatively related to the profit share	$d(WN/P)/dm < 0$
Wage-led growth	**Capital accumulation rate inversely related to the profit share**	$dg/dm < 0$
Profit-led growth	**Capital accumulation rate positively related to the profit share**	$dg/dm > 0$

Source: Blecker (2002, p. 134).

$$g^i = \gamma + g_u u + g_m m \qquad (3.6c)$$

This investment function allows a wide typology of growth regimes relevant for our discussions, presented in Table 3.3, based on Blecker (2002, p. 134). The key to see which of all these regimes holds is in the reaction of investment to changes in the profit margin and capacity utilization. The 'exhilarationist' regime requires a strong effect of the profit margin on investment, overcompensating for the fall in consumption due to lower wages. If not, a higher profit share might stimulate investment and growth and even the profit rate, but fail to stimulate aggregate demand, capacity utilization and employment (the conflictive stagnationism). The above-mentioned work by Blecker is important because it relaxes the restraint on savings by workers. The creative jargon used to name different regimes has been replaced by more standard (and less literary) denominations.

It might be useful to explain some features of Table 3.3. For a better understanding, u means capacity utilization, m represents the profit share, r represents the profit rate, WN/P is the total wage bill deflated by the price label (it represents the total real labour income), and g represents the rate of growth of the capital stock. Consider the following two cases: conflictive stagnationism, and cooperative exhilarationism. In the first, aggregate demand (with the CU as a proxy) is positively correlated with the real wage, but the profit rate is positively correlated with the profit share, represented by m (the rise in aggregate demand is not enough to compensate the fall of unit margin), so that companies will not be interested in stimulating demand through higher wages (as in the cooperative stagnationism); on the contrary, they would push for a secular stagnation. In the case of a cooperative exhilarationism, even though aggregate demand is ruled by the profit share (through its impact on the profit rate and investment), there is the chance of a 'concordance of interests' in the sense that the wage bill might increase without compromising the evolution of economic activity.

The second line of critique came from Marxists and Sraffians who have taken Vianello's point to an extreme by saying that in the long term, the effective capacity utilization rate should be equal to its normal or standard level, achieving a 'fully adjusted position'. In the Kaleckian model, capacity utilization is endogenous and not necessarily equal to its normal value. As an example, we consider the model of Duménil and Lévy (1999) as a leading case in the Marxist tradition. The idea is that the macroeconomic consequences of individual behaviour are not as each investor wished, so that it cannot be called a long-term equilibrium position. Then we have the problem of finding the mechanism that brings the short-term CU to its long-term normal level. In Duménil and Lévy's opinion, when the actual CU is higher than the normal rate, inflation grows. Duménil and Lévy then reinterpret the parameter g as a proxy of firms' capacity to borrow, which is reduced in an inflationary context. This impacts negatively on investment, falling to a level lower than at the start. In the end, there is neither a paradox of thrift nor a paradox of costs, according to the classical (and neoclassical) view. In these models, both u_n and r_n are exogenous parameters, of a unique and unmodified value.

The reader might ask, after all, what are these 'normal' values? Regarding the normal rate of profit, the definition of Pivetti is very clear: '[the normal rate of profit] corresponds to the rate of return on capital which would be obtained by firms using dominant or generally accessible techniques, and producing output at levels regarded as normal at the time the capacity was installed' (Pivetti 1991, p. 20). Lavoie (2014, p. 372) has a similar definition, in which the normal rate of profit is generated (for a given mark-up) when the economy 'is running at its normal rate of capacity utilization'. As for the determination of the normal degree of utilization (which need not be a full utilization level), there is much less agreement. Kurz (1990 [1986]) argues that it is a cost-minimizing degree; Steindl (1976 [1952]) argued that it was an expectation of the state of the economy in some future time; Auerbach and Skott (1988, p. 51) say that it is an optimal level that firms will try to achieve, while Skott (2012) includes a myriad of factors that affect it (habits and conventions; changes in the degree of competition, demand volatility, managerial constraints or bottlenecks, etc.).

The criticism by Bhaduri and Marglin and Kurz about the a priori over-shooting effect is well taken, since it cannot be logically rejected. Actually, that was Rowthorn's original point: capacity utilization has an influence by itself and by its positive impact on the profit rate. The investment function they propose, however, does not enjoy unanimous support.

The main critiques were Mott and Slattery (1994, p. 72) and Lavoie (1995b, pp. 799–800). As a first point, the profit margin might not neces-sarily correlate with the profit share in the presence of overhead labour. Secondly, the profit rate conveys more information than the profit margin or the profit share about the financial state of the company. The profit margin might reflect movements in the interest rate (an argument put forward by Pivetti (1991)), reducing its usefulness as a repayment indica-tor. But that does not answer those that question the long-term divergence between the effective CU rate and profit rate with its normal values. Accepting it to be a long-term equilibrium requirement, Lavoie (1995b, 1996) explores the conditions for the model to converge to such a fully adjusted position without losing its distinctive Kaleckian features, the paradox of costs and paradox of thrift. He does that by endogenizing the normal capacity utilization rate through a process of hysteresis, in which 'the new fully adjusted position depends *on the adjustment process during the transition*' (Lavoie 1996, p. 132, italics in the original). Post-Keynesian characteristics are preserved in the long run as well as in the short run, in opposition to what, for instance, Duménil and Lévy hold.

Other 'more radical' replies have been those by Chick and Caserta (1997) among others, who say that the behavioural parameters and norms are so variable that a long-term analysis with fully adjusted positions, in which the CU equals its normal value, is not very relevant. Another interpretation is that of Hicks (1974, p. 19), Dutt (1990, p. 59) and Palumbo and Trezzini (2003, p. 128) in which firms do not target a particular rate but a range, in a conventional way, so that as long as the CU rate stays within that range, its discrepancy with some normal value is not a problem.

3.4   RECENT CRITIQUES

These extensions and modifications of the basic Kaleckian model have not convinced the critics, as expected. The heart of the debate about Kaleckian models of growth and distribution concerns the existence of the mere possibility of getting a certain parameter configuration under which we can obtain a stagnationist (or wage-led) regime. All critiques and arguments presented against Kaleckian models discard this possibility, allowing only for a negative relationship between investment and the real wage (no paradox of costs). Without closing the front on the convergence of the effective rate of profit and/or capacity utilization towards its normal values, or the endogeneity of these, the new battlefield refers to the issue of the stability conditions in Kaleckian models. Being somewhat unfair to other participants in the debate, it is still the case that the main critiques on both fronts have come from Peter Skott. Skott has spelled out his critique of the Kaleckian approach in the following detail (Skott 2010, p. 110):

> This paper challenges the Kaleckian approach. I shall argue (i) that there are good theoretical reasons to rule out steady-growth deviations between actual and desired utilization rates. (ii) that the theoretical case for (quantitatively significant) adaptative changes in desired utilization is weak. (iii) that the Kaleckian specification implies long-run variations in utilization rates that have no counterpart in the data, and (iv) that existing econometric studies have been badly misinterpreted.

The discussions about different approaches to Say's Law might serve as evidence about the existence, not just of alternative theories, but also opposite 'interpretations' of the reality, ways of apprehending the object of analysis, the economy. Where some economists emphasize the importance of short-term phenomena, the impact of unstable moods and expectations, others put the focus on the study of long-term 'regularities', trends, with the subsequent disagreement about how far away one should look for those regularities. It is not a matter of the capabilities to identify such regularities between the mist of fluctuations and events that plague the passage of time; it is rather a matter of whether one believes those regularities exist at all. The former issue (the capability to understand the object of analysis) refers to an *epistemological* concern; the second is an *ontological* divide, a 'vision' thing in the terms of Schumpeter (1954). I have come to the conclusion that no agreement is likely to be achieved when the same phenomenon is observed with different glasses, or different mindsets, to be more precise. These thoughts apply, in particular, to Skott's point (i). Just as Skott (and some Sraffians, to name others) finds theoretical reasons to dismiss the study of long-term deviations of the actual rate of utilization from its norm or desired level, others consider the discrepancy between those two variables to be a regular feature of different economies, and therefore a worthwhile assumption or possibility.

Notwithstanding that difference of 'vision', for the purposes of debate some sides are willing to retreat a little in order for a discussion to take place. In their response to Skott, Hein, Lavoie and Van Treeck (2012, pp. 145–148) highlight the fact that firms might actually be interested, not on one strict level of desired or normal capacity utilization, but on a range of values, in order to take account of potential 'surprises', so that there is a corridor of stability, in a sense. Dallery and Van Treeck (2011) argue that a firm and its stakeholders may have different objectives, which may be mutually incompatible (for instance, regarding accumulation and dividends policies between shareholders and managers, or regarding profits and wages between the two mentioned and workers), so that all objectives might not be realized even in a long-run equilibrium.

As for Skott's point (ii), the following quotation reflects his position: 'Adjustment in the target [expected or normal utilization rate] would only be justified if the experience of low actual utilization makes firms think that low utilization has now become optimal, and neither Amadeo nor Lavoie present an argument for this causal link' (Skott 2012, p. 118). In the case that such lack of convergence is due to random and non-systematic shocks, Skott goes on, these should not change the targets. Skott emphasizes that firms would change their investment decisions instead of changing the desired utilization rate.

However, a strong rebuttal of his claim came from an unexpected direction. Duménil and Lévy (2012) analyse the data of capacity utilization in the manufacturing sector for the United States (more on this in the next paragraph) and concluded that we can observe a clear decreasing trend in its level. They use a Whittaker filter, and with unit root tests they reject the null hypothesis of stationarity, having evidence of a downward-drifting trend. This trend is used as a new 'center of gravitation', but not a constant one. The declining trend might reflect technical-organizational (or 'institutional') transformations.

Skott argues in turn that small parameter changes lead to relatively large variations in capacity utilization rates that have no counterpart in the macroeconomic data. Skott is not alone in raising this point: Dallery (2007) also questions the empirical relevance of the Kaleckian argument by developing a simple model and evaluating the parameter configuration that would assure the stability, and its empirical relevance. That basic model is based on equations, (3.5), (3.6b) and (3.8), without overhead labour. However, the findings by Skott as well as Dallery may be hard to generalize themselves, because they are based on extremely stylized models without a public sector, without a foreign sector, without a financial sector, without workers' savings, and so on. Moreover, in order for the reader himself (or herself) to have an idea about the magnitude of the actual changes in the capacity utilization, we present Figure 3.3, extracted from the website of the Federal Reserve of the United States, which casts doubts on the alleged stability of the capacity utilization rate as argued

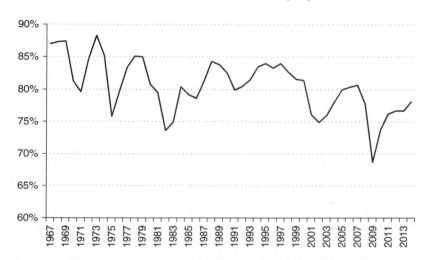

Source: Board of Governors of the Federal Reserve System (US), Capacity Utilization: Total Industry [TCU], retrieved from FRED, Federal Reserve Bank of St. Louis https:// research.stlouisfed.org/fred2/series/TCU/, 25 September 2015.

Figure 3.3   Capacity utilization in the US

by Skott. The findings by Duménil and Lévy (2012, Figure 1) are also conclusive, in my view.

During the boom the industry seems to operate at stable levels, though there appear to be some considerable fluctuations. But that does not imply that we can safely assume that the normal use is a target that companies have sustained in a prolonged way. On one side, the average utilization rates are not equal for all the boom periods, so it does not seem unreasonable to assume that firms are satisfied with a range, more than with a fixed determined utilization rate. Besides, cyclical fluctuations have not been stable, so that past cycles are not a precedent for future ones. There is also empirical evidence which goes against Skott's stylized fact. For example, Michalis Nikiforos (2012), while criticizing the economic rationale put forward by Kaleckian economists to defend the endogeneity of the capacity utilization rate, argues that by taking into account the existence of economies of scale at the firm level, 'the normal rate of capacity utilization is endogenous and positively related to the level of the demand for the product of the firm' (p. 18), a proposition for which he finds empirical support. Similar conclusions are reached by Schoder (2011) in his study of the US manufacturing sector and its subsectors.

The other front of attack to Kaleckian models opened by Skott is the stability issue, and short- and long-run effects. As in all critiques, 'the economy is "exhilarationist" and profit led in the long run' (Skott 2010, p. 114). However, the stationary solution is unstable in the model presented, a 'Harrodian' model in which investment as a share of capital is determined not only by the present and past value of the capacity utilization rate, but also by the own lagged values of investment. The main characteristic of the Harrodian approach is that investment has a low short-term sensitivity to changes in aggregate demand, and a larger one in the long run (Skott 2010, p. 120), being itself the only variable that reconciles the normal use of capacity. Skott recognizes that in certain cases the instability of the steady state might be a reflection of more complex short-term, local, instability issues, representing fluctuations around a long-term path. To attenuate instability, Skott proposes adjustment mechanisms in which prices react faster than output to disequilibrium (in fact, he assumes a given output level, with firms focusing on the growth rate itself, without noting the apparent incompatibility of both in the long run), or mechanisms in which the employment rate is a relevant factor, since he assumes full employment.

The Kaleckian response points to different aspects. First, a distinction between different types of stability; secondly, and more importantly, even in instability cases as contemplated in Skott's models, we can preserve the distinctive characteristics of Kaleckian models, such as wage-led growth and aggregate demand. The works of Hein, Lavoie and Van Treeck (2011, 2012) and Lavoie (2010a) develop these arguments, and we are going to sum up what their lines of reply are, following their expositions. Lavoie (2014, pp. 377–386) also has a neat discussion of the topic.

Kaleckians usually assume Keynesian stability, which requires that savings react more strongly than investment to changes in the rate of capacity utilization. In the space (u, g), it requires that savings be steeper than investment. Figures 3.4a and 3.4b exemplify Keynesian stability and instability. g^s and g^i are taken from equations (3.5) and (3.6), depicting the growth of savings and investment related to the capacity utilization rate.

Harrodian instability, even though it might be very difficult to distinguish from the Keynesian, has a different theoretical underpinning. Repeating equations (3.5), (3.8) and a simple investment function in (3.9):

$$g^s = rs_p \qquad\qquad (3.5)$$

$$r = \frac{mu}{v} \qquad\qquad (3.8)$$

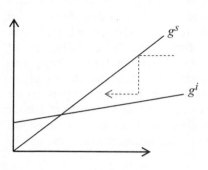 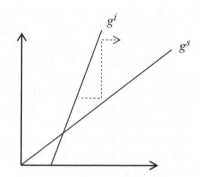

Source: Hein, Lavoie and Van Treeck
(2011, p. 591).

Figure 3.4a   Keynesian stability   *Figure 3.4b   Keynesian instability*

$$g^i = \gamma + \gamma_u(u - u_n) \tag{3.9}$$

For Keynesian stability to hold,

$$s_p \frac{m}{v} > \gamma_u$$

Even if that condition is fulfilled, Harrodian instability might arise. What do we mean by Harrodian instability? It means that γ (reinterpreted as a sort of trend rate of sales growth) increases whenever the capacity utilization rate is above its normal value. When the level of utilization is consistently above the normal level, firms expect a higher trend of sales growth, and γ increases. So, even in the case of Figure 3.4a, the g^i is consistently shifted upwards. All the 'solutions' to this instability problem proposed by Skott and others focus on reducing the value of γ.

Skott (2010, pp. 115–126) mentioned several mechanisms for dealing with instability. Some of them are similar to the Kaldor and Robinson models described above, in which higher rates of utilization go hand in hand with higher profit margins (thus giving rise to forced savings). That seems totally counterintuitive, since in those cases the bargaining power of labour should be strengthened, not weakened. Another mechanism is that, instead of rising margins, firms curtail their expansion plans in situations of full employment or near full employment, for the very precise motive we mentioned above: a more combative labour force and a more conflictive environment. In this variant, capitalists themselves are the ones that restrict employment. He refers (2010, p. 120) to the 'political business cycle' described by Kalecki, and even though that point is well taken, it seems very unlikely that this is the channel by which that cycle takes place. It is more likely to have rising wage shares, falling profit margins and a chorus of business voices chanting for austerity and central bank intervention, than to see firms restricting their hiring plans. Hein, Lavoie and Van Treeck (2011, p. 604) note that Skott's formulations seem to exclude Kaleckian results by assumption. And if we allow labour force growth (by encouraging immigration, for instance) the 'near full employment' level at which firms reduce their hiring plans might not be relevant at all.

3.5   THEORETICAL UNDERPINNINGS OF EMPIRICAL APPLICATIONS

With the major shifts in income distribution observed in developed and developing countries since the mid-1970s, combined with the slowdown in economic growth suffered by the former economies (and some of the latter group), it seems natural that Kaleckian economists have turned to utilize the theoretical framework presented above in order to empirically study a significant number of countries. In the next sections I want to give the reader a glimpse of how this rather large body of literature was carried out, and present as an example my own econometric work on one country, Argentina. But before reviewing this applied work, it is better to describe the theoretical models behind the two main alternative approaches used in the empirical literature when it comes to the macroeconomic regimes of different economies. That is what we will do in this section.

There are two distinguishable strands in the literature when it comes to corroborating empirically the validity of the Kaleckian model of growth. The first, and more popular, takes income distribution as exogenous, and evaluates how changes in distributional parameters affect the components of private GDP (consumption, investment and the balance of trade). Differences arise because of differences in the explanatory variables in each function, but a specific direction of causality can be established a priori. This is what Hein and Vogel (2008) have done, and this will be presented next.

The other strand applies what has been termed a 'systems approach', in which the determination of income distribution is equally endogenous. Usually, it is corroborated via a VAR model, its addition transforms the Vector Auto-Regressive regression into a Vector Error-Correction model, or VEC[3], in case there is a cointegration relationship between some or all

BOX 3.1   EXTENSIONS OF THE KALECKIAN MODEL

The basic Kaleckian model has been extended to study different issues of empirical and theoretical relevance, to try to see if its main characteristics are preserved. Without claiming to be exhaustive, the reader may find here a review of those extensions.

First, the one-sector model analysis has been extended to a two-sector model, in which the profit margin of the consumption-goods sector depends, among other parameters, on the profit margin of the investment-goods sector. Lavoie and Ramírez-Gastón (1997) show that an increase in the profit margin of any sector, as well as the desired profit rates, brings about a lower accumulation rate. However, the latter does not necessarily imply lower sectorial profit rates. Another work which also designs a two-sector model, in the context of a stock-flow consistent modelling, is Kim (2006), who finds that both the paradox of thrift and the paradox of costs might disappear according to the initial situation of income distribution and the monetary policy, reinforcing the concept of 'path dependency'. When we introduce conflicting claims, the results are more complex. For instance, a push by workers for higher wages which does not bring about a fall in profitability expected by firms (meaning that firms do not lower their mark-ups) reduces financial wealth, and as long as their holders have an important propensity to consume (for instance, pensioners), that has an effect on consumption, output and employment. To quote Kim: 'In conclusion, what has a positive effect on economic activity is not an increase in nominal wages in itself, but the strong bargaining position of labour unions to refrain the profit share' (p. 20).

Lavoie (2009) and Carvalho and Rezai (2015) analyse a different sectoral splitting, this time among workers, to incorporate into the framework the increase in wage inequality observed since the 1980s, reflected in the widening *personal* income inequality. Allowing for different types of workers (white collar/blue collar, or managers/workers) adds a level of complexity to the standard results, and has important implications for understanding empirical findings. For instance, Carvalho and Rezai come to the conclusion that, while many studies have found the US economy to be 'profit led' (as the survey in Table 3.5 will show), the growing disparity among wage earners, with bonuses and managerial salaries going through the roof while the income of average workers has stagnated, is a more likely explanatory variable: increasing the 'labour share' while not taking into account this inequality leads to contradictory results. On the contrary, redistribution in favour of low-wage earners unequivocally increases aggregate demand. Lavoie (2009) reaches a similar conclusion regarding the importance of the labour share as a suitable indicator.

Secondly, the Kaleckian model has been extended so as to include financial or monetary variables. The most important works on these issues have been Lavoie (1993, 1995a) and Hein, especially (Hein 2006; Hein and Ochsen 2003). Lavoie's articles were among the first on the topic, and he tackles the issue of the influence of the interest rate on aggregate demand. Hein's work goes further in the topic, adding the importance of the debt/capital coefficient of firms, giving rise to other paradoxical conclusions (Hein 2006, p. 347). To start with, we must take account of rentiers' propensity to consume and the dividend ratio of firms. If rentiers save a big proportion of their (interest) income, redistribution in their favour has dampening effects on activity and growth. If the mark-up reacts to increases in the interest rate, firms might defend their profit share and might protect their internal source of funds for investment, but labour income will fall, and with it economic activity, in a wage led-case. But when we allow the debt/capital ratio to change, we have strange results. For instance, in the case described above, with rentiers saving a lot and firms reacting to interest rate changes, accumulation slows down, but with this the ratio becomes unstable (the denominator falls, or fails to keep up with the increase in the numerator). Firms raise their mark-ups, but activity falls, investment falls and debt burden increases. Hein and Stockhammer (2011), in turn, develop a macroeconomic model with conflicting-claims-spurred inflation and a significant role for monetary and fiscal policy which includes several Kaleckian features such as the investment function and the endogeneity of capacity utilization. Rochon and Setterfield (2012) go a step further, analysing the impact of different monetary policy rules with 'post-Keynesian' inspiration, for the real interest rate (either to be at zero, or to keep up with productivity growth). They search for conditions to maintain high growth with low inflation within a model with inflation triggered by a distributive struggle, coming to the conclusions that different wage targets (i.e. a real wage, or wage share) have different implications for the conduct and the effect of monetary policy.

The Kaleckian approach has further been extended into a stock-flow consistent modelling methodology by Godley and Lavoie (2007a), who develop an impressive model, incorporating firms' investment decisions, profit distribution, banking policy, nonperforming loans reserve, public sector financing policy, and so on. We must also mention the literature dealing with 'financialization', a phenomenon frequently used to explain the crisis of 2008 in the US and that spread globally. One of the first works in that line was Palley (1996), who revisited the subject in 2008, 2010 and 2013 (Palley 2008, 2010, 2013). A summary can be found in Hein and Van Treeck (2010), while Hein himself has written more recently in 2012 and 2015, applying a number of the elements mentioned above (Hein 2012, 2015). The move towards shareholder-value orientation has given shareholders more influence in dividends and investment policy, and also weakened the traditional 'growth-oriented vision' of managers (Stockhammer 2005; Hein 2012, p.39). And by hurting investment, it affects productivity. The same impact may have a greater power of shareholders vis-à-vis workers, since that would diminish the impact of the real wage on the diffusion of new technologies and labour-saving productivity (Hein 2012, p.73).

Thirdly, the subject of technical progress has been present from the very beginning in this type of model. Rowthorn (1989 [1981]) spends a good deal of his article analysing the effects of technical progress, both when it is labour saving as well as capital saving, in line with the 'Kaldor–Verdoorn Law'. Kurz (1990) emphasizes the fact that among the effects of technical progress, in its various shapes, might be the change of distributive regime, as well as the deepening of expected patterns within each typology. Lavoie (1992, Chapter 7), Cassetti (2003) and Ono and Oreiro (2006) do something similar. The first two studies also deal with distributive conflict, based on a theory of inflation originating out of conflictive distributive claims.

On a different vein, Naastepad (2006) and Storm and Naastepad (2012) distinguish between a demand regime and a productivity regime, which might render the picture more complex and rich. A similar path was taken by Setterfield and Cornwall (2002) and Hein and Tarassow (2010).

Allain (2015), in turn, brings forth the impact of autonomous public expenditures. In the short run, the wage-led characteristics can be retained. In the long run, as will be seen in the stock-flow model later in this book, the economy will tend to grow at the rate of growth of public expenditure. And when public expenditure and taxation, instead of being exogenous, acquire the character of automatic stabilizers, distribution ceases to be an influential variable in the rate of growth, though higher real wages do have an impact on the level of variables (output, capital stock, etc.). You and Dutt (1996) present another model of public deficit, debt and income distribution. Government debt may positively impact output via the receipt of interest payments, and an expansionary fiscal policy might not worsen public debt sustainability in the presence of a large multiplier effect. The rise in output, in turn, can reasonably counteract the increased inequality due to higher interest rate payments. In general, income distribution worsens when debt grows faster than output, because workers are assumed not to receive payments in debt service concept, while capitalists are.

Blecker (2002) makes a summary of different topics tackled by Kaleckian models up to that date. He includes topics such as tax policy and progressiveness in the taxation structure, the implications of workers' savings for the model, and international trade, an aspect that he discussed on other occasions (such as Blecker 1999) as does Missaglia (2007), who adapts the determinants of the mark-up to adjust it to international competition. Blecker (1999) manifests that the fulfilment of Marshall–Lerner conditions for a devaluation that improves the balance of trade makes the economy more likely to behave like an exhilarationist regime. Cassetti (2012) goes into detail on the matter, by analysing under which conditions that proposition holds, when we add the possibility of wage and profit claims. Blecker also argues that, in a Kaleckian context, the effectiveness of devaluations in regards to an improved trade balance might undermine the other typical role of a devaluation, that is, the rise in national income and employment.

the endogenous variables. That was the method adopted by Onaran and Stockhammer (2004, 2006).

3.5.1 Exogenous Distribution

This model does not include financial markets, nor technical progress, so that labour productivity and the capital–potential output ratio are constant. It depicts an open economy with no government that depends on imported inputs for production purposes and produces a single tradable product, apt for consumption and investment. Finally, the nominal exchange rate is determined by the monetary policy, so we can treat it as an exogenous variable.

The pricing function is similar to equation (3.3), but including the impact of imported inputs. Thus, with a little bit of algebra, we can build the following price equations, each equal to the other:

$$p = (1 + \theta)\left[\frac{w}{y} + p_f e \mu\right] \tag{3.10}$$

$$p = (1 + \theta)\frac{w}{y}\left[1 + \frac{p_f e \mu}{w/y}\right] = (1 + \theta)\frac{w}{y}(1 + z) \tag{3.10a}$$

In these equations, θ describes the mark-up rate, w is the nominal wage rate, y is output per unit of labour, p_f is the foreign price level, e is the nominal exchange rate and μ represents unit imported inputs. z, in turn, expresses the ratio between unit material costs (composed of imported inputs) and unit labour costs:

$$z = \frac{p_f e \mu}{w/y}$$

It can be shown that, with the previous definitions, the profit share of aggregate income is given by:

$$m = \frac{1}{\dfrac{1}{(1 + z)\theta} + 1}$$

A higher ratio between material costs and unit labour costs implies a higher profit share, for a given mark-up. And a higher mark-up also implies a higher profit share, given the aforementioned ratio. The same holds for a higher (more depreciated) nominal exchange rate. What about the *real* exchange rate?

The real exchange rate is:

$$e_r = \frac{e p_f}{p}$$

In dynamic terms, we have:

$$\hat{e}_r = \hat{e} + \hat{p}_f - \hat{p}$$

If we take the derivative of e_r with respect to the profit margin θ and the nominal wage w, we can see that each is negative, so the overall derivative $\frac{\partial e_r}{\partial m}$ is a priori undetermined.

All these parameters are exogenous, so in actual terms we must speak of a constant profit share; and when we perform the simulations, it will be assumed that the parameter that moves is the mark-up, except in the case of the trade balance, where the effect is undetermined, as we have said.

In order to analyse the effect of changes in income distribution on economic activity we must study the equilibrium in the goods market of an open economy. The equality between savings and investment plus net exports is an identity, but they have different determinants. For a steady state to be achieved, we must make sure that the saving rate (normalized by the capital stock, $\sigma = S/K$) is equal to the sum of the accumulation rate ($g = I/K$) plus net exports ($b = NX/K$).

In this model we include savings not only from profits but from wages as well, unlike in equation (3.5), though the saving propensity out of profit income (s_p) is higher than that out of the latter (s_w). With u representing capacity utilization, υ being the capital–output ratio, Y symbolizing income and P being gross profits, we have equation (3.5a):

$$\sigma = \frac{s_p P + s_w(Y - P)}{K} = [s_w + (s_p - s_w)m]u/v \qquad (3.5a)$$

The most common investment function used in the empirical literature, and the one we will adopt in this part of the chapter, is equation (3.6c), a linearized version of the formula proposed by Bhaduri and Marglin (1990). Repeating it here for convenience:

$$g^i = \gamma + \gamma_u u + \gamma_m m \qquad (3.6c)$$

In this formulation, γ represents autonomous investment, due perhaps to some assessed sales trend, or 'animal spirits'. Investment reacts to capacity pressures (measured by capacity utilization) and profitability. We need now to check the balance of payments, for which we adopt a very simple formulation, in which the balance of trade (the only element included in this model) depends positively upon the real exchange rate (as a measure of competitiveness) and negatively on capacity utilization (representing demand). The real exchange rate, in turn, also depends on distributive variables, which are captured here by the profit share. We have thus equation (3.11):

$$b = NX/K = \psi e_r(m) - \phi u, \ \psi \text{ and } \phi > 0 \qquad (3.11)$$

Keynesian stability conditions require that savings react more strongly to variations in demand (represented by capacity utilization) than investment and net exports, combined. Otherwise, with investment reacting more strongly than savings to changes in demand, there would be a never-ending self-reinforcing expansion or depression, with no possibility of achieving a macro equilibrium. Ruling out issues with Harrodian stability, for the model to be stable the parameters must fulfil the following inequality:

$$[s_w + (s_p - s_w)m]1/v - \gamma_u + \phi > 0$$

The equilibrium values of capacity utilization and accumulation rate, in turn, are:

$$u^* = \frac{\gamma + g_m m + \psi e_r(m)}{[s_w + (s_p - s_w)m]\dfrac{1}{v} - g_u + \phi} \tag{3.12}$$

$$g^* = \gamma + \frac{\beta[\gamma + g_m m + \psi e_r(m)]}{[s_w + (s_p - s_w)m]\dfrac{1}{v} - g_u + \phi} + g_m m \tag{3.13}$$

This study tries to analyse the effect of income distribution on economic growth. The independent variable in this model is m, and the impact of a change in it on the equilibrium levels of utilization and growth are:

$$\frac{\partial u^*}{\partial m} = \frac{g_m - (s_p - s_w)\dfrac{u}{v} + \psi\dfrac{\partial e_r}{\partial m}}{[s_w + (s_p - s_w)m]\dfrac{1}{v} - g_u + \phi} \tag{3.14}$$

$$\frac{\partial g^*}{\partial m} = \frac{g_m\left(\dfrac{s_w}{v} + \phi\right) + (s_p - s_w)\left(g_m\dfrac{m}{v} - g_u\dfrac{u}{v}\right) + g_m\psi\dfrac{\partial e_r}{\partial m}}{[s_w + (s_p - s_w)m]\dfrac{1}{v} - g_u + \phi} \tag{3.15}$$

Stability conditions require that the denominator be positive. The effects shown in equations (3.14) and (3.15) might go in one way or the other, depending on the sign of the numerator. Regarding the impact on capacity utilization, the increase in the profit share has a positive effect through its impact on investment (g_m), a negative impact through consumption ($(s_p - s_w)\frac{u}{v}$) and an undetermined effect on the balance of trade ($\psi\frac{\partial e_r}{\partial m}$). The latter depends on the source of change: it is assumed that lower wages favour net exports, while higher profit margins decrease them. The effect on accumulation is equally undetermined, and it crucially depends on the relative size of the coefficients g_m and g_u. It may well be possible that the sign of equation (3.14) be positive, while equation (3.15) is negative.

3.5.2 Endogenous Distribution

A different route was followed by Onaran and Stockhammer (2004, 2006). In their papers, Onaran and Stockhammer question the exogenous charac-

Table 3.4   List of equations of the Onaran and Stockhammer (2004, 2006) model

A. Investment	$g_t = a_0 + a_1 u_{t-1} + a_2 m_{t-1} + a_3 n x_t$
B. Capacity utilization	$u_t = b_1 g_t + b_2 m_t$
C. Profit share	$m_t = c_0 + c_1 u_t + c_2 L_{t-1}$
D. Net exports	$nx_t = d_1 u_t + d_2 m_t$
E. Employment	$L_t = e_0 + e_1 g_t + e_2 \Delta u + e_3 L_{t-1} + e_4 m_t + e_5 n x_t$

Source: Onaran and Stockhammer (2004).

ter of distribution, and argue instead in favour of a simultaneous approach to analysing these matters, where distribution, demand and capital accumulation are all endogenous variables and determine each other. In order to do so, they perform a Structural VAR approach (SVAR). However, they do not try a non-theoretical econometric model; quite the contrary. What characterizes the SVAR approach, that is, what gives it the character of 'structural', is that one can impose contemporaneous restrictions on the interaction of the variables and then execute hypothesis testing in order to corroborate or reject their empirical pertinence. These restrictions are based on a theoretical model, and in Onaran and Stockhammer's work, they serve the purpose of estimating many of the same hypotheses included in the work of Hein and Vogel. Onaran and Stockhammer emphasize that, even if one imposes contemporaneous restrictions on the behaviour of the variables, in the long run one can still observe, in this methodology, values opposed to the contemporaneous effects.

The restrictions imposed on the contemporaneous interactions of the variables represent the theoretical core of the model. A full list of these is presented in Table 3.4, but data characteristics and other econometric issues will not allow us to test them all, as will be explained in due course.

Equation A is similar to equation (3.6c), with lagged variables to reflect an accelerator process, and it includes net exports as an explanatory variable. The rationale of this specification, according to Onaran and Stockhammer, is to test the relevance of an export-oriented strategy for investment growth (in the 2006 article, they test this model for South Korea and Turkey). Accumulation, in turn, also affects capacity utilization, as well as the profit share, though in the latter case the sign of b_2 is a priori undetermined: if it is positive, one can say that the demand regime is profit led (a much simpler expression than the original denomination 'exhilarationist'): if it is negative, then one can characterize the system as wage led.

Even though it is not the objective of this chapter to explore in depth the determinants of income distribution, the SVAR approach forces us to

BOX 3.2   EMPIRICAL ESTIMATIONS OF KALECKIAN
          MODELS (AND TWO MORE)

Table 3.5 provides a survey of diverse studies that tested empirically one or another version of the Kaleckian models, with different econometric techniques and time spans. In the table we only distinguish whether they applied the single estimation method or the simultaneous equation approach (i.e. VAR or VEC models). This table is inspired by and based on Hein and Vogel (2008, pp. 488–489), but more recent studies have been added. In terms of countries analysed, the reader can find a summary in Appendix D of Onaran and Galanis (2012).

Results differ considerably across studies, depending on the specification of the regressions, the period under analysis, the frequency of the observations, and so on, though in general terms they found a majority of wage-led countries. Perhaps one exception is the USA, where most of the studies (though not all) found it to be profit led, but these studies did not include measures of consumer indebtedness, for example, that may blur the clear-cut picture between profit-financed investment and wages-financed consumption. The point made by Carvalho and Rezai (2015) mentioned above is also pertinent.

Onaran and Galanis (2012) adopt a somewhat novel approach, asking a novel question. They adopt the single equation methodology of Hein and Vogel (2008), but they also develop a 'global multiplier', which takes account of a point usually forgotten in the austerity recipe aiming at 'gaining competitiveness' for countries in crisis (and one can safely say that there are many in that situation nowadays): that if all (or many) countries lower their wages at the same time, even though some might react positively by themselves, that effect is nullified by the aggregate impact of global austerity. That result holds for the Euro Area and for 15 out of 20 members of the G20. As they put it:

> the most novel finding of this paper is that even if there are some countries, which are profit led, the global economy is wage led. Thus, a simultaneous wage cut in a highly integrated global economy leaves most countries with only the negative domestic demand effects, and the global economy contracts. Furthermore some profit-led countries contract when they decrease their wage-share, if a similar strategy is implemented by their trading partners. (Onaran and Galanis 2012, p. 42)

The reader may ask whether only Kaleckian models have found this inverse relation between income inequality and economic growth. The answer is no, and we want to emphasize two recent studies by international organizations, the IMF and the OECD, that stand in contradiction to the economic policies recommended by such institutions. Ostry, Berg and Tsangarides (2014) show not only that lower income inequality is associated with more sustained and faster growth rates, but also that *redistributive policies* do not have a significantly detrimental impact on economic performance. Similar conclusions were obtained in another IMF paper by Dabla-Norris et al. (2015). Pursuing more egalitarian economic policies seems a win–win objective.

Cingano (2014), in turn, finds that increased inequality has a detrimental impact on future growth rates, analysing OECD countries since the mid-1980s. The explanation he draws falls in line with the above-mentioned work by Galor and Zeira (1993), by stressing the negative impact that both relative and absolute income inequality have on skills acquisition and 'human capital development'.

Table 3.5 Survey of empirical applications of the Kaleckian growth model

Author	Countries	Econometric method	Closed economy	Open economy
Bowles and Boyer (1995)	France, Ger., Japan, UK and USA	Single equation	All wage led	France, Ger., Japan: wage led; UK and USA: profit led
Gordon (1995)	USA	Single equation	Profit led	Profit led
Onaran and Stockhammer (2004)	France, UK and USA	SVAR	Not estimated	Not significant
Onaran and Stockhammer (2006)	Turkey and South Korea	SVAR	Not estimated	Wage led, Turkey in short term, South Korea in long term
Naastepad (2006)	Netherlands	Single equation	Wage led	Wage led (but only marginally)
Naastepad and Storm (2006)	France, Ger., Italy, Japan, NL, Spain, UK, USA	Single equation	France, Ger., Italy, Spain, NL, UK: wage led; Japan, USA: profit led	France, Ger., Italy, Spain, NL, UK: wage led; Japan, USA: profit led
Ederer and Stockhammer (2008)	Austria	Single equation	Wage led	Wage led in 1960, profit led in 2005
Hein and Vogel (2008)	Austria, France, Ger., NL, UK and USA	Single equation	Austria, France, Ger., UK and USA: wage led; NL: profit led	France, Ger., UK and USA: wage led; Austria and NL: profit led
Ederer, Onaran and Stockhammer (2009)	Euro Area	Single equation	Wage led	Wage led
Stockhammer and Stehrer (2011)	Australia, Can., Ger., Finland, Fr., Ireland, Japan, Lux., NL, Sweden, UK and USA	Single equation	Ger., Fin., France, Irl., Lux., NL, Sweden: wage led; Australia, UK: profit led; Japan, USA: not significant	
López G. (2012a)	France, Ger., Japan, Spain, UK and USA	VEC	Not estimated	France, Germany, Japan, Spain, UK and USA: wage led
López G. (2012b)	Mexico	VEC	Not estimated	Wage led

Source: Author's elaboration based on Hein and Vogel (2008, pp. 488–489).

take a look at them, and the variables we have chosen do not seem unreasonable. In equation C, higher capacity utilization is assumed to impact positively, and the employment level in a negative way, due to increased bargaining power of workers. The equation for net exports is a standard one, in which they are explained by capacity utilization (a higher level may imply higher imports) and the profit share, in order to reflect the competitiveness of the economy, so that one expects in principle that d_2 be positive. In case it is not, or if it turns out to be not significant, there are grounds to sustain that devaluations and income transfers that devaluations carry along with them are not sufficient (or must be exceedingly large) to impact positively the trade balance.

Equation E, finally, explains the movement in employment, and uses as explanatory factors the lagged values of that variable (in order to reflect an hysteresis process), accumulation, change in capacity utilization, and two variables that might capture the effects of an export-oriented development strategy: the profit share and net exports. The former also pretends to represent the neoclassical hypothesis according to which a regressive income distribution is a requisite for stimulating employment.

3.6   SOME ARGENTINEAN HISTORY

Besides being the country of origin of this author, Argentina seems both an exciting and challenging country to study from an empirical perspective, due to the dramatic and sudden changes experienced in the post-war era, the period of time under investigation in this chapter. In the first decades of the post-war period, a development strategy based on the expansion of the manufacturing sector coexisted with higher labour shares (though not at the same level as in industrialized economies). But starting from 1976, with the last military dictatorship, there began a complete turn in economic orientation, with a deindustrialization process which went hand in hand with regressive developments in income distribution. Just to show an example, Figures 3.5 and 3.6 show the growth rate and the profit share from 1950 to 2006. The reader may rest assured that this is not the electrocardiogram of any person nor the result of some lie detector or the register of seismic movements in a fault line, or at least it has not been copied from there.

While there were some periods of relative stability in the economic front (particularly the years between 1964 and 1974), starting in 1976 one can observe a widening of the business cycle and an acceleration in its frequency, reflecting a violent increase in macroeconomic volatility. Before that year, the average rate of growth was 3.48 per cent (1950–1975), while

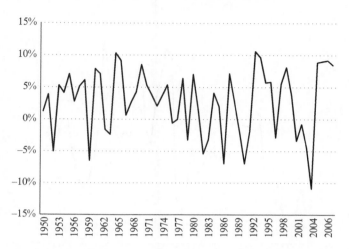

Source: Coremberg et al. (2007) for 1950–1992; Dirección Nacional de Cuentas Nacionales for 1993–2006.

Figure 3.5   *Growth rate in Argentina*

between 1976 and 2001 (the last year of the currency board) the average was 1.50 per cent, but the standard deviation of the growth rate increased 50 per cent in the last period.

When we look at (functional) distribution, 1976 is also a striking year. During the early Peronist years (1950–1955) the profit share fluctuated between 52 and 56 per cent (in the year after a disastrous harvest). It took 19 years, until the next Peronist government (Perón's third and last term, followed by his wife and vice-president for almost two years before the 1976 coup) to reach that level again. And in 1976, everything blew up. The profit share increased from 54 to 71 per cent in one year, a rate of increase of 30 per cent. After that, it remained above 60 per cent, in spite of some fluctuations, for the whole period except the early years of the currency board period (starting in 1991, which stopped a couple of hyperinflationary episodes). In 2002, when Argentina abandoned the currency board and the peg to the dollar, it jumped again above 70 per cent, and then started to decline.

The early Peronist government gave impulse simultaneously to a redistribution of income in favour of workers and an industrialization process (Gerchunoff and Llach 2000, pp. 181–187; Basualdo 2006, pp. 34–37). In its last years, inflation started to pick up, and the diagnosis differed according to the interpretation. The official line, in accordance with the

Source: Graña and Kennedy (2008).

Figure 3.6   Profit share in Argentina

guidance of the IMF, was that there was an excess demand that required tight monetary and fiscal policies coupled with a devaluation to improve the trade balance (Basualdo 2006, p. 56). These policies were directly aimed at lowering the real wage and domestic demand. We can see then, that from early on a more equal distribution of income (that never got even close to the values of developed countries in terms of its progressiveness) was seen as an obstacle to the economic development of the country.

These 'stabilization' programmes were adopted from time to time, for example during the Frondizi presidency between 1958 and 1962, and in the government of Maria Estela Martínez de Perón, Perón's widow and president between 1974 and March 1976. In between, some governments allowed for higher real wages either directly or by compensating negative impacts of devaluations on food prices, for instance.

The major shift in income distribution brought about by the military dictatorship established in 1976 took place through political repression, trade and financial openness, exchange rate policies, deindustrialization, and so on (Canitrot 1981; Feldman and Sommer 1986; Basualdo 2006, Chapter 3). Many of these economic policies (in particular, trade and financial openness), and others such as the privatization of vast parts of the productive structure, continued until 2001.[4]

This profit-led strategy was maintained for a period of 25 years. Was it effective in fostering economic growth? Is a more unequal income distribution a requirement for achieving and sustaining higher investment rates for longer periods? I am certainly not the first person to try to answer these questions. Argentinean economists have long been interested in the effects of income distribution on economic activity, though only recently have there appeared studies that deal with this question in a more formal econometric manner, in particular Lanata Briones and Lo Vuolo (2008, 2011). Lavagna (1978a, 1978b) and Lindenboim, Kennedy and Graña (2005, 2006, 2011), in turn, find a constant (on average) investment rate (but not stable), for long periods of time, amid substantial shifts in the wage–profit income distribution, in different macroeconomic settings.

Panigo et al. (2007) have found a significant and positive influence of the wage share on private investment for the period 1970–2005, though in a larger macroeconometric model published by the Ministry of Economy and Production (in which Panigo also took part (Panigo et al. 2009)), they found that both capacity utilization and the *profit* share were significant and positive explanatory variables of private investment for the period 1970–2007. Lanata Briones and Lo Vuolo (2008, 2011) find that the Argentinean economy had between 1960 and 2008 a wage-led demand regime, but its characteristics were not homogeneous during the period. In the first period, which goes from 1960 to 1981, the wage share drives private consumption and it created an important accelerator effect driving as well investment. For the second period, the results also indicate a wage-led demand regime, but with much more nuanced characteristics, up to the point that one could say they are not significant. There occurred a change of regime, based on the openness of the capital account and the deregulation of the financial sector, which led Basualdo (2006) to affirm that financial valorization took over as the main profit source mechanism. Cibils and Allami (2008) reach similar conclusions regarding the period 1990–2007. Finally, Onaran and Galanis (2012) found that, domestically speaking (i.e. looking only at consumption and private investment), Argentina was a wage-led economy for the period 1970–2007, but the positive impact of an increase in the wage share on net exports was of a magnitude sufficient to turn the country into a profit-led economy. However, they do mention (as we did earlier) that if we include the effect of a simultaneous global contraction, the economy recovers its wage-led characteristics, and the same holds if only its trading partners (and not the whole world) follow the same path. What results do we get?

3.7   EMPIRICAL ESTIMATION

The data were taken from different sources and we did take care in ensuring their consistency. Data on GDP, private consumption and private investment were taken from Coremberg et al. (2007) and the National Direction of National Accounts; the data on the trade balance were obtained from Ferreres (2005) and the same National Direction; while the data on wage and profit shares, as well as employment, were taken from Graña and Kennedy (2008). Finally, data regarding the evolution of world demand were taken from the Conference Board Total Economy Database.

Whichever methodology we use, we must first see if there is evidence of unit roots in the variables, that is, if the variables to be used are integrated. And indeed they are, at least most of them. However, they do not have the same order of integration. For instance, the logarithm of employment has one unit root (it is $I(1)$), but the level of employment has two unit roots. The profit share does not show evidence of a unit root, but real gross profits do, as well as real labour compensation. The balance of trade does not have a unit root at first glance, but when we look more closely it actually has one, for the period 1982–2006, but not for 1950–1981.

If all variables had the same order of integration, we should be searching for the presence of cointegration between them. If we found such a relation, a term must be included in order to avoid omitting relevant variables (that relationship, in this case). That term is called the error correction term. Since the variables to be used in the VAR do not have the same order of integration, we do not have to bother with that problem, but some equations of the components of GDP do have the same order and we will approach them carefully. Let's start with them.

3.7.1   The Model of Hein and Vogel

The proxies to measure distribution used in different specifications change in different equations according to different authors, as shown in Table 3.2. Hein and Vogel (2008) use for the consumption function both compensation of real employees and gross operating surplus, adjusted for the compensation of the self-employed. Onaran and Galanis (2012) adopt a similar specification, and we will follow their lead. However, our data have some differences from them, in particular for the period 1993–2005 in which they adjust real gross profits for the compensation of the self-employed. However, when it comes to the investment function and net exports, most studies tend to use the profit share.

3.7.1.1 Private consumption

Following Hein and Vogel (2008) and Onaran and Galanis (2012), the effect of a change in distribution on aggregate consumption was estimated according to the following equation:

$$C = f(W, \Pi) \qquad (3.16)$$

where C is private consumption, W is real labour compensation and Π is real gross profit. The (logs of the) three variables were found to be $I(1)$, and we could not reject the existence of a long-run relationship between them, so we estimated an Error Correction Model with the following specification:

$$d[\log(C_t)] = c + \beta_1 d[\log(W)_t] + \beta_2 d[\log(\Pi_t)] + \beta_3 d[\log(W_{t-1})]$$

$$+ \beta_4 d[\log(\Pi_{t-1})] + \beta_5 d[\log(C_{t-1})] \qquad (3.17)$$

In order to obtain the long-run elasticities of consumption with respect to real wage compensation and real profits, we have to divide the coefficients β_1 and β_2 by one minus the coefficient of the lagged dependent variable, β_5.

The results show that real wage compensation was a significant explanatory variable of private consumption at a 95 per cent level of confidence, but that was not the case for real gross profits. Even more, the coefficient β_2 was very small and negative, though the short-run impact was positive (but equally insignificant). The Wald test showed that the coefficients were jointly significant, with an adjusted R^2 of 0.2776. A dummy variable for the year 1993 had to be included in order to control for the normal distribution of errors. Table 3.6 summarizes the findings.

In order to calculate the direct partial effects of changes in distribution on consumption, coefficients β_1 and β_2 were divided by one minus β_5 in order to get the long-run elasticity of consumption with respects to profits and wages. After that, the direct partial effects of changes in the wage share were calculated in the same way as Hein and Vogel (2008) and Onaran and Galanis (2012), according to the following condition:

$$\frac{\frac{\partial C}{Y}}{\partial m} = \beta_2 \left(\frac{C}{\Pi} \right) - \beta_1 \left(\frac{C}{W} \right)$$

With the above-mentioned adjustments, β_2 is worth -0.00933, while β_1 is worth 0.115032. For the terms in parentheses, we used the average value of each ratio during the period, which was 1.289 in the case of $\frac{C}{\Pi}$ and 1.939

Table 3.6   Results of the consumption function estimation

Parameter	Coefficient	t statistic	Probability
c	0.014485*	1.930572	0.0595
β_1	0.105177**	2.013342	0.0497
β_2	−0.008530	−0.161158	0.8726
β_3	0.065466	1.523126	0.1343
β_4	0.032052	0.531002	0.5979
β_5	0.085675	1.290225	0.2032
R^2	0.350979		
$R^2_{adjusted}$	0.269852		
F		4.326262	0.00145
DW		2.03032	

Note: * significant at 90% confidence; ** significant at 95% confidence.

Source: Author's calculations.

in the case of $\frac{C}{W}$. Based on these data, *a 1 per cent increase in the profit share would lower GDP, considering only its impact on consumption, by 0.23508 per cent.*

3.7.1.2   Private investment

Which specification would be suitable to analyse the impact of the profit share on private investment? Hein and Vogel (2008) relate the change in investment with the previous *level* of the profit share and the previous logarithm of GDP, as a measure of capacity utilization. Onaran and Galanis use the contemporaneous logarithm of the profit share and GDP. In both cases, though, they use an Error Correction Model. In that way, Onaran and Galanis for instance incorporate contemporaneous and previous effects of GDP and profit share on investment.

   Given the fact that both investment and GDP are $I(1)$, in our formulation, changes in investment are related to (contemporaneous and past) changes in the profit share, and to contemporaneous and past changes in GDP. The logic is that changes in GDP *accelerate* (or deter) investment. This is not the accelerator principle per se (since it relates the *level* of investment to the *change* in GDP), but it comes close. One can assume that there is a necessary level of investment in order to cover for depreciation of the capital stock, and that investment above that level is stimulated by how fast the economy is growing. The contemporaneous and lagged effect of the profit share is included to reflect the Keynesian idea that expectations are formed on the basis of today's circumstances, if there are no reasons

Table 3.7   Results of the investment function estimation

Variable	Coefficient	t statistic	Probability
c	0.140563	0.567686	0.5729
α_1	2.5320720***	8.357637	0.0000
α_2	−0.314988	−0.878394	0.3841
α_3	0.057361	0.182769	0.8557
α_4	0.375582*	1.746825	0.0871
α_5	−0.016998	−0.720802	0.4745
R^2	0.709715		
$R^2_{adjusted}$	0.673429		
F		19.55912	0.0000
DW		1.866924	

Note: * significant at 90% confidence; *** significant at 99% confidence.

Source: Author's calculations.

to expect a change, and to allow previous profitability expectations to materialize in the investment decisions of firms. The specification of the investment function is as follows:

$$d[\log(I_t)] = c + \alpha_1 d[\log(GDP_t)] + \alpha_2 d[\log(m_t)] + \alpha_3 d[\log(GDP_{t-1})]$$

$$+ \alpha_4 d[\log(m_{t-1})] + \alpha_5 d[\log(I_{t-1})] \tag{3.18}$$

In this case, α_2 does *not* represent the long-run elasticity of investment with respect to the profit share, because the profit share is not an integrated variable. The total impact of the profit share is given by the sums of α_2 and α_4, divided by one minus the coefficient of the lagged endogenous variable, α_5. But first, Table 3.7 shows the results of the regression, which was jointly significant, with a high R^2. A dummy variable for the year 1991 was used in order to control the normality of errors.

As expected, GDP has a significant long-run relationship with investment, but the impact of the profit share is more nuanced. Only past changes in the profit share seem to have a significant impact (at a 90 per cent level of confidence) on investment. More recent changes actually impact negatively, according to the sign of α_2, though it is not a significant coefficient, and smaller in value than α_4. Remembering that we have to correct for the value of the lagged endogenous variable, the direct partial effect on investment is given, then, by:

$$\frac{\partial \frac{I}{Y}}{\partial m} = \frac{\alpha_2 + \alpha_4\left(\frac{I}{Y}\right)}{1 - \alpha_5}$$

The average value of the ratio $(\frac{I}{Y})$ during the period was 0.154171. The ratio of the coefficients is 0.059581. Therefore, the impact on GDP through higher investment would be 0.009186 per cent.

3.7.1.3 Trade balance

In the presentation of the model we mentioned that, theoretically speaking, the effect of a higher profit share on net exports was in principle ambiguous, since both a higher profit margin and a higher nominal wage impact negatively on the real exchange rate. However, changes in the nominal exchange rate cause an improvement in the profit share and also in international competitiveness. In this case, the profit share would affect positively the trade performance. Domestic demand is expected to have a negative influence on net exports, and world economic activity is expected to have a positive effect.

As we have mentioned, the behaviour of net exports varies according to the period we select, since starting in 1982 we can identify the presence of a unit root. Therefore, we will run two regressions, one for 1950–1981 and the other for 1982–2006. For the first, we use the following specification, including a term to correct for autocorrelation in the first period:

$$\frac{NX_t}{GDP} = c + \varepsilon_1 d[\log(GDP_t)] + \varepsilon_2[\log(GDP_t^f)] + \varepsilon_3 m_t + \varepsilon_4 AR(1) \quad (3.19)$$

For the second period we follow Hein and Vogel (2008, p. 499) and include the lagged values of net exports and the profit share:

$$\frac{NX_t}{GDP_t} = c + \gamma_1 d[\log(GDP_t)] + \gamma_2[\log(GDP_t^f)] + \gamma_3 m_t + \gamma_4 m_{t-1}$$

$$+ \gamma_5 \frac{NX_{t-1}}{GDP_{t-1}} \quad (3.19')$$

Why have we found a change in 1982? One reasonable explanation is that it was only with the debt crisis in the early 1980s that the new character of the foreign constraint became binding. The current account was no longer the dynamic and autonomous factor of the balance of payments; it was rather the capital and the financial account.

The results are shown in Tables 3.8–3.10.

Table 3.8   *Results of the trade balance function estimation 1950–1981*

Variable	Coefficient	t statistic	Probability
c	−0.0540703**	−2.392924	0.0245
ε_1	−0.031147	−1.037436	0.3095
ε_2	0.116603	0.885204	0.3845
ε_3	0.000686**	2.063790	0.0496
ε_4	0.540703***	3.125719	0.0045
R^2	0.414841		
$R^2_{adjusted}$	0.321215		
F		4.43085	0.007626
DW		1.639746	

Note: ** significant at 95% confidence; *** significant at 99% confidence.

Source: Author's calculations.

Table 3.9   *Results of the trade balance function estimation 1950–1976*

Variable	Coefficient	t statistic	Probability
c	−0.033014	−1.468786	0.1574
ε_1	−0.027767	−0.74540	0.4647
ε_2	0.025185	0.224809	0.8244
ε_3	0.000569	1.28270	0.2143
ε_4	0.459642*	1.94089	0.0665
R^2	0.275489		
$R^2_{adjusted}$	0.130586		
F		1.901203	0.14964
DW		1.915557	

Note: * significant at 90% confidence.

Source: Author's calculations.

It seems that during the first period the profit share was a (positive) significant influence on the balance of trade. The coefficient of the GDP has the expected sign, but it is strangely not significant.

However, these results should not be taken at face value, since we detected a structural break in the regression in 1976 (the Chow test gives a probability of 0.00031, and no breaks were detected in 1964), so if we run again the regression for the period 1950–1976, the profit share is no longer

Table 3.10   Results of the trade balance function estimation 1982–2006

Variable	Coefficient	t statistic	Probability
c	−0.064417*	−1.983845	0.0627
γ_1	−0.278540***	−6.699556	0.0000
γ_2	−0.029837	−0.126280	0.9009
γ_3	0.001049	0.939697	0.3598
γ_4	0.000147	0.208151	0.8374
γ_5	0.806507***	12.38438	0.0000
R^2	0.918982		
$R^2_{adjusted}$	0.896477		
F		40.83451	0.0000
DW		2.104011	

Note: * significant at 90% confidence; *** significant at 99% confidence.

Source: Author's calculations.

a significant variable, and the results are much less robust. The equation itself is not significant. These results are shown in Table 3.9, and will be the ones considered for the total estimation, with the above-mentioned caveat.

As for the second period, the profit share is not significant and the impact is also much reduced. The GDP is the most relevant variable, with the expected sign. We could not corroborate cointegration relationships and we did not find structural breaks in the expected years (1989 and 1992; there were too few observations to test for a break in 2002). However, the regression has a strangely high R^2.

Without forgetting the low significance level of the variable that interests us, we can point out that, on average, *during the period 1950–1976 the increase in the GDP (through an improved trade balance) given a 1 per cent increase in the profit share would have been only 0.000569 per cent.*

For the second stretch of years analysed, we have to adjust the impact of the profit share (given by γ_3 and γ_4) by one minus the value of the endogenous variable. *The effect increases substantially but is still small, around 0.006181 per cent of GDP.* Even though the results showed the expected signs, we do not have evidence to sustain that a regressive income distribution (a restraint on labour costs) had been a requirement to improve the export position in an economically significant way.

3.7.1.4   Summing up

To conclude the testing of the Hein and Vogel model, let's sum up our findings: *an increase of 1 per cent in the profit share would reduce GDP*

0.23508 per cent through its impact on consumption; would increase GDP 0.009186 per cent through its impact on investment; and would increase it again 0.006181 per cent (using the most recent values) through its impact on net exports. In total, it would have a negative impact of 0.219713 per cent of GDP.
We now turn to perform the Structural VAR.

3.7.2 The Model of Onaran and Stockhammer

Given the aforementioned characteristics of the data about the trade balance, we refrain from including it in the VAR, so we are left with a system of four variables: investment, GDP, profit share and employment. The first two variables and employment are estimated in logarithms, which are all $I(1)$, while the profit share is stationary. We worked with the first difference in the integrated variables, and left the profit share untouched. The tests performed in order to choose the number of lags to be used concluded that one lag was enough. We will estimate equation (3.20):

$$Bx_t = \Gamma_0 + \Gamma_1 x_{t-1} + \in_t \tag{3.20}$$

Matrix B captures the contemporaneous effect of interactions between the variables, but is not estimable in a straight way, since restriction must be imposed on its parameters. In other words, we must assume that several elements of that matrix are equal to zero, so that it can be identifiable. According to the manual of the software we used, Eviews (Quantitative Micro Software 2004, p. 721), we cannot put restrictions on the elements of the diagonal of B, that is, we cannot assume they are equal to one. The contemporaneous effects we chose to test are represented in the following matrix:

$$B = \begin{bmatrix} b_{11} & b_{12} & b_{13} & 0 \\ 0 & b_{22} & b_{23} & 0 \\ 0 & 0 & b_{33} & 0 \\ 0 & b_{42} & b_{43} & b_{44} \end{bmatrix}$$

This matrix regulates the contemporaneous effects, but there are no restrictions on the long-term behaviour, so that we could observe behaviour opposed to that postulated. The expected signs of the coefficients outside the diagonal are:

- $b_{12} > 0$, representing an accelerator effect;
- $b_{13} > 0$, representing the impact of profit over investment (if negative, it would imply that investment and profit share are inversely related, adding strength to the wage-led hypothesis);

Inequality, growth and 'hot' money

- b_{23}, ambiguous, if negative, it implies a wage-led demand regime; if positive, a profit-led regime;
- $b_{42} > 0$, this hypothesis implies that the labour market is ruled by what happens in the goods market. If not, labour market (de)regulation would be more relevant as a determinant of the employment level. The former view is in agreement with Panigo, Toledo and Agis (2008), the latter with Gasparini (2005);
- $b_{43} > 0$, to test for the neoclassical hypothesis about the labour market, in the sense that a greater profit share is a stimulus for increasing employment.

The procedure is as follows: first we estimate a standard VAR, obtaining residuals and coefficients on the lagged variables. These residuals are used to estimate the coefficients of matrix B. Both groups of coefficients are used, later, to calculate the impulse–response functions of the system to external shocks. We have estimated the VAR with a constant term, to capture long-term effects. Since some of the variables are in difference we present the results of the contemporaneous effects according to the sign and the significance of the coefficients (Table 3.11).

The results are significant. Almost all coefficients have the expected sign, except for b_{43}, though it is the least significant of all the coefficients.

Figure 3.7 shows the simulations based on the impulse–response functions, and Table 3.12 sums up the results of the hypotheses.

Table 3.11   Results of the SVAR estimation

Coefficient	Sign	Probability
b_{12}	+	0.0000
b_{13}	−	0.0010
b_{23}	−	0.0016
b_{42}	+	0.0000
b_{43}	−	0.0919
Log likelihood	130.0860	
Test LR of overidentification: Chi square (1)	0.024047	0.8768

Source: Author's calculations.

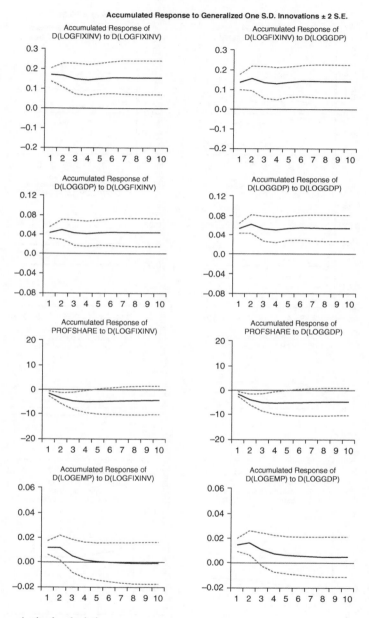

Source: Author's calculations.

Figure 3.7 Impulse–response function

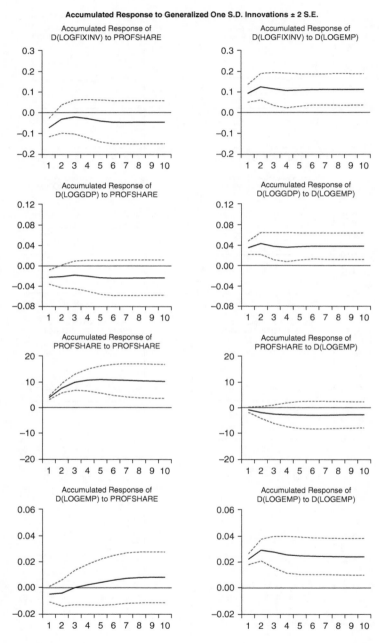

Figure 3.7   (continued)

Table 3.12   Hypotheses tests

Hypothesis	Results
$\frac{\partial L}{\partial g}$	Positive and significant in the short run, insignificant in the long run
$\frac{\partial L}{\partial u}$	Positive and significant in the short run, insignificant in the long run
$\frac{\partial g}{\partial m}$	Negative and significant in the short run, not significant in the long run
$\frac{\partial u}{\partial m}$	Negative and significant in the short run, not significant in the long run
$\frac{\partial m}{\partial L}$	Negative in the short and long run, though not significant
$\frac{\partial L}{\partial m}$	Negative in the short run and positive in the long run, though not significant

Source: Author's calculations.

3.8   A RELEVANT CONTRIBUTION AND A WAY FORWARD

In this chapter, we presented the Kaleckian model of growth, highlighting as its main contribution the rejection of a necessary negative relation between the real wage and economic growth, and actually the likelihood of *positive* relations between the two, seen from a demand-side perspective. We explained some criticisms that this type of model aroused, some lines of defence and reviewed some extensions that allowed us to tackle a multitude of real world events and features, beyond the basic version presented initially.

We also surveyed a number of empirical estimations of different versions of Kaleckian models, and performed our own attempt to show the reader the feasibility and the relevance of this line of literature in order to increase our understanding of developed and developing economies alike. Our results for Argentina contradict, for instance, the dominant view according to which it is through real wage and wage share repression that the economy will find a path of sustainable and equitable growth, and a number of studies reinforce this claim for other countries as well. Quite the contrary, it looks like more progressive regimes of income distribution are a necessity when we aim to achieve long-run stable economic growth. The main message of Kaleckian models does not lack empirical support.

However, there are still areas to be included and analysed in the Kaleckian literature. As an example, in our research the change in the behaviour of the balance of trade in Argentina around 1976 supports the view that in the last three decades covered in this study the balance of trade might have reduced its relevance as a binding factor of short-term growth. This might at first glance appear in contradiction with a major strand of the literature, the balance of payments-constrained approach, developed initially by Thirlwall (1979). These types of models (a thorough review is given in McCombie and Thirlwall 2004) posit that the balance of payments is the main constraint to economic growth. These demand-led growth models are quite diverse in the subjects with which they deal, from financial flows to debt sustainability to foreign aid. However, an implicit assumption in the way they are presented is the existence of the relative version of the Purchasing Power Parity. In this model, the real exchange rate is basically fixed and prices do not affect trade performance. But if we relax that assumption, then we have to integrate the effects of changes in income distribution into those models, and that is exactly what Blecker (1999) did. By doing so, Blecker cleared the way to cover what is one of the main neglected issues in Kaleckian growth models: the omission of foreign debt.

We mentioned some works by Kaleckian economists that touch upon the topic. A name that comes to mind quickly is Bhaduri (2004), who emphasizes the danger associated with capital inflows (and the corresponding debt creation) not associated with a rise in investment and consumption, since these inflows might be just feeding financial bubbles. However, he does not go too deeply into an analysis of the interaction between financial flows, investment and distribution. La Marca (2005, 2010) develops Kaleckian models of growth and distribution, adding an analysis of the conditions for the sustainability of the current account. But the current account imbalances (driven by or reflected in capital inflows/outflows) can have important effects before they are corrected, if they are corrected at all.

The results regarding the change in the binding relevance of the trade balance in the late 1970s and early 1980s are not limited to Argentina. The global simultaneity and the timing of changes coincident with a tendency towards a change in the regulation of financial markets and a push for loosening capital controls indicate that the explosion of financial flows around the globe might be a force to reckon with. We hope it is clear by now why we emphasize the Kaleckian framework to study the issue: it is a framework that rejects the negative association in the long run between real wage and investment, allowing for the possibility of a positive relation. And, having shown the importance that financial flows have had since the 1970s and the impact they have had in developing countries, the Kaleckian model provides us the flexibility to integrate this feature into a comprehensive economic model, able to deal with distribution, growth and foreign debt. That is what we will do in the next chapters.

NOTES

1. See Lee (1998), Downward and Reynolds (1996) and Downward and Lee (2001), among others. Another procedure, usually adopted, is a variant of normal prices or full-cost pricing, called target-return pricing. This implies a mark-up over total costs with the aim of achieving a profit rate for a standard level of CU. The mark-up is determined according to the investment and financing policies of the firm (see Harcourt 2006, Chapter 3; Lavoie 2014, Chapter 3). Therefore, and with u_s y r_s representing standard levels, the price function becomes:

$$p = \left(\frac{u_s + f}{u_s - r_s v}\right)\frac{w}{y_v} \qquad (3.3')$$

Putting this into (3.2) and solving for r, we have the following linear equation on u:

$$r = [(f + r_s v)u - (u_s - r_s v)f]/v(u_s + f) \qquad (3.4')$$

2. The condition is that $dS/dr > dI/dr$ evaluated on the *ED* curve. Below, we present some recent discussions about the stability of Kaleckian models.
3. Enders (2010) provides an easy introduction to the topic, while Greene (2011) and Juselius (2006) develop a more thorough explanation.
4. A study about market deregulation can be found in Azpiazu (1999), while Damill and Keifman (1992) analysed trade liberalization in the late 1980s and early 1990s.

4. An integration of the real and the monetary economy[1]

4.1 PUTTING TOGETHER DISTRIBUTION WITH MONEY FLOWS

The way we choose to begin the study of the effect and interaction between international financial flows, investment decisions, economic growth and income distribution is by adopting an approach in which 'you follow the money'. We integrate real and financial flows into a single comprehensive framework, a 'monetary theory of production', in terms of Keynes (1933), or a 'monetary analysis', in terms of Schumpeter (1954). Money, credit, debt, loans, assets are an integral part of the analysis and appear each step of the way. Firms have to recover their monetary expenses; households get paid in money and invest in money-denominated assets; producers are paid in money, money that comes from somewhere and goes somewhere else. Perhaps Marx (1867) was the first to actually develop a theory in which you follow the money, when he explained the 'commodity circulation' chain (in which a commodity is sold to buy other commodities) and the 'capitalist circulation' chain (in which money is employed to produce a good to be sold at a profit). Or perhaps it was Quesnay, with his Tableau Economique, which later inspired Marx himself to create the 'reproduction scheme', which tracks buys and sells between different sectors of the economy.

In that way, Marx developed a 'social accounting matrix' (SAM), in which one can see the flows that drive the economy. We plan to use a kind of SAM for our modelling purposes in this chapter, the 'Stock-Flow Consistent' (SFC) approach, and we will spend some time explaining what it is about, before we develop a two-country open economy SFC model, with households, firms, banks, governments, trade of goods and financial assets. Later on we will show the results of some simulations we performed with that model, drawing some conclusions which will help us in the later stage of this book when we try to estimate a Kaleckian model with foreign private debt for a couple of countries. But let's not skip stages.

4.2 ORIGINS, DEVELOPMENT AND THEMES REGARDING SFC MODELLING

Not all SAM models can be considered SFC models. They have been thoroughly used for planning purposes, in applied Computed General Equilibrium (CGE) models, which provide a complex description of the real economy and the interaction between different sectors, as the remarkable works of Pyatt and Round (1985) and Robinson (1989, 2006) show. However, their main weakness lies in the integration of the real with the financial economy, in which every real transaction has a financial counterpart. That requires at least a discussion of the financial structure of the economy.

Caverzasi and Godin (2013, p. 5) and Godley and Lavoie (2007a, p. 23) date the roots of SFC modelling to the work of Morris Copeland (1949), which was the basis for the Flow-of-Funds Account provided by the Federal Reserve ('Federal Reserve Bureau Z.1 Release'). Copeland's intention was to track the origin and destiny of money used in the purchase of national production. The tool can be called 'Luca Pacioli squared', in the sense that it relied not on double-entry bookkeeping (an invention more important for mankind than the wheel, according to Davidson (1982, p. 287)), but on quadruple-entry bookkeeping: to each transaction corresponds both a seller and a buyer, and also an asset and a liability, a key distinction that was not taken into account in the original presentations of the United Nations' System of National Accounts (1952).

Copeland's plea to integrate the financial and the real analysis fell on deaf ears in the mainstream. It was the work of a research project in Yale and a group of economists in Cambridge that responded to that call and developed a type of modelling that fulfils the following requirement according to Tobin (the leader of the Yale or 'pitfalls' approach): '(i) Precision regarding time . . . (ii) Tracking of stocks . . . (iii) Several assets and rates of return . . . (iv) Modelling of financial and monetary policy operations . . . (v) Walras's Law and adding-up constraints' (Tobin 1982, pp. 172–173).

These definitions make up the core of SFC modelling nowadays. The 'pitfalls approach' owes its name to Brainard and Tobin (1968). These models (one can include Tobin and Buiter (1976) and Backus et al. (1980)) present in different versions a detailed account of equilibrium wealth allocation and disequilibrium adjustments, after households have made their consumption decisions. Their important innovation is the integration of saving and portfolio decisions (Tobin 1982, p. 187). These are models of flows and stocks equilibrium, and can be seen as general SF equilibrium models (Dos Santos 2002, p. 64). However, production and financing decisions by firms are not explicitly included in these sorts of models, while the public sector deficit is exogenous, and those are omissions the other strand of pioneering SFC works delved into, without the assumption of intertemporal maximizing behaviour as in most CGE models, not to speak of the modern Dynamic Stochastic General Equilibrium (DSGE) framework.

The SFC approach is associated with the work of Wynne Godley and the Cambridge Economic Policy Group or 'New Cambridge School', in the late 1970s. Examples of this line of research are Cripps and Godley (1976) and Godley and Cripps (1978, 1983). Their work theorized directly over macroeconomic aggregates, usually conflating the private sector, splitting it from the government and the foreign sector, with the objective of deriving robust empirical regularities from the most aggregate possible level, and with fewer required behavioural hypotheses (Dos Santos 2002, pp. 71–72). This aggregative level led them to propose a stable private expenditure to wealth ratio, a stock-flow norm, which established an association between public deficit and foreign trade, the so-called 'twin deficits'. It is worth mentioning that in New Cambridge models the budget deficit is endogenous to the state of economic activity. They were also quite explicit in the financing role of banks. But they did not go into the portfolio allocation decisions, since, when you put together households, banks and firms, the only real debt is government debt. They also downplayed the role of monetary policy.

A natural progression is the development of the current Godley-type models, the modern version of stock-flow models, which conflates an analysis of income determination and production decisions with portfolio allocation. Seminal articles are Godley (1996, 1999a), while the major oeuvre is Godley and Lavoie (2007a). Why the emphasis on stocks and flows? Because this provides the dynamic link to integrate finance and the real economy as they evolve through time: a stock of wealth, capital and liabilities determines a flow of output, money, assets and liabilities given behavioural assumptions, affecting different prices (and therefore distribution), and ending up at the end of the period with another stock.

This requires a water-tight accounting, which Tobin interpreted as Walras's Law. It is not the case, however. Walras's Law states that excess demand across all markets must be equal to excess supply, and usually a price mechanism is inserted which assures a market clearing in those markets, in the Arrow–Debreu style. SFC models do not go so far, they just claim that there cannot be any black hole in the system-wide accounting. To better explain what they mean, we must first say that SFC models start by presenting the balance sheet of the economy, with one sector's liability being another sector's assets. The sole exception is usually the capital stock (and housing, in models that contemplate it). They proceed next by depicting the transaction and revaluation matrix that tracks all flows occurring in the economy during a certain period, as well as the capital gains due to asset price changes. The system-wide accounting implies that the accounts of the nth sector of the economy are completely determined by the accounts of the other $n - 1$ sectors.

This matrix also provides us with the 'sectoral budget constraints'. 'While consistency is required at the accounting level, it is also required at the behavioural level' (Godley and Lavoie 2007a, p. 14). These budget constraints are important in a number of senses, the most relevant here being that they remind us not only of things that cannot happen, but also of things that should not or are not likely to happen. In other words, they can help to identify unsustainable processes, deviations of long-term norms, leverage build-up, and so on.

The accounting is indispensable but not sufficient, obviously. Budget constraints are part of the equations, but not the only part. Behavioural relations are postulated as in any other model. That is why the SFC framework is called a 'methodology which will make it possible to start exploring rigorously how real economic systems, replete with realistic institutions, function as a whole' (Godley and Lavoie 2007a, p. 4). The behaviour of the sectors, institutions and actors involved is up to the modeller to describe, but there is something which is always present in SFC models, and which Godley emphasized consistently: the presence of buffers. Inventories, banking deposits, bank discounts, central bank advances, Treasury bills. I still do not think that this has anything to do with Walras's Law. For instance, what is an excess supply in the checking accounts 'market'? In the inventories market? Walras's Law is interwoven with the neoclassical visualization of markets, which requires a market-clearing price, with agents having initial endowments, with complete future markets (in the Arrow–Debreu version), and so on. SFC models do not share that approach.

How does one usually proceed with SFC models? After defining the level of aggregation, and the behavioural relations, the model is solved. As Caverzasi and Godin said (2013, pp. 8–9), SFC models can be solved analytically and numerically, and in this author's experience, both ways go hand in hand. The latter is achieved in a tiring but simple way: values of parameters and exogenous variables are calibrated, either through econometric studies, by empirical regularities or by steady-state requirements. However, there are some requirements that need to be fulfilled and that provide a guide to the calibration: in a steady state all flows and stocks grow at the same rate. This implies the existence of stock-flow norms which should be respected and which are of invaluable help in the calibration. Dos Santos and Zezza (2008) is an example of analytical solutions.

Kinsella, Godin and Tiou Tagba-Aliti (2012) and Kinsella and O'Shea (2010) develop algorithmic methods to solve SFC models, and different softwares provide other alternatives. In a different vein, Carrión Alvarez and Ehnts (2014) present a novel approach to SFC modelling using graph theory, which allows for the study of regime changes, for instance. They show the usefulness of that approach by casting model SIM (Godley and Lavoie 2007a, Chapter 3) in graph theory.

The level of aggregation in SFC models depends on the nature of the problem to be tackled. New Cambridge models, as we have said, aggregated households, banks and firms into one sector. In recent times, however, the level of sectoral differentiation tends to follow, at the most basic level, the institutional design of National Accounts, in which there are households, firms, banks and government (and a central bank, usually separated from the former). Beyond that point, the researcher can split households (Zezza (2008) between the top 5 and the bottom 95 per cent; or different households owning different assets; or different expectations about asset prices, as Lavoie and Daigle (2011)); firms (Kim (2006) splits a consumption good and a capital goods sector); Valdecantos (2012) develops a model with 'agricultural and non-agricultural' production plus a third one; Caiani, Godin and Lucarelli (2012) also use three sectors (more on that paper later); banks (Fontana and Godin (2013) model a commercial bank and two investment banks to analyse the impact of securitization); and the rest of the world (one, two or more countries).

It is true, though, that SFC models do not usually deal with microeconomic issues, and theorize about aggregates. Post-Keynesian approaches are not homogeneous in terms of their viewpoints regarding micro foundations, and a recent and thorough review of the topic, going well beyond the subject of this thesis, can be found in King (2012). However, this direct theorizing about macro aggregates reveals a conviction in the relevance of *emergent phenomena*, novel properties that arise when individual agents interact (Hodgson 2007, p. 220). As Lawson (2007, p. 257) puts it:

> A strata of reality can be said to be emergent, or as possessing emergent powers, if there is a sense in which it (1) has arisen out of a lower strata, being formed by principles operative at the lower level, and (2) remains dependent on the lower strata for its existence but (3) contains causal powers of its own which are both irreducible to those operating at the lower level and (perhaps) capable of acting back on the lower level.

The usual analogy one can resort to, is that when dealing with a health issue, one goes to a medical practitioner, not a biologist or a chemist, even though as living beings we are composed of elements and other forms of life which are the object of study of these specialists. It just so happens that

BOX 4.1   SHORT REVIEW OF THE SFC LITERATURE

The literature on SFC modelling is expanding at an exponential rate. The author has counted close to 100 papers that use SFC methodology, so there is no point in pretending to be exhaustive. Therefore, we have chosen to do a review of subjects tackled by SFC models, mentioning some relevant articles on the topic, some of the conclusions and the issues explored. The selection is admittedly arbitrary, and the reader can find another survey in Caverzasi and Godin (2013, pp. 16–27), though there will be some inevitable overlap with this review.

To start with, there are two very interesting articles by Godin, writing alone or as co-author, besides those we have already mentioned from this prolific author. In Godin (2012) he mixes employment policies such as Employment of Last Resort (ELR) (see Wray (1997, 2000) and Papadimitriou (2008) for an introduction to the subject) with savings in energy consumption. ELR is an employment programme which offers a job to anybody willing to take it at a certain wage, somewhat lower than that ruling in the market. When the jobs offered correspond to productive activity which reduces energy consumption, effective demand rises by effect of the ELR programme, but not only that, it also increases more in the consumption-goods sector, while diminishing the energy demand.

In Caiani, Godin and Lucarelli (2012), in turn, he models the introduction of an innovative sector financed with borrowing in a Schumpeterian fashion, and is able to reproduce the dynamics postulated by Schumpeter (1934), with an initial period of inflation and later disinflation (and deflation), and a displacement of all capital goods by new and more productive equipment, both in the capital-goods sector and in the consumption-goods sector.

Since almost by definition SFC integrates the real and the financial sides, it is no surprise that there are a myriad of models analysing different aspects of banking and financial markets. We will name just a few. Dafermos (2012) analyses different channels through which liquidity preference (by households, firms and banks) affects the real economy, according to different asset allocation, credit rationing and uncertainty. Le Heron (2009) analyses banking behaviour, adopting a Taylor Rule and a New Keynesian Phillips curve, and two government fiscal rules: one concerned with public expenditure and the other concerned with a balanced budget. It is shown that in the presence of more prudent and cautious bank lending in the context of increasing borrower and lender risk, a policy rule concerned with public expenditure acting as an automatic stabilizer actually fulfils its purpose, while a policy that aims at balancing the budget exerts a destabilizing impact on the economy. This result also holds in Le Heron (2012), were he models a generalized crisis in the state of confidence of banks, firms and households. Monetary policy has a limited stabilizing effect in a normal Taylor Rule, but even less when the central bank is only concerned with inflation and not with employment (or the output gap).

Lavoie (2008) provides a framework, built on the basis of Chapter 11 of Godley and Lavoie (2007a), to analyse the impact of different developments associated with the rise of 'financialization', defined as an 'increasing role of financial motives, financial markets, financial actors and financial institutions in the operation of the domestic and international economies' (Epstein 2005, p. 3). An intention of firms to finance investment through retained profits (achieved through an increased mark-up) instead of equity financing, leads the economy to an inflationary path, which causes losses to the holdings of financial assets of households, bringing down economic activity. Similar effects are achieved if firms decide to increase their dividend payments: there is a subsequent increase in inflation which reduces consumption out of wealth. Van Treeck (2009) goes further into the issue of share-holder value orientation, affirming that actually firms' investment decisions are tempered by dividends claim of shareholders. It takes into account rentiers' pro-pensity to consume and to borrow against financial wealth, so that, when dividend payments are increased for example, economic activity might experience some stimulus but at the expense of a more fragile financial system, because firms have a deteriorated balance sheet and rentiers are more indebted. Hein (2009) distin-guishes several 'growth regimes' according to the impact of higher rates of return demanded by shareholders, and whether they are transmitted into prices, and the response of investment to firms' own source of finance, among other motives. Other models that deal with financial fragility in an SFC framework are those of Dos Santos (2005), Kinsella (2011) and Passarella (2012), who also provides a survey of past literature.

Distributive conflict is modelled in Dallery and Van Treeck (2011). They model a firm and its stakeholders that may have different objectives, which may be mutu-ally incompatible (for instance, regarding accumulation and dividends policies between shareholders and managers, or regarding profits and wages between the two mentioned and workers), so that all objectives might not be realized even in a long-run equilibrium.

Dafermos and Papatheodorou (2011) present an SFC model to study the increase in inequality in both personal and functional income distribution observed since the 1970s, by distinguishing 'classes' within the household sector, such as supervisory workers (and unemployed), non-supervisory workers and capital owners. The model includes government transfers for the unemployed, but also rent payments for housing purposes on houses of different quality (high and low). Through simulations, they track how changes in functional distribution (a rise in wages of non-supervisory workers, for instance) and in rental variables (rent, interest rates) translate into changes in personal distribution, by developing ine-quality indexes. Zezza (2008) integrates distributive analysis with the develop-ment of the housing sector to model the trajectory of the US economy since the 1970s, by distinguishing between the top 5 and the bottom 95 per cent of house-holds in terms of income. This is another example of the flexibility in terms of sectoral aggregation that SFC models offer. Finally, Belabed, Theobald and Van Treeck (2013) develop a three-country SFC model to analyse the interaction between functional and personal income distribution, and current account imbalances.

The housing bubble in the US was related to the change in 'originate-to-distribute' in banking strategy and to securitization. Fontana and Godin (2013) include a commercial and two investment banks to analyse derivatives inflation and banking fragility, according to relative portfolio preference of banks and house-hold income distribution (the authors distinguish between workers and capitalists, that have claims on both types of banking). An expected increase in house prices, for instance, leads initially to a decrease in household leverage (since the value of their net worth increased) but later that fosters more borrowing. Eatwell, Mouakil and Taylor (2008) also depict, in an SFC model, mortgage-based securities (MBS) in the broader context of shadow banking to analyse the crisis of 2008. By comparing the results they get with stylized facts of that event, they reach the conclusion that the chain of events resembles more a story in which the leading factor was not the interaction of housing price expectation with household leverage, but with banking leverage. This is because higher housing prices, and higher securities prices, encourage banks to continue to extend mortgage lending and to produce more MBS in an 'inflating balloon', as the authors quote approvingly of Shin (2009). This has the important conclusion of putting the focus not on mortgage lending, but on the financial innovations associated with the development and exponential growth of MBS and generally asset-based securities markets since the 1990s. Pilkington (2008) develops an SFC framework to understand the interaction of shadow-banking institutions, outside the regulatory powers of the central bank, with the other sectors of the economy in order to clarify the potential (and actual) fragilities that might arise.

We mentioned Le Heron (2009) as a paper that compares the relative efficacy of monetary and fiscal policy as stabilizing forces. Models depicting the implications of different fiscal policy regimes are Godley and Lavoie (2007b), Martin (2008) and Ryoo and Skott (2013). The first two papers are quite similar, and extend the conditions under which the debt to GDP ratio is stable in the long run, even in the presence of a Non-Accelerating Inflation Rate of Unemployment (NAIRU). In this model 'fiscal policy is, in theory, capable of achieving full employment at some target inflation rate' (Godley and Lavoie 2007b, p.96). Ryoo and Skott (2013) present a more general paper in which capital accumulation is accounted for, and with different tax rates according to source of income (wage, corporate or property income), though they do not go into discussions of inflation. They still hold, though, that fiscal policy is a preferred instrument to achieve full-employment growth without exerting destabilizing influences on the dynamics of public debt, since it is (in a closed economy) a private sector asset which renders interest services and therefore can sustain demand (to some extent, think of pension funds).

Godley (1999c) set the benchmark in SFC models to analyse matters of open economies. The world comprises two countries that trade goods and financial assets (government bonds). Chapter 12 of Godley and Lavoie (2007a) extends this model to allow for flexible and fixed exchange rates, a simple version is in Godley and Lavoie (2005). The results question many established views regarding monetary policy in open economies, such as the Mundell–Fleming model. For instance, the so-called 'trilemma', which says that it is not possible to have stable (or fixed) exchange rates, control of the interest rate and free movements of capital, actually does not hold in theory. The key to understand this is to remember that, even when capital may flow freely between countries, assets are not perfect substitutes between each other, so that a country might be able to have a fixed exchange rate and still control its interest rate, as long as it has foreign reserves. It also posits that what is a violation of the 'rules of the game' in fixed exchange rate Mundell–Fleming models, that is, sterilization of foreign exchange purchases, is actually required for the central bank to keep the interest rate at the level of choice. Lavoie (2006a) develops an SFC model of a currency board, dwelling deeper on the subject. Finally, Lavoie and Daigle (2011) extend Chapter 12 of Godley and Lavoie (2007a), modelling exchange rate expectations according to the post-Keynesian literature. More will be said on that paper later in this chapter.

Regarding the treatment of open economy matters, there are three lines of research that we want to highlight here: models about Euroland; models about economic structure issues in an open economy; and models about the international financial system. On the Euroland case, Godley and Lavoie (2007c) develop a model of three countries, of which two have a fixed exchange rate regime, akin to the arrangements in the Eurozone. They point out the deflationary bias of the Eurozone arrangements that, in the case of substantive current account imbalance and with an unaccommodative behaviour of the central bank, the deficit country would be forced to adopt a restrictive fiscal policy, absent expansionary policies or resource transfers from the surplus country.

Lavoie and Zhao (2010), in turn, study what might be the effect of a diversification of China's foreign reserves, currently held mostly in US Treasury bonds. The model contains a fixed exchange rate (ER) (between China and the US) and two flexible ERs: Europe with China and with the US. If China chooses to build up reserves in Euro-denominated bonds instead of dollars (though unlikely nowadays, there was a debate about that topic years ago), the economic activity of the Eurozone might actually be hurt, since the euro would appreciate substantially against the two currencies. In a similar model, Mazier and Tiou-Tagba Aliti (2012) argue in favour of a more flexible exchange rate of the yuan in order to realign current account imbalances.

Regarding the issue of economic structure, Pérez Caldentey (2007) develops a model used to analyse the performance of the Caribbean economies. The conclusion reached is that if the fiscal stance (government expenditure divided by the marginal tax rate) is above the income elasticities ratio of exports and imports, the economy will certainly hit the foreign constraint, ending up in a balance of payments crisis due to an increased external debt. The result is similar to the balance of payment-constrained growth models of Thirlwall (see McCombie and Thirlwall (2004) for a collection of essays on the topic). The aforementioned work by Valdecantos (2012) aims to show the implications of such conditions in a model resembling the economic structure of Argentina, with an agricultural sector driven by supply constraints and in which prices are market clearing (in the real world, commodities prices are determined at world market level, so the assumption is not unreasonable). A recent paper by Michelena (2014) analyses the general reduction in import tariffs fostered by global organizations such as the World Trade Organization, and emphasizes the importance of the adaptation capability of the domestic economy in order to protect employment and, eventually, avoid balance of payments crises arising from sustained current account deficits. Finally, Valdecantos and Zezza (2012) develop alternative closures representing different alternatives of reform of the current international financial system, according to whether a greater preponderance is given to Special Drawing Rights (SDR) of the IMF in settling imbalances, or whether a reform akin to Keynes's original BANCOR Plan is adopted, which implies that no national money plays the role of international payment means. Their results show that in that setting more room is given to national governments to pursue expansionary domestic policies, while the BANCOR mechanism (that essentially penalizes creditor countries) prevents in fact the pursuit of export-led, or beggar-the-neighbour growth strategies.

As a last topic, we mention the important work developed by Wynne Godley at the Levy Institute, where he developed an SFC model of the US economy which led him to predict many features of what turned out to be the 2008 financial crisis, like Godley (1999b), Godley and Izurieta (2004) and Godley and Zezza (2006). The reader may also be interested in Kinsella and Tiou Tagba-Aliti (2012), who estimate the recessionary impact of austerity in Ireland; and also may notice an SFC model developed to study the Greek economy, which can be found in Papadimitriou, Zezza and Nikiforos (2013, 2014).

the interaction of these organisms gives rise to phenomena which demand its specificity as entity of analysis.

Notwithstanding what has just been said, there is a recent line of research that tries to bring SFC models closer to agent-based modelling, adopting microeconomic behaviour from the latter (though not necessarily optimizing, in the mainstream sense). That is the plea of Bezemer (2011), to combine models of agent interaction with a thorough description of sectors' balance sheets. For a review of agent-based modelling, the interested reader might check Tesfatsion and Judd (2006) and Borrill and Tesfatsion (2010), among others. Caiani et al. (2015) try to develop a 'benchmark' agent-based SFC model. Among the articles that can also be mentioned are Cincotti, Roberto and Teglio (2010), which investigates the interplay of credit and firm dividends with output and prices; Kinsella, Greiff and Nell (2011), in which the authors replicate empirical regularities of income inequality arising out of competition and innovation; Seppecher (2012a, 2012b), in which by developing a software named JAMEL, the author aims to show the possibility to account for gross intrasectorial flows and stocks; and Caiani et al. (2014), who develop an agent-based SFC model to analyse the impact of innovation on the structure of production processes, the evolution of industrial market structures, and employment dynamics.

4.3 GETTING INTO MY MODEL: SECTORS, ASSETS AND LIABILITIES

After this rather long introduction, it is time to present the SFC open-economy model which allows for trade and financial transactions between two economies. In this chapter we extend the model of Chapter 12 of Godley and Lavoie (2007a), adding, among other things, features presented in Lavoie and Daigle (2011) related to exchange rate expectations. The model is very long, the number of equations is high, and we will focus on the economics behind the model rather than present each and every one of the equations involved, a more pedagogical way of illustrating the rationale and the logic behind the model. To start with, one of the defining characteristics of the model is that one country has the possibility of issuing debt denominated in both currencies, a typical feature of developing economies; therefore the name we assign to the countries in our model: 'USA' and 'Argentina'. Not only that: we include as well foreign lending to firms in a foreign currency. The focus will be on what happens to the developing country, which will also be called 'Greece' at times, leaving aside the effects on the USA (or Germany) as long as they are not necessary for the presentation of the argument.

The model presents a world composed of two countries ('USA' and 'Argentina'), with five sectors in each: households, firms, banks, government and the central bank, which is split from the government for explanatory purposes. Each country produces one good, apt for consumption, investment and export purposes. They only use labour and imports as input for their only product, with a fixed-coefficient production function, that is, in which there is no substitution between inputs. Countries sell goods to each other (well, actually firms do that), and also financial assets. The asset structure of each country is presented in Table 4.1.

Households allocate their wealth in deposits (M), cash (H) and short-term bills, which only last one period. There are three types of these bills: the American government issues bills denominated in dollars (B^u); the Argentinean government issues bills denominated in pesos ($B^{\$a}$), that can be acquired by households of both countries, and it also issues bills denominated in dollars ($B^{\$u}$) that can only be acquired by residents in the US. All holdings are expressed in the domestic currency, so, for instance, $B^{\$a}_{hu}.xru$ represents the holdings of Argentinean bills denominated in pesos (the upper-script a) by American households (the lower script hu), translated into dollars by multiplying it by the American exchange rate. It is just unfortunate that dollars and pesos share the same symbol. It used to be the case that Argentina had a different name for its currency, the Austral, but that was foregone in 1991. And just a useless clarification in order to tamper nationalistic outrage: by 'American' we refer to US households, even though Argentinean households are also American, *strictu senso*. The sole asset of firms is their capital stock; their sole liability, the loans they take from banks (Argentinean firms can borrow from Argentinean banks in pesos and from American banks in dollars; loans have a one-period lifespan), and the difference is their net wealth. Banks, in turn, lend to firms, take deposits, invest in bills and take advances from the central bank according to their circumstances. Their profits accumulate to make their net wealth. For simplicity, banks and firms are assumed to issue no equities and pay no dividends. The central bank issues cash (its liability), grants advances to banks and buys government bills. In the case of the

Table 4.1 *Balance sheets*

	USA					Argentina				
	Households	Firms	Banks	Gov.	Central bank	Households	Firms	Banks	Gov.	Central bank
Capital stock		$+K_u$					$+K_a$			
Cash	$+H_u$				$-H_u$	$+H_a$				$-H_a$
Deposits	$+M_u$		$-M_u$			$+M_a$		$-M_a$		
Advances			$-A_u$		$+A_u$			$-A_a$		$+A_a$
Bills USA	$+B_{hu}^u$		$+B_{bu}^u$	$-B^u$	$+B_{cbu}^u$	$+B_{ha}^u.xra$				$+B_{cba}^u.xra$
Bills Arg. '\$a'	$+B_{hu}^{\$a}.xra$					$+B_{ha}^a$		$+B_{ba}^a$	$-B^{\$a}$	$+B_{cba}^a$
Bills Arg. '\$u'	$+B_{hu}^{\$u}$								$-B^{\$u}.xra$	
Loans '\$a'							$-L_a^a$	$+L^a$		
Loans '\$u'		$-L_u^u$	$+L^u$				$-L_a^u.xra$			
Wealth	$-V_{hu}$	$-V_{fu}$	$-V_{bu}$	$+V_{gu}$	$-V_{cbu}$	$-V_{ha}$	$-V_{fa}$	$-V_{ba}$	$+V_{ga}$	$-V_{cba}$
Σ	0	0	0	0	0	0	0	0	0	0

Argentinean central bank, it also holds American bills $(B_{cba}^u.xra)$, which constitute its reserves, and a sort of net wealth.

Balance sheets are like a photo, they reflect a moment in time. Tables 4.2a and 4.2b track all the flows that occur in one period, one for each country. They provide the dynamic link, they capture a sequence. A plus sign represents an income or a source of funds, and a minus sign represents an expenditure or a use of funds. For instance, investment of net wealth in bills is represented by $-B$, while the proceeds of that sale are noted as $+B$, and so forth. We separate the columns of firms and banks to differentiate between current transactions (which do not affect the firms' capital) and capital transactions (which do).

The first five rows represent the components of the GDP: consumption, government expenditure, investment, exports and imports. Investment is recorded with a plus sign in the current column (tracing the sale of the capital good) and a minus sign in the capital column (recording the use of funds for patrimonial increase). The following rows register wages payments, tax payments and depreciation allowance. The latter, from the point of view of the firm, is a source of funds coming from its own capital, thus the positive sign. Then come interest payments on bills (to domestic and foreign residents, banks and central banks), on deposits, on loans and on advances. Taking all these movements into account, we can compute profits of firms, banks and central banks. The latter are transferred to their respective government, while banks' and firms' profits are a source of funds for increasing their net wealth.

In the final rows, we present the net increment in their holdings of the aforementioned financial assets, which from their point of view is a use of their money and thus is recorded with a minus. From the receiver's point of view it is a source, and we compute it with a plus sign. The same logic holds for banks' and central banks' holdings of bills. We also record the increase in firms' borrowing and banks' lending.

4.4   THE ECONOMICS BEHIND IT

In Appendix A to this chapter the reader will find a list of all the equations that comprise the model. Many are self-explanatory: real and nominal sales, GDP, nominal imports and exports, nominal capital stock, depreciation allowance, taxes, supply and demand from some assets, and so on. But instead of explaining each and every equation, we find it better to explain some of them, the most important, that convey the theory and behavioural guidance of the model. Because, after all, identities are just that, tautological truths that do not explain anything until we attach a theory describing

Table 4.2a   Transaction matrix USA

| | USA | | | | | |
| | Households | Firms | | Banks | | Government | Central bank |
		C	K	C	K		
C	$-C_u$	$+C_u$					
G		$+G_u$				$-G_u$	
I		$+I_u$	$-I_u$				
X		$+X_u$					
IM		$-IM_u$					
[Y]		$[Y_u]$					
W	$+W_u.N_u$	$-W_u.N_u$					
T	$-T_u$					$+T_u$	
DA		$-DA_u$	$+DA_u$				
Int.							
D	$+r_{mu(-1)}.M_{us(-1)}$			$-r_{mu(-1)}.M_{us(-1)}$			
B^u	$+rb_{u(-1)}.B^u_{hus(-1)}$			$+rb_{u(-1)}.B^u_{hus(-1)}$		$-r_{bu(-1)}.B^u_{s(-1)}$	$+rb_{u(-1)}.B^u_{cbus(-1)}$
B^{Sa}	$+rb_{a(-1)}.B^{Sa}_{hus(-1)}.xru$						
B^{Su}	$+rb_{u(-1)}.B^{Su}_{hud(-1)}$						
A				$-ra_{u(-1)}.A_{us(-1)}$			$+ra_{u(-1)}.A_{us(-1)}$
L^a							

87

Table 4.2a (continued)

	USA						
	Households	Firms		Banks		Government	Central bank
		C	K	C	K		
L^u	$-rl_{u(-1)} \cdot L^u_{us(-1)} - F_{fu}$	$-rl_{u(-1)} \cdot L^u_{us(-1)}$ $-F_{fu}$		$+rl_{u(-1)} \cdot L^u_{us(-1)}$			
F_f			$+F_{fu}$				
F_{cb}						$+F_{cbu}$	$-F_{cbu}$
F_b				$-F_{bu}$	$+F_{bu}$		
Ch.							
H	$-\Delta H_u$						$+\Delta H_u$
M	$-\Delta M_u$				$+\Delta M_u$		
B^u	$-\Delta B^u_{hus}$				$-\Delta B^u_{bus}$	$+\Delta B^u$	$-\Delta B^u_{cbus}$
B^{Sa}	$-\Delta B^{Sa}_{hus(-1)} \cdot xru$						
B^{Su}	$-\Delta B^{Su}_{hud}$						
A					$+\Delta A_{us}$		$-\Delta A_{us}$
L^a							
L^u	$+\Delta L^u_u$				$-\Delta L^u$		

Table 4.2b Transaction matrix Argentina

		Argentina					
	Households	Firms		Banks		Government	Central bank
		C	K	C	K		
C	$-C_a$	$+C_a$					
G		$+G_a$				$-G_a$	
I		$+I_a$	$-I_a$				
X		$+X_a$					
IM		$-IM_a$					
[Y]		$[Y_a]$					
W	$+W_a.N_a$	$-W_a.N_a$					
T	$-T_a$					$+T_a$	
DA		$+DA_a$	$+DA_a$				
Int.							
D	$+r_{ma(-1)}.M_{as(-1)}$			$-r_{ma(-1)}.M_{as(-1)}$			
B^u	$+rb_{a(-1)}.B^u_{has(-1)}.xra$						$+rb_{a(-1)}.B^u_{cbas(-1)}.xra$
B^{Sa}	$+rb_{a(-1)}.B^a_{has(-1)}$			$+rb_{a(-1)}.B^a_{bas(-1)}$		$-r_{ba(-1)}.B^{Sa}_{s(-1)}$	$+rb_{a(-1)}.B^a_{cbas(-1)}$
B^{Su}						$-B^{Su}_{mıa(-1)}.r_{ba(-1)}.xra$	
A				$-ra_{a(-1)}.A_{as(-1)}$			$+ra_{a(-1)}.A_{as(-1)}$
L^a	$-rl_{a(-1)}.L^a_{as(-1)}$	$+DA_a$		$+rl_{a(-1)}.L^a_{as(-1)}$	$+rl_{a(-1)}.L^a_{s(-1)}$		

89

Table 4.2b (continued)

	Households	Firms		Banks		Government	Central bank
		C	K	C	K		
L^u	$-rl_{uA(-1)}.L^u_{aS(-1)}.xra$						
F_f		$-F_{fa}$	$+F_{fa}$				
F_{cb}						$+F_{cba}$	$-F_{cba}$
F_b				$-F_{ba}$	$+F_{ba}$		
Ch.							
H	$-\Delta H_a$						$+\Delta H_a$
M	$-\Delta M_a$				$+\Delta M_a$		
B^u	$-\Delta B^u_{has}.xra$						$-\Delta B^u_{cbas}.xra$
B^{Su}	$-\Delta B^a_{has}$				$-\Delta B^a_{has}$	$+\Delta B^{Sa}$	$-\Delta B^a_{cbas}$
B^{Sa}						$+\Delta B^{Sa}_{hat}.xra$	
A					$+\Delta A_{as}$		$-\Delta A_{as}$
L^a			$+\Delta L^a_a$		$-\Delta L^a$		
L^u			$+\Delta L^a_{us}.xra$				

Argentina

which variables are independent, which variables are dependent, what is their logic, how do they behave. The SFC approach is a modelling methodology, not a theory in itself.

4.4.1   Prices and Wages

When we explained the Kaleckian model of growth, we used a mark-up over costs function to depict the pricing behaviour of firms. At first we only considered labour costs, but in the Hein and Vogel model we presented, costs included labour and imported inputs. This reflects a long-standing tradition in economics, actually dating back to the period when the discipline was called 'political economy': prices are set to recover costs, at least. From that phrase, some thoughts come to mind, in order to explain the pricing behaviour implicit in our models. A more thorough review is to be found in Lavoie (2014, pp. 156–175) and the aforementioned book by Lee (1998).

First, we used the word 'set'. Prices are set by firms, according to their objectives. They are not the result of an auction process, they are not set to clear the market, they are not short-run profit maximizing. To cover costs is the primary objective of a firm. One may add growth projects, investment financing, shareholder satisfaction, all factors which interact with each other in a complex, not always complementary way.

All this leads us to the following point: in order to achieve these objectives, prices are administered, and are set before transactions occur (Lavoie 2014, p. 157), before the firms know what the demand (and even actual costs) is. Prices are more stable because of this: firms want to avoid price wars; they want to maintain longer-term relations with clients; they have 'margins of safety' like inventories and/or planned excess capacity in order to respond to predicted or unpredicted short-run peaks in their demand, and so on.

And in an open economy framework, as in our model, one also has to consider the influence of the exchange rate on the pricing behaviour of firms. In that setting, the mark-up charged over costs can function as an accommodating factor that attenuates the impact of fluctuations in the exchange rate on domestic prices. This is consistent with stylized facts that show that the pass-through from devaluations to prices is smaller than one, so that the real exchange rate moves together with the nominal, and that usually it is the latter that has the most decisive influence on the former (Taylor and Taylor 2004). A different but compatible explanation is set up in Amiti, Itskhoki and Konings (2014), who emphasize the empirical fact that, in an increasingly globalized global value chain, large exporters are at the same time large importers, so that they internalize variations in nominal exchange rates.

It should be pointed out that most of the post-Keynesian theory of pricing determination, the one we presented above, is said to hold for manufacturing goods. Commodity products are said to reflect supply and demand conditions (Kalecki himself made that distinction). However, even in the financialized context in which many commodity prices are set today, there is still a preponderant role for strategic pricing behaviour by different actors in the chain, as exemplified by several price-rigging cases discovered since 2012.

These thoughts help to defend the following specification for the sales price, as will be computed in our model:

$$p_{su} = \frac{(1 + \pi_u).(W_u.N_u + IM_u + rl_{u(-1)}.L^u_{us(-1)})}{S_u}$$

$$p_{sa} = \frac{(1 + \pi_a).\left(\begin{array}{c} W_a.N_a + IM_a + rl_{a(-1)}.L^a_{as(-1)} \\ + rl_{u(-1)}.L^u_{as(-1)}.xra \end{array}\right)}{S_a}$$

The equations say that sales prices (p_{sa} or p_{su}, depending on whether they refer to Argentina or the US) are set on the basis of a mark-up (π) over unit costs (that is why the sales level appears in the denominator). Nominal costs are composed by the wage bill (nominal wages times the employment level), nominal imports and interest servicing, which is a cost like any other concept. Since Argentinean firms borrow both from Argentinean and American banks, the interest corresponding to loans from the latter are reflected in the term $rl_{u(-1)}.L^u_{as(-1)}.xra$, which reads as: the interest rate of the previous period, times the amount borrowed last period from US banks (expressed in dollars) times the current exchange rate.

Let's analyse each component of the equation, starting with the mark-up. It is exogenous in this model, to a certain extent. As we have said, it is a well-known phenomenon that the pass-through from the exchange rate to prices is lower than unity, and particularly so in the last 25 years or so (McCarthy 2007; Da Silva and Vernengo 2008; Nogueira Junior and León-Ledesma 2010). In this model, this is achieved through changes in the mark-up: a depreciation raises the mark-up, because firms do not lower their prices in line with the fall in the exchange rate, increasing their profit margins. The opposite happens with appreciations, which is a way firms have in order to retain market share. Therefore the function:

$$\pi = \pi_0 + \pi_1.\left(\frac{\Delta(xr_{(-1)})}{xr_{(-1)}}\right)$$

A higher coefficient π_1 would mean that the country is more exposed to international competition, so in case of an appreciation of the exchange rate (a *negative* change in the exchange rate) the mark-up absorbs part of the impact and prices do not rise by the extent they should (Arestis and Milberg 1993–94; Ampudia Márquez 2011). Mendieta-Muñoz (2013), however, stresses that this mark-up adjustment, though certainly relevant in the short run, might exacerbate inflation arising out of a distributive struggle, so that the diminution of the pass through in the short term might be eroded in the longer term, particularly in Latin American economies.

Since exports are sales, their price is equal to domestic sales prices. This implies that exporters set the price of their good, while quantities are determined by the import country. The import function is a traditional one, in which imports depend on relative competitiveness, domestic demand and the productive structure, which implies by itself a certain level of imports relative to GDP.

In a typical Keynesian manner, the level of employment (one of the two components of the wage bill) is determined by the level of output, given the productivity level (more on this below). But what about wages? What is its relation with employment? The reader surely knows at this time about the famous Phillips curve, which noted a downward-sloped relationship between nominal wages and unemployment for the United Kingdom, and in which the line measuring wage inflation cut the horizontal axis (unemployment) at the so-called 'natural' rate of unemployment (Phillips 1958).[2] In later usage the natural rate became the 'Non-Accelerating Inflation Rate of Unemployment', which was devoid of a 'labour market-clearing' sense. It did not posit full employment; it just assumed that, unemployment being at that rate, inflation would not accelerate.

The reader may also be aware that in the late 1960s and 1970s monetarist theories developed by Milton Friedman, and later new classical economics fostered by Lucas, defended the existence of a long-run (and in Lucas's case, even a short-run) vertical Phillips's curve, in which unemployment could not deviate from the NAIRU except for the shortest of periods. However, the empirical evidence, particularly since the 1990s, defends the existence of a horizontal Phillips curve, for a relevant range of unemployment rates. That holds not only for the US, as found in Barnes and Olivei (2003), Lye and McDonald (2008), Stock and Watson (2010) and Peach, Rich and Cororaton (2011), but also in Canada, Japan, the United Kingdom and the Euro Area, as can be seen in IMF (2013, Chapter 3) and López-Pérez (2015), among others. This is tantamount to saying that there is not a NAIRU, at least not as an attractor of the unemployment rate (Storm and Naastepad 2012). How do we model such horizontal segment?

We do so by focusing on nominal wage demands. Our equations

draw heavily on Godley and Lavoie (2007a), especially Chapter 11 (pp. 386–388). Workers demand wage adjustment according to the divergence between past real wage and targeted real wage. Wage demands are backward looking:

$$W = W_{(-1)} + \omega_0 \cdot (w^T_{(-1)} \cdot p_s - W_{(-1)})$$

This target real wage reflects the demand pressure from the labour market, exemplified by the rate of change of the employment volume, but in a non-linear way. If the employment rate is within certain bands, whatever its actual value, workers will demand a certain real wage, determined by what they judge a 'reasonable' increase in the employment volume (or whatever the reader wants to call it), $EMP^\#$, equal to 3 per cent. If it is below the bands, then the relationship between real wage demand and employment change is linear, and the same if it is above the top band. Our Phillips curve has a flat middle segment. Its bands are determined by institutional factors, with scope for the influence of political actors. The equation that represents this Phillips curve is the following:

$$w^T = \omega_1 + \omega_2 \cdot (EMP + z_1 \cdot [EMP^\# - EMP] - z_2 \cdot bandb + z_3 \cdot bandt)$$

The z_1 dummy variable will be equal to one if the change in employment is within the flat segment, otherwise it will be zero. The same holds for the z_2 dummy variable (if the change in employment is below the value accepted by workers) and for z_3 (if it is above).

The employment level is determined by output and labour productivity. The latter factor reacts to changes in the real wage, weighted by a coefficient q. We have omitted in this formulation the Kaldor–Verdoorn effect which states that productivity itself responds to the rate of growth of the economy, even though we are a firm believer in its relevance (see the abovementioned volume by McCombie, Pugno and Soro (2002)). We can only offer a clumsy excuse for its omission in this model. The Kaldor–Verdoorn effect sets in motion a cumulative growth process, in demand-led growth models such as this, by incorporating increasing returns to scale. In our model, that implies an unstable, explosive behaviour, which deprives it from a steady state. Rowthorn (1989 [1981]) has already noted that the introduction of such features severely restricts the stability conditions of Kaleckian models, and the same argument applies this time. The effect of real wage growth (or restraint) on productivity has substantial empirical support of its own, such as in Storm and Naastepad (2009, 2012) and Vergeer and Kleinknecht (2007, 2011, 2012), though in the 2011 article they do not find strong evidence of a Kaldor–Verdoorn effect.

4.4.2   Investment, Consumption and Savings

The review of the literature in Chapters 2 and 3 has shown that the defining feature of demand-led growth models is the positive and substantial reaction of investment to changes in aggregate demand, one characterization being the accelerator principle. That is the investment function we adopt in this model:

$$gk = \gamma_0 + \gamma_1.(\Delta y_{(-1)}/y_{(-1)})$$

The growth rate of the capital stock depends on past output growth rate plus an exogenous term. However, investment also covers depreciation, so in proper terms the capital stock is:

$$k = k_{(-1)}.(1 - \delta + gk)$$

where δ is the depreciation rate (assumed constant and exogenous). Firms demand loans to cover their financial needs (principal and interest of past loans, investments) not covered by the depreciation allowance and their past profits. In this model Argentinean firms can borrow in the Argentinean and in the American banking system, in different currencies. The dollarization of firms' balance sheets is a well-known factor in developing and emerging economies, partly due to the low development of their financial system, the relatively higher level of interest rates vis-à-vis the international rate (Mantey 2013), and the increasing influence of transnational corporations, who guide the borrowing and investment decisions of their affiliates.

What about consumption and savings? Tables 4.2a and 4.2b serve as an introduction, because we can deduce from them the regular income of households: the wage bill, and interest payments on their financial assets. They pay taxes on that regular income. They have capital gains (due to the movement of the exchange rate, since bills last one period) for the holdings of financial assets denominated in a foreign currency. For instance, see the case of American households: they have two types of Argentinean bills, one denominated in pesos and the other denominated in dollars. American households only see a capital gain on their holdings of bills in pesos, not on their holdings of bills in dollars. Their regular income minus their taxes plus their capital gain constitutes their disposable income. Only definitions, so far.

Households consume according to their disposable income and their accumulated wealth. However, their consumption patterns are not derived from an optimizing plan, from maximizing utility, nor a forecast of future events by means of rational expectations. Households act according to conventions in a context of uncertainty, in which the present and the recent past influence more than proportionally their expectations of future conditions.[3] That is why, in this model, households consume a proportion of their *expected* real disposable income, with a kind of habit formation called adaptive expectations:

$$yd^e = yd_{(-1)} + \beta(yd_{(-1)} - yd^e_{(-1)})$$

Financial and real-estate wealth has been increasingly important in influencing households' consumption habits, and we do reflect that here. The consumption function we adopt is as follows:

$$c = \alpha_1.yd^e + \alpha_2.v_{h(-1)}$$

But the fact that households base their consumption decisions on their *expected* real disposable income, with room for possible mistakes in their expectations, implies that households might err in the forecast of the financial wealth they will invest in different assets. But before that we want to highlight an important factor. In the steady state, with no mistaken expectations, there is a stable relation between wealth and disposable income, equal to $V_h^* = \alpha_3.YD^*$, with $\alpha_3 = \frac{(1-\alpha_1)}{[1-(\frac{1}{1+gr})\cdot(\frac{\alpha_2}{1+gr})]}$, where *gr* is the growth rate of disposable income and consumption. This long-run *norm* will have a substantial effect on *government debt*, as we will show later in the simulations. A detailed analysis is found in Godley and Lavoie (2007a), appendix 3.4.

4.4.3 Financial Investments

How do households invest their wealth? To start with, they allocate not any kind of wealth: they invest their *expected* wealth:

$$V_h^e = V_{h(-1)} + YD^e - C$$

Given that all financial assets last one period in this model, there is no impediment for households to reallocate their whole wealth, not just new savings. And in order to do that, they compare different rates of return, plus the relevant risk of the specific asset. Ruling out banking default, deposits do not carry any risk. We only consider two types of risk: currency risk, which can cause capital gains or losses according to exchange rate movements; and sovereign risk, which questions directly the repayment capacity of the debtor, the government. Different risks apply to different assets. When a country issues debt denominated in its own currency, in the case of a crisis that can lead to depreciation, the corresponding asset faces currency (or depreciation) risk for foreign investors. Sovereign risk is particularly relevant for countries that have debt denominated in a foreign currency. In our model, sovereign risk is relevant only relative to Argentinean bills denominated in dollars. Another implication is that investors know that there is no possibility of government defaulting on their debt denominated in domestic currency. We present the equations describing the portfolio decisions of American households, which have recourse to a greater array of financial assets than their Argentinean peers. But a clarification regarding the notation is needed: the variable $B_{hud}^{\$a}$ represents the demand of Argentinean bills denominated in pesos ('$\$a$') by American households ('*hud*'), while the variable $B_{hud}^{\$u}$ represents the demand, by the same households, of Argentinean bills denominated in dollars ('$\$u$'). As we said earlier, it is just unfortunate that dollars and pesos share the same symbol.

$$M_{ud}^n = V_{hu}^e.(\lambda_{10} + \lambda_{11}.rm_u + \lambda_{12}.rb_u + \lambda_{13}.[rb_a + dxru^e] + \lambda_{14}.[rb_u - \varphi])$$

$$B_{hud}^u = V_{hu}^e.(\lambda_{20} + \lambda_{21}.rm_u + \lambda_{22}.rb_u + \lambda_{23}.[rb_a + dxru^e] + \lambda_{24}.[rb_u - \varphi])$$

$$B_{hud}^{\$a} = V_{hu}^e.(\lambda_{30} + \lambda_{31}.rm_u + \lambda_{32}.rb_u + \lambda_{33}.[rb_a + dxru^e] + \lambda_{34}.[rb_u - \varphi])$$

$$B_{hud}^{\$u} = V_{hu}^e.(\lambda_{40} + \lambda_{41}.rm_u + \lambda_{42}.rb_u + \lambda_{43}.[rb_a + dxru^e] + \lambda_{44}.[rb_u - \varphi])$$

$$H_{ud}^n = V_{hu} - M_{ud}^n - B_{hud}^u - B_{hud}^{\$a} - B_{hud}^{\$u}$$

There are many things to develop here. First things first. The first and the last equation show notional demands for cash and deposits; that is why they have an upper-script 'n'. By notional we denote the amounts that investors plan to demand a priori without any consideration as to whether that amount will be effectively demanded, ignoring any shortage that might arise. Why do we split between notional and actual demands for these two assets in particular? The explanation lies in the first term in the portfolio equations: households allocate their expected wealth, with cash demand being the buffer stock that absorbs mistaken expectations between actual and expected wealth. But at times these divergences can be so huge that the notional demand for cash becomes negative. In that case families decrease their deposits to cover the difference.

Portfolio allocation is done according to Tobinesque rules. All the values of the λ coefficients must respect the adding-up constraints set in Godley and Lavoie (2007a, pp. 328–329). And just like them (pp. 325–328), we also have an implicit demand for money which has a negative rate of return equal to the inflation rate, incorporated in the values assigned to the λ. Households compare the rates of return on deposits, on the US government debt and on the different types of Argentinean government debt. It is assumed that the interest rate that Argentina pays for its debt denominated in dollars is equal to the American interest rate, but investors are still concerned about the prospect of default on that debt. What are the determinants of those risks in our model? Let's deal first with currency or depreciation risk.

When dealing with financial markets, post-Keynesians have emphasized the importance of the divergence of views regarding the future. Keynes himself, in Chapter 17 of the General Theory, stressed the need of heterogeneous beliefs regarding the future of the interest rate in order to trace a smooth liquidity preference function. And we do model heterogeneous beliefs regarding the future path of the exchange rate, in line with a broad literature in which we can mention Harvey (1993, 2009), Moosa (2003, Chapter 8), De Grauwe and Grimaldi (2006, Chapter 2) and Rossi (2010); our own model owes more to Lavoie and Daigle (2011). This line of literature, which questions or nuances (if not refutes) the importance of rational expectation agents in the foreign exchange market, has also received some support from mainstream authors such as Frankel and Froot (1990), Cutler, Poterba and Summers (1990), Spronk, Verschoor and Zwinkels (2013) and Chutasripanich and Yetman (2015), among others.

In the exchange markets there is a proportion of 'fundamentalist' traders that act according to some rule and a proportion of 'chartist' traders, who follow past movements trying to predict future ones. In the case of the 'fundamentalist' traders, they expect the exchange rate to move according to the divergence between its past value and some benchmark, $xra^{\#}$. This value does not arise from an equilibrium process nor is it directly related to any real fundamental; instead I think of it as a market convention, as what 'fundamentalist' traders *believe* the exchange rate should be worth. It may sound obvious, but I still prefer to state clearly that there is nothing religious in naming these types of traders 'fundamentalist'. The 'chartist' traders, in turn, try to anticipate the market and guess where the next period value will be based on trend and past behaviour analysis. In our model (as well as in Lavoie and Daigle (2011)) they assume that the exchange rate will move as it has moved in the period before, in a proportion given by parameter ξ. This is shown in the following equations. Notice as well that:

$$dxru^e = - dxra^e$$

$$dxra^e = \chi^f.dxra^{ef} + \chi^c.dxra^{ec}$$

$$dxra^{ef} = \zeta.\left(\frac{xra^\# - xra_{(-1)}}{xra_{(-1)}}\right)$$

$$dxra^{ec} = \xi.(\Delta(xra_{(-1)}/xra_{(-1)})$$

The repayment capabilities are the major concern behind sovereign risk, and that is captured by the parameter ϕ. Since investors are concerned with the repayment by Argentina of its debt in dollars, a standard measure is to assume that risk moves in line (at a given proportion) with the *rate of change* in the ratio of (past) Argentina's foreign debt denominated in dollars to its nominal GDP also expressed in dollars. The fact that the variable that influences the perception of risk is the rate of change of that ratio, and not its level, reflects for instance differences observed in the European crisis where countries with lower public debt were perceived as riskier than other economies with higher debt, because their situation was quickly deteriorating, as in the case of Spain or Ireland. Our indicator of choice should not be confused as an endorsement of the Reinhart and Rogoff (2010) thesis, by which a higher public debt is associated with (and in early writings, causes) lower rates of growth. For instance, we focus here only on debt denominated in a foreign currency, a key factor to differentiate responses to financial crises (Nersisyan and Wray 2010).

4.4.4 Interest Rates, Deposits and Loans

A recent article by researchers at the Bank of England (McLeay, Radia and Thomas 2014) has joined the long-standing ranks of post-Keynesian economists who defend a causality relationship running from loans to deposits and not the other way around (Kaldor 1982; Rochon 1999; Lavoie 2006b, 2014). This view is part and parcel of the Banking School and can be traced back at least to Adam Smith, and was present in such diverse authors as Thomas Tooke, Joseph Schumpeter, Dennis Robertson and Keynes, in particular in his Treatise on Money. The banking system as a whole is not constrained by (deposit) reserves to lend. Quite the contrary, it creates those very reserves by lending and crediting the loan in the borrower's account. What is the purpose of deposits, then? Well, they are a means (among others) to fund other deposits. When the borrower borrows (sorry for the redundancy), the bank credits his savings account. The borrower is free to move that money to other banks, which may end up with more reserves. Therefore the need for the first bank to find money (attracting other deposits, or borrowing from other banks or the central bank) to fund that runaway deposit. The reader may find other similar explanations in Bindseil (2004) and Borio and Disyatat (2009), to quote from two central bankers. How do we express this in our model? Banks give all the loans that firms demand from them. If deposits are more than enough (together with their accumulated profits or net wealth) to fund those loans, the remaining is invested in government bills. If deposits fall short of the credit demand by firms, they ask for advances from the central bank.

The other trademark of post-Keynesian monetary economics is the setting of the short-term interest rate by the central bank. This feature is also recognized by practitioners, as explained in the aforementioned papers of Bindseil (2004) and McLeay, Radia and Thomas (2014). Even though changes have occurred in the way central banks operate since the 2008 crisis (Lavoie 2010b), this is still a valid representation of short-term interest rate setting in the real world. Loans are granted at a mark-up over the base rate (the bills rate), and advances have a penalty rate attached to them. There is no room for crowding out effects of public borrowing on the terms and conditions of lending to the private sector. The deposit rate is equal to the bills rate. And real government expenditure is assumed to grow at a fixed rate.

4.4.5   Closures

In the fixed exchange regime, if investors do not want American bills, the Argentinean central bank has to intervene and buy all the remaining American bills, otherwise the dollar would plummet and the peso would rise. In the flexible exchange regime, Argentinean foreign reserves are fixed and the exchange rate equalizes demand and supply of bills. However, this does not mean that bills alone are the sole factor in the determination of the exchange rate: all the variables play a role here. Imports and exports affect income; GDP growth affects investment, loans and interest rate payments. That is the beauty of stock-flow methodology: it is a macroeconomic structural model, with no account holes, and with a simultaneous and consistent determination of flows, stocks and prices. The disadvantage is that in models this large stability analysis becomes almost impossible, and one can only infer about it by reading actual tendencies and not by looking at mathematical conditions. Another point to be made is that flexible exchange rate regimes do not need actually to have constant reserves. The level of reserves just needs to be independent of the performance of the balance of payments. In Godley and Lavoie's book, for instance, there is a 'Lequain's closure', in which reserves increase with the interest received on the reserves of the previous period. We observe in the real world that countries like the United Kingdom or Brazil, which allegedly let their currencies float in accordance with market conditions, also experience big movements in their foreign reserves, contradicting the textbook description.

In SFC models there is always one redundant equation. In this model, it is the supply of Argentinean government bills to the central bank. There are two ways it can be described: either the government supplies whatever the central bank asks, or supplies what the other sectors reject. Given the tight accounting of SFC, the fulfilment of both equations is assured. The last caveat to notice, and as has already been pointed out by other authors, since in the flexible exchange rate regime there are possibilities of capital gains on Argentinean foreign reserves (a constant stock of US bills in dollars) due to exchange rate movements, the balance of payments is not equal to zero by definition (Godley and Lavoie 2007a, p. 453).

4.5   SIMULATIONS

4.5.1   Consumption, Savings and Fiscal Policy

Having described SFC models in general, and having presented our own model, it is time to taste the pudding and perform the experiments that we judged relevant and informative. Simulations run during a hundred periods called 'years', starting from a fictional 1950 to 2050. Shocks were introduced in the 'year' 1960, and the results are compared with a base-line scenario. In it, at the end of 2050 GDP was increasing, in the flexible exchange rate regime, at 3.04 per cent in Argentina and 3.03 per cent in the USA, with the Argentinean peso slightly depreciating around 0.08 per cent annually, real wages going up 0.03 per cent in Argentina and 0.04 per cent in the USA, there is some deflation at around 0.4 per cent per period, and the accumulation rate proceeds at 2.9 per cent. In the fixed exchange rate regime, in turn, GDP grows in both countries at 3.03 per cent, the real wage rate grows at 0.04 per cent, deflation is also at 0.04 per cent and accumulation moves at 2.9 per cent per period. The debt to GDP ratio grows but at a decreasing trend in both regimes, rising by less than 0.1 per cent per period and stabilizing asymptotically. In our opinion, however, these values should not be given much importance. What matters in our view is to examine the impact of the shocks compared with the baseline, the base-line itself being of secondary importance. The reader should be reminded, though, that the names 'Argentina' and 'USA' are purely fictional; the calibration does not intend to match the characteristics of either of these two countries, except for the fact that the Argentinean government and Argentinean firms borrow in dollars, while neither the US government nor American firms borrow in pesos.

In the first experiment I increase the coefficient α_{1a} by 10 per cent, which represents the propensity to consume of Argentinean households out of their disposable income. As expected in a model that imposes no constraint on the supply side, we observe that real GDP is higher after the change, the short-term impact being higher than in the long run, but still positive. The paradox of thrift holds both in the short and in the long run. However, we can see a fall in real and nominal household wealth, which slightly counteracts the increased propensity to consume. In other words the coefficient α_3, the wealth to disposable income ratio, becomes smaller. But that is not the only implication.

Higher consumption and less saving is matched, all things equal, by two features: one is a deterioration in the external performance, and we do observe the deterioration in the trade and current account of Argentina, attenuated in the flexible exchange rate regime precisely by the depreciation of the peso (though this does not mean that the exchange rate moves necessarily in the same direction as the current account, as I will show later). The other important feature is the fall in the public sector borrowing requirements of the Argentinean government, which is basically the issue of new bills. We therefore have a lower ratio of debt to GDP (though foreign debt denominated in dollars is a higher proportion of total debt). To put it in layman's terms: fewer households' savings imply that households lend less to (or borrow more from) the rest of the world; and they lend less to government, which by itself is asking for less debt since its income has increased (due to higher GDP). This is shown in Figure 4.1.

Let us look now at the effects of a higher rate of growth of public expenditures. The model is very sensitive to changes in this parameter. We increased the relevant coefficients by 5 per cent in the case of a fixed ER regime and by 4 per cent in the case of the flexible regime, and even in the latter case, in what refers to the rate of growth of American public expenditures, we did not have values for the last 15 periods, though the sample was big enough to draw some conclusions.

Both increases are expansionary for the country that implements them and for the other as well, due to the stimulus for imports. However, the net impact on the balance of trade depends on the ER regime. The flexible ER regime reflects higher output due to an improved balance of trade, which in turn is caused by a depreciation of the exchange rate. The rate of growth of capital stock also has the same behaviour: in both cases it is positive, but it is greater in the flexible ER regime. Instead real consumption is slightly higher in the fixed ER regime than in the other. The reason: sustained depreciation increases the mark-up and lowers real wages, also due to inflationary pressure from more highly priced import goods, something ruled out in our fixed ER model. However, given the parameters of our

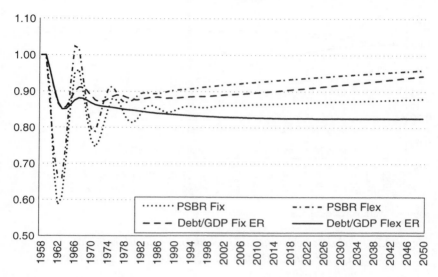

Source: Author's calculations.

Figure 4.1   *Public sector borrowing requirements and debt/nominal GDP ratio in Argentina after an increase in the propensity to consume out of disposable income*

simulations and the magnitude of the changes, the fall in the real wage is very small and the trade balance impact prevails over losses of consumption expenditure due to lower wages. The opposite of a depreciation is a run-out of foreign reserves in Argentina, in the fixed ER case. Our model corroborates the positive impact of expansionary fiscal policies. Whether it is in the best interest of one country to let its currency appreciate in the context of a fiscal stimulus in the other economy depends on the reaction of its balance of trade to changes in the exchange rate. As said above, we calibrated the model in such a way that it fulfils the so-called Marshall–Lerner conditions, that is, the balance of trade is strongly affected by the exchange rate. That may not be the case in many economies, including Argentina itself (Zak and Dalle 2014).

In recent times financial blogs have started to use as a guide to estimate the future movements of corporate profits the 'Kaleckian equation', which basically says that profits are equal to corporate investment minus household savings plus the budget deficit plus the current account surplus (Kalecki 1971). Can we observe something like that here? Paraphrasing Barack Obama: yes, we can. Figure 4.2 shows the evolution of the loans to firms' net wealth ratio, and the ratio (net of depreciation allowance) of

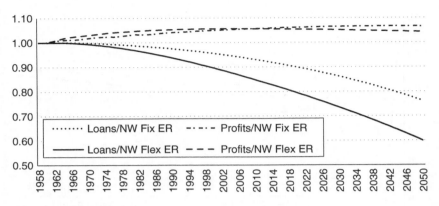

Source: Author's calculations.

*Figure 4.2   Loans to net wealth and profit to net wealth ratios of
Argentinean firms after an increase in the rate of growth of
public expenditures*

profits to net wealth. Compared with the baseline, we observe the expected
result: the loans to net wealth ratio goes down, the profits to net wealth
ratio goes up. Also the former ratio falls even more in the flexible ER
regime than in the fixed, even though the magnitude of the change is lower.
We attribute this to the increase in the mark-up and the higher price level
observed when the ER is allowed to float. Government deficits crowd in
private savings, instead of crowding them out.

4.5.2   Interest Rates, Portfolios, Capital Flight, Devaluations and Expectations

In what refers to monetary policy I conducted basically three experiments:
I raised the interest rate on American bills (and Argentinean bills denominated in dollars), I raised the interest rate on bills denominated in pesos, and
I raised both at the same time. In the first stage, we will present the results
on the second experiment (an increase of 50 bps in r_{ba} from 3 per cent to
3.5 per cent). The very short run movements are as expected, the medium to
longer run not, but they do offer a lot of insight, this notwithstanding. It is
a supply and demand story. Let us start with the fixed ER regime. Figure 4.3
presents selected variables, and their reaction to such an increase, during the
first five years. We beg the reader to stay with us during the explanation,
because it is a difficult graph to read and the explanation is a little technical.
   Argentinean public sector borrowing requirements (PSBR, which

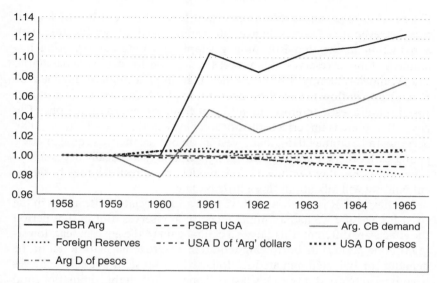

Source: Author's calculations.

Figure 4.3   *Reaction to an increase of 50 bps in the interest rate on bills in pesos in a fixed ER*

includes the fiscal deficit plus the repayment of debt) escalate, with a small alleviation in the second period, as interest rates take a greater toll in the government budget. The demand for bills in pesos, from American and Argentinean households increases slightly, except for the latter in 1961. The American demand for US bills decreases also in a low magnitude initially, though later it will grow together with household wealth.

What declines steadily is the US PSBR. Greater interest payments to US households imply greater income and smaller deficits (this effect is actually small: the American debt is barely 2 per cent lower in the last period of the simulation compared with the baseline). The supply of American bills goes down, and the supply of Argentinean bills goes up. In the first year, with the increase in the demand of Argentinean bills (and the small decline in the demand of American bills) foreign reserves increase, but later they go down as well. The Argentinean central bank sells the dollars in exchange for pesos, but now there are fewer pesos in circulation than the amount required to keep the interest rate at the desired level, so the central bank buys the bills the government is issuing with the pesos required to keep the interest rate. That is how the increased PSBR is 'financed'. However implausible this might seem (and it does seem unrealistic to us), there is one good, relevant and important feature: the outflow of foreign reserves, even in a fixed exchange rate regime, need not go together with a reduction in the domestic money supply. As long as Argentina has (enough) foreign reserves, this process can go on for ever (Lavoie 2001). The Mundell–Fleming theorem, which is in itself a modern-day view of Hume's specie-flow mechanism, does not apply. A country can have (and sustain) a domestic interest rate different from the international one. The key is that there is imperfect substitution between the assets (Lavoie 2000; Serrano and Summa 2015), that investors do not see them as equal or competing with others. Capital controls might not be theoretically necessary to accomplish this, there are none in our model, but in reality it may be different, and we will talk about this a little bit later.

In a flexible ER regime, in 1961 we have an appreciated ER, just as in the fixed ER closure we had an initial increase in reserves. But in that period the effects are different: this causes a capital gain to the government, lowering (in one period) its borrowing requirements, together with a fall in the demand for bills denominated in dollars. In a sense, it actually achieves what it tried to do. But this only lasts for one period, in this simulation, and later the effect is reversed. Figure 4.4 shows this.

The attentive reader may ask what happens with the expectations about the movement of the exchange rate. There are two cases. In the fixed ER closure, given that we chose to set an exchange rate level equal to what fundamentalist traders think it should be, there are no expectations of depreciations (I do model this case below). In the flexible exchange rate regime the values obtained for the baseline are below the 'fundamental' ER. As the actual ER depreciates in the simulation, it gets closer to the fundamental value, and expectations about its future movement become more optimistic (i.e. the expectation of depreciation is reduced, though in an attenuated way because of the chartist traders).

Some more remarks are important here. In my model the impact of an increase in the Argentinean interest rate on output is slightly positive. Output is less than 2 per cent higher in the last period compared with the baseline (in the fixed ER closure, it is 1 per cent higher) because interest receipts increase disposable income and with it consumption. In the flexible ER we should also add the impact of a positive trade balance. Think of interest payments received by pension funds, combined with an increasingly aged population, and the idea of a positive impact of a higher interest rate does not seem so counterintuitive, though I do not endorse it because of multiple other concerns (like household borrowing, for instance). I did not include a negative check of the interest rate on the investment function, but that is also being contested in numerous papers (see for instance Chirinko 1993 and Sharpe and Suarez 2014).

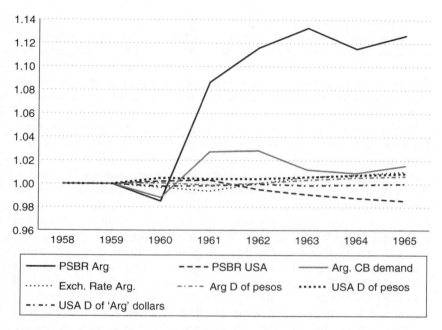

Source: Author's calculations.

Figure 4.4 *Reaction to an increase of 50 bps in the interest rate on bills in pesos in a flexible ER*

Finally, what happens when such increase in the Argentinean interest rate goes hand in hand with an increase in the American interest rate? Sparing the reader more complicated graphics, we can confidently say that, given the parameters of our model, both PSBRs (American and Argentinean) go up. The Argentinean government even has to pay more for its bills denominated in dollars. The behaviour we observed previously is attenuated: depreciation is more nuanced, and Argentina even has a gain in its foreign reserves. Due to the cost effect of interest payments on loans (that also rise together with the base rate) the real wage is somewhat decreased as a by-product. This counteracts the effect of interest receipts for a long time, especially the fixed ER closure.

What are the effects when we change the portfolio decisions of households, the proportion by which they allocate their wealth among different assets? For example, what happens when American households worry about the evolution of the Argentinean economy and increase their holdings of domestic bills at the expense of the others? And what if, on top of this, they have doubts about its solvency in dollars and sovereign risk rises?

In the fixed ER regime, private financial flows to Argentina fall, and so do foreign reserves. However, as mentioned earlier, the 'rules of the game' of a gold standard do not apply: nobody plays by the rules. Domestic credit is increased by the central bank, as long as it has foreign reserves to defend the exchange rate. We will show later what happens when it does not defend the exchange rate. So far, the situation is not good. But what about that in a flexible ER?

Several things are noticeable here. First, the exchange rate depreciates. Does the story end there? No. Depreciation of the peso has certain effects on Argentina, and it is interesting to track them. In this simulation, depreciation increases prices in Argentina and decreases them in the US, via two effects: increasing the cost of imports (and in the Argentinean case, the burden of interest payments plus the cost of paying back debts on foreign loans); and it increases (decreases) the mark-up. Profits in Argentina increase, in the US they decline. Still, having decided in real terms how much to invest, price increases force Argentinean firms to borrow more, and American firms to borrow less, which means that Argentinean banks demand fewer bills, and American banks demand more. Real consumption also stays the same, but nominal consumption increases (even though the real wage falls). One would assume that both expected and actual nominal wealth fall in tandem (remember, expectations about disposable income are backward looking in this model, and so they do not change initially). But that does not happen. Expected nominal wealth does fall, and with it the Argentinean demand for bills and deposits. But depreciation also causes a capital gain on Argentinean households' holdings of foreign bills (and the opposite goes for US households), which increases their actual disposable income. In the first period, therefore, they increase their cash holdings, the central bank buying the bills that foreigners, locals and banks do not. This is how the interest rate is kept at its target. In the USA, on the contrary, the central bank sells the bills the agents demand. This result shows that the money supply is determined by the preference of the agents, not set by the central bank (Lavoie 2001).

The capital account surplus is reduced as well as the current account deficit. PSBR in Argentina relies more on domestic financing than foreign. The Argentinean real wage declines initially, which impacts on real consumption, but as the exchange rate stabilizes, it returns to normality, though at a higher price level. What happens with the expectations about the exchange rate? Keeping in mind that a positive $dxra^e$ implies that the Argentinean ER is expected to depreciate, that variable diminishes. Initially, chartist traders increase substantially their expectations of an exchange rate depreciation, but the opposite happens with the fundamentalists: now the exchange rate is at a higher level, close to (or above) the value they judge appropriate. A similar story happens when there is a capital flight from Argentinean households.

There was an experiment, though, in which nothing happened and that is a lesson. We modelled a change in the portfolio allocation of American households: they buy more Argentinean bills denominated in pesos than in dollars. And nothing happened. There was no change relative to the baseline scenario. No more foreign reserves, no peso appreciation. And in a sense, that is not unrealistic: the same amount of dollars keeps flowing into the country. The difference is that, when buying bills in dollars, it is the government that sells those dollars to the central bank, while if investors buy bills in pesos they sell their dollars themselves to the central bank (in our model at least; in reality there is a different route). But this also has implications for a capital flight: there is no big difference between being indebted in your own currency or in a foreign currency when financial investors leave the country. Because, just as they sell dollars when they flow in, they buy dollars when they flow out. This holds more for a developing country, but the argument is solid: if there is a good degree of convertibility between the domestic currency and a foreign currency (and nowadays, that is a fact), even if a developing country has most of its debt denominated in its own currency, it is still liable to a balance of payments crisis due to a capital outflow, because investors will demand the international currency, and if that country does not have enough it might be forced to implement capital controls or even default. Ebeke and Lu (2014) have found that, effectively, foreign holdings of local currency government bonds have increased in the post-Lehman crisis period. However, the authors find that this has led to *increased volatility* in government yields. The key issue here is that of *convertibility*, or asset substitution, as we mentioned before: if it is easy to sell one currency for the other, then developing countries are liable to balance of payments problems even in the face of flexible exchange rates and a high share of public debt denominated in its own currency. There are nuances, however, and they are important.

We differentiated between households' regular income and disposable income by noticing that the disposable income definition included tax payments and capital gains on the holdings of financial assets denominated in a foreign currency due to movements in the exchange rate. And here comes the point. Let's assume a flexible exchange rate regime in a scenario capital outflow and a depreciation of the peso. If the Argentinean government has a high proportion of its debt denominated in dollars when facing a capital outflow and a depreciation of its currency, it will have to sell more pesos for the same debt denominated in dollars. That is, it will face a capital loss. However, if most of its debt is denominated in pesos, the capital loss will be borne by investors, not by the government. This is a relevant feature.

With fixed exchange rates, the danger is even greater, because the government has to provide the dollars demanded by investors who drop bills denominated in pesos when they leave the country. In the next chapter we will discuss in more depth the policy implications of this result for developing countries.

A simplifying assumption that we have maintained in this analysis is that, for bonds denominated in dollars, Argentina pays the same interest rate as the United States. That is clearly not realistic. Bonds of developing countries usually pay a premium over the risk-free asset. Higher interest rates on domestic liabilities than the earnings on foreign assets can give rise to a Ponzi dynamics, independent of the currency in which it is denominated. Another assumption that we adopted for ease was that the Argentinean government granted all the bonds that were required, and that whatever remained loose was bought/sold by the Argentinean central bank. However, in the real world, the government has more ample room to decide, in normal times, how much to borrow and under what conditions, which obviously include currency denomination. But as we have seen, the effect on the exchange rate of financial inflows either to buy bonds in pesos or in dollars does not vary too much, if the central bank has room (meaning reserves) to control the interest rate.

It is also interesting to see what happens when *firms* change their funding decisions. Suppose Argentinean firms start to borrow more in the US. In the simulation with the flexible ER regime, we increased that proportion from 20 per cent to 30 per cent of their total borrowing requirements, while in the fixed ER closure we raised it to 50 per cent. Let us start with the latter. The current account of Argentina deteriorates, but aggregate demand does not deteriorate and prices do not change. Remember, the ER does not move. But what happens to the banking sector and private debt is quite revealing. Figure 4.5 shows selected variables of the balance sheet of American banks. The lines corresponding to banks' profits and banks' net wealth should be read in the secondary (right hand) axis; the others, in the left-hand axis.

The increase in borrowing by Argentinean firms forces US banks to sell all their holdings of bills. They face a sudden change in their asset composition. They would sell even more bills than what they have (the pointed line representing notional demand of bills goes into negativity). But since they cannot do that, they are forced to ask for advances from the central bank to fund their lending (the line that, starting from zero, goes up initially and then returns to zero around 1970; notional and actual demand of bills are the same after 10 periods). The central bank accepts that, but in order to keep its balance sheet it is forced to sell the bills it holds. Who buys them? The Argentinean central bank, of course. It must, if it wants

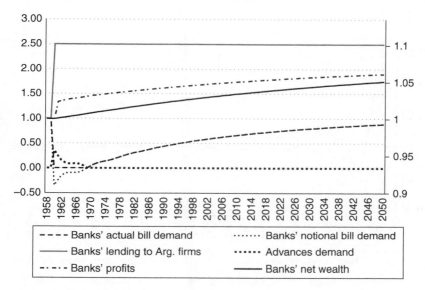

Source: Author's calculations.

Figure 4.5   *Behaviour of selected variables in the balance sheet of*
              American banks

to preserve the exchange rate. Foreign reserves increase substantially, and
their rhythm is only reduced when banks start to invest their increased
profits in bills, the equivalent of parking them in the central bank, as we
see nowadays. That is why banks' profits and net wealth increase: lending
goes up.

The opposite happens in Argentina. Lending goes down, pulling down
profits and net wealth. They invest what they do not lend in bills, which
are sold by the central bank to sterilize its purchase of foreign reserves.
I believe that this situation represents appropriately the run-up to the
Asian crisis, as told by Kregel (1998): an explosion of foreign borrowing
in a context of stable ER and increased reserves, triggered by financial
liberalization in those countries and increased reserves. When something
went wrong, those reserves were not enough, because private debt had
also escalated. This description also fits with our concerns regarding debt
denomination which were mentioned above and which will be discussed
further in the next chapter.

In the flexible exchange rate the situation is as one should expect by now.
The exchange rate appreciates, there is an inflow of capital, and the current
account deteriorates, but not as much as in the fixed ER closure. American

Source: Author's calculations.

Figure 4.6   Impact in Argentina after a 10 per cent devaluation in a fixed ER regime

banks are also forced to borrow from their central bank in order to keep pace with their lending.

When Argentina actually devaluates while keeping its fixed exchange regime, households face two different effects: on one side, their real wage is diminished. On the other, they enjoy a once-in-a-lifetime capital gain on holdings of foreign bills (not actually true, of course; devaluations are common events, but in our model this episode occurs once in 100 years). In the real world, the people who suffer mostly from the former are not those who enjoy the latter. What prevails in the outcome? Figure 4.6 shows us.

The graph shows us that real disposable income spikes first, driving later consumption with it. Remember that expected disposable income is backward looking. But real wealth falls due to the impact of a higher price level on the other assets. In the medium run, disposable income realigns itself with the real wage, albeit in a somewhat cyclical fashion due to the correction mechanism in the expectations described above. Real exports increase, foreign reserves increase, bills demands by American households and the Fed decline.

But what if a devaluation is expected but does not occur? Assume that $xra^{\#}$ increases 10 per cent: fundamentalist traders now believe that the Argentinean ER is worth 10 per cent less. The demand for bills denominated in pesos falls, and the demand for bills denominated in dollars, issued both by the American and the Argentinean governments, increases. This is not corrected over time, since neither the exchange rate nor the value judged by the trader changes. The impact of the higher demand for American bills is indeed responsible for the fall in foreign reserves. And in the flexible ER regime? It does translate into a small depreciation of the peso, which slightly reduces the PSBR of the American government. Argentineans demand more American bills, but their demand represents less (in marginal terms, admittedly) and so interest payments fall. Argentinean real exports increase a little, and so firms profit.

4.5.3 Distribution Issues

In our model, does a higher wage demand (say, a higher ω_1) bring higher growth? No. Does a higher mark-up (say, a higher π_0) cause higher growth? Again, no. Both together? No. Figures 4.7 and 4.8 show Argentinean real GDP and its (real) components (other than real public expenditure) for the first five years after the change (in 1960), in the case of higher wage

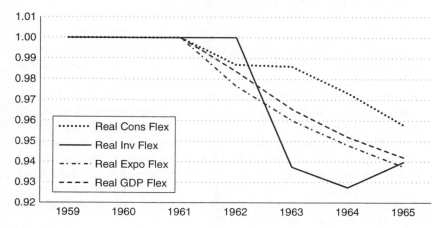

Source: Author's calculations.

Figure 4.7 Effect of an increase of 20 per cent in the real wage targeted by Argentinean workers

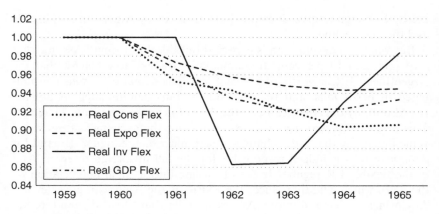

Source: Author's calculations.

Figure 4.8   Effect of a 20 per cent increase in the mark-up of Argentinean firms

demand and higher mark-up, only in the flexible exchange rate regime, for reasons of space. There is a stark resemblance between these results and the implications of the Hein and Vogel (2008) model presented in the previous chapter, particularly in the reaction of the real exchange rate to changes in distributive variables. The timing of changes will show that exports are the main driving force in this context.

In the case of an increase in ω_1 in the fixed ER regime there is actually a very slight increase of real consumption in the year 1962, but the fall in real exports is substantial, dragging down first real GDP and afterwards real investment. The effect of the latter is much more pronounced than in the flexible ER.

Two well-established facts are that investment tracks GDP, and it does so with wild fluctuations. That is the essence of the accelerator principle. Why does real consumption fall so hard, even if the real wage increases as it does? Because to the depressing effect of falling real GDP on employment, one has to add precisely the effects of real wages on productivity: a higher real wage stimulates productivity. The real wage bill (real wage times the employment level, which is a good proxy for the real wage rate) actually falls, even though the wage share rises, because productivity increases only a fraction of the amelioration in the real wage.

Table 4.3 summarizes the impact of some shocks on a few selected variables, particularly shocks to the propensity to consume out of disposable income of Argentinean households, and the rate of growth of public expenditure of the Argentinean government.

Table 4.3   Summary of shock responses

Shock on	Effect on	Argentina		USA	
		Flexible ER	Fixed ER	Flexible ER	Fixed ER
Propensity to	Real output	+	+	+	+
consume in	Real wage	–	–	+	+
Argentina	Current account	–	+	+	+
Public	Real output	+	+	+	+
expenditure	Real wage	–	–	+	+
in Argentina	Current account	–	+	+	+

Source: Author's elaboration.

We performed experiments moving the flat segment of the Phillips curve for 'USA'. We did not find major noticeable changes in the variables. But we did not want to finish the paper without any finding that might propose some solution, even in this highly sketched model, for a great scourge of our times, which is the situation in the European 'periphery' of Greece, Spain Ireland, and so on. And we do have interesting findings.

4.5.4   Something to Say about Europe

Even though no European country has a central bank and cannot print its own currency, at least that is what the treaties say, we can think of a fixed ER as a proxy for a monetary union, and to treat, in our case, Greece as 'Argentina' and Germany as the 'USA'. And given what we saw, the high sensitivity our results have to changes in external competitiveness, one might be tempted to say that a good and viable solution for Greece would be a German 'inflation', meaning by that an increase in its real wage. Even more, let us make German imports even more sensitive to this deterioration in its price-competitiveness by increasing, precisely, its price-elasticity. The results are not as encouraging as one would like.

We increased by 10 per cent the price-elasticity of German imports e_1 and also ω_{1u}, which in this case, making use of our imagination, corresponds to the wage aspiration of German workers. As expected, Greek exports improve, and GDP follows, but not that much, because there is another depressing force: consumption. The increase in German wages is translated into export prices, and even though there is some 'substitution' between German and Greek production, it is of little magnitude for the consumption basket of Greek workers who see their real wages go down due to higher import prices. A moderate increase in German wages might solve the trade balance problem, but does not improve the situation of

Greek workers. There are some imports that are not easily replaceable, and others which are not replaceable at all. Something else must change for the Greek economy (measured by real GDP) and the situation of Greek workers to improve at the same time. It is not mostly a problem of price-competitiveness; it is more a problem of economic structure (Felipe and Kumar 2011; Gaulier and Vicard 2013; Schroeder 2015; Storm and Naastepad 2015). Where can we find the solution?

One idea is to invest more in Greece, let's say by raising autonomous investment. And yes, this does have positive effects: Greek employment increases, GDP as well, and the PSBR falls. But the trade balance deteriorates together with the current account. Notice that in this case we do not have twin deficits: we have a public surplus and external deficit, because the former is not as big as the private deficit. Twin deficits are not an economic necessity, as the IMF programmes want us to believe. So how can we solve them? The ideal world is a Marshall Plan that changes the economic structure of Greece and makes it less dependent on imports. We model this by increasing γ_{0a} (which stands for autonomous investment) and at the same time increasing e_0 10 per cent, that is, the propensity of the German economy to import from Greece. Figure 4.9 shows what happens. Real GDP in Greece increases, employment increases, consumption increases, the current account improves and public sector borrowing falls, for both

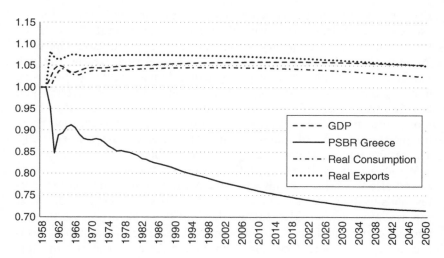

Source: Author's calculations.

Figure 4.9   Effect after an increase in autonomous investment in Greece and German propensity to import from Greece

factors. Even though Germany experiences a fall in its in GDP, in the long run it starts to improve due to higher imports of a booming Greece. Our conviction in the necessity, if Greece is going to stay in the euro (a big if), of a Marshall Plan instead of limited changes in relative prices does not come just from these results, but is also based in empirical literature, such as Felipe and Kumar (2011) and Papadimitriou, Zezza and Nikiforos (2013). Our simulations, although limited in their characteristics, give us a little more confidence in advancing these solutions.

4.6 CONCLUSIONS

The chapter presented a model developed with a methodology, the stock-flow consistent approach, which allows the modeller to 'follow the money'. Our model had a good number of macroeconomic features associated with post-Keynesian economics, with some of them having been endorsed by international organizations (like the IMF, in the case of a Phillips curve with a flat segment) and public institutions (like numerous central banks, in the case of the endogenous money theory) because, well, they have been repeatedly corroborated in the real world!

The simulations we performed gave us diverse conclusions, in spite of the simplistic nature of some of our assumptions. In order to save space, we highlight just two points.

First, the behaviour of the exchange rate depends on the financial positions of the different sectors (including the government), the portfolio allocation and exchange rate expectations of traders, and is not strictly related to the behaviour of the current account of the balance of payments. The exchange rate (in a flexible exchange rate regime) or the reserves equilibrate the demand and supply of funding that a country and its agents require and/or demand, according to the currency in which this funding is offered/required. In different simulations, a current account surplus for one country coexisted either with a depreciating exchange rate or an appreciating one. If any causality can be observed, one could say that the movement of the exchange rate influences the trade balance much more than the other way around. However, this does not mean that the exchange rate plays an equilibrating role on the balance of trade or the current account; on the contrary.

Secondly, our results show that different exchange rate regimes might each have positive and negative consequences under different circumstances. We therefore find ourselves in agreement with Palley (2003) in the sense that an active management of both exchange policy and capital mobility can avoid the dangers associated with the passivity of the government in face of the disruptive consequence each extreme case might have. The set of rules for this management can (and should) be designed to achieve different targets in terms of employment, output, inflation and balance of payments performance: it is not easy, but it can be done, even in an open-economy context.

The model presented here, however, is not suitable to perform econometric analyses. In the next chapter we will develop a one-country model that will help us to establish the empirical relevance of demand-led (and Kaleckian) models of growth, adding the impact of foreign debt and using many of the corollaries obtained in the simulations performed above.

NOTES

1. This chapter presents an enlarged and revised version of Bortz (2014).
2. See Humphrey (1985) for a history of (earlier than) the Phillip's curve.
3. Chapter 3 of Lavoie (2014) thoroughly explains the post-Keynesian theory of consumer choice.

APPENDIX A: LIST OF EQUATIONS OF SFC MODEL

(1u) $s_u = c_u + i_u + g_u + x_u$

(1a) $s_a = c_a + i_a + g_a + x_a$

(2u) $S_u = s_u.p_{su}$

(2a) $S_a = s_a.p_{sa}$

(3u) $y_u = s_u - im_u$

(3a) $y_a = s_a - im_a$

(4u) $Y_u = S_u - IM_u$

(4a) $Y_a = S_a - IM_a$

(5u) $p_{yu} = \dfrac{Y_u}{y_u}$

(5a) $p_{ya} = \dfrac{Y_a}{y_a}$

(6u) $p_{mu} = ps_a.xr_u$

(6a) $p_{ma} = ps_u.xr_a$

(7u) $IM_u = im_u.p_{mu}$

(7a) $IM_a = im_a.p_{ma}$

(8u) $X_u = x_u.p_{su}$

(8a) $X_a = x_a.p_{sa}$

(9u) $C_u = c_u.p_{su}$

(9a) $C_a = c_a.p_{sa}$

(10u) $I_u = i_u.p_{su}$

(10a) $I_a = i_a.p_{sa}$

(11u) $G_u = g_u.p_{su}$

(11a) $G_a = g_a.p_{sa}$

(12u) $p_{su} = \dfrac{(1 + \pi_u).(W_u.N_u + IM_u + rl_{u(-1)}.L^u_{us(-1)})}{s_u}$

$$(12a)\ p_{sa} = \frac{(1 + \pi_a).\left(\begin{array}{c}W_a.N_a + IM_a + rl_{a(-1)}.L^a_{as(-1)} \\ + rl_{u(-1)}.L^u_{as(-1)}.xra\end{array}\right)}{s_a}$$

$$(13u)\ \pi_u = \pi_{0u} + \pi_{1u}.\left(\frac{\Delta(xr_{u(-1)})}{xr_{u(-1)}}\right)$$

$$(13a)\ \pi_a = \pi_{0a} + \pi_{1a}.\left(\frac{\Delta(xr_{a(-1)})}{xr_{a(-1)}}\right)$$

$$(14u)\ W_u = W_{u(-1)} + \omega_{0u}.(w^T_{u(-1)}.p_{su} - W_{u(-1)})$$

$$(14a)\ W_a = W_{a(-1)} + \omega_{0a}.(w^T_{a(-1)}.p_{sa} - W_{a(-1)})$$

$$(15u)\ w^T_u = \omega_{1u} + \omega_{2u}.(EMP_u + z_{1u}.[EMP^\#_u - EMP_u] - z_{2u}.bandb_u + z_{3u}.bandt_u)$$

$$(15a)\ w^T_a = \omega_{1a} + \omega_{2a}.(EMP_a + z_{1a}.[EMP^\#_a - EMP_a] - z_{2a}.bandb_a + z_{3a}.bandt_a)$$

$(16ui)\ z_{1u} = 1$ if $bandb_u < EMP_u < bandt_u$

$(16uii)\ z_{2u} = 1$ if $bandb_u > EMP_u$

$(16uiii)\ z_{3u} = 1$ if $EMP_u > bandt_u$

$(16ai)\ z_{1a} = 1$ if $bandb_a < EMP_a < bandt_a$

$(16aii)\ z_{2a} = 1$ if $bandb_a > EMP_a$

$(16aiii)\ z_{3a} = 1$ if $EMP_a > bandt_a$

$$(17u)\ EMP_u = \Delta(N_{u(-1)}) \big/ N_{u(-1)}$$

$$(17a)\ EMP_a = \Delta(N_{a(-1)}) \big/ N_{a(-1)}$$

$(18u)\ w_u = W_u/p_{su}$

$(18a)\ w_a = W_a/p_{sa}$

$(19u)\ N_u = y_u/pr_u$

$(19a)\ N_a = y_a/pr_a$

$(20u)\ pr_u = pr_u.(1 + g_{pru})$

$(20a)\ pr_a = pr_a.(1 + g_{pra})$

$$(21u)\ g_{pru} = q_u.\left(\Delta(w_{u(-1)}) \big/ w_{u(-1)}\right)$$

$(21a)\ g_{pra} = q_a \cdot \left(\Delta(w_{a(-1)}) \Big/ w_{a(-1)} \right)$

$(22u)\ im_u = \varepsilon_o \cdot \left(\dfrac{p_{yu(-1)}}{p_{mu(-1)}} \right)^{e_1} \cdot y_u^{e_2}$

$(22a)\ im_a = \mu_o \cdot \left(\dfrac{p_{ya(-1)}}{p_{ma(-1)}} \right)^{\mu_1} \cdot y_a^{\mu_2}$

$(23u)\ x_u = im_a$

$(23a)\ x_a = im_u$

$(24u)\ K_u = k_u \cdot p_{su}$

$(24a)\ K_a = k_a \cdot p_{sa}$

$(25u)\ k_u = k_{u(-1)} \cdot (1 - \delta_u + gk_u)$

$(25a)\ k_a = k_{a(-1)} \cdot (1 - \delta_a + gk_a)$

$(26u)\ i_u = k_{u(-1)} \cdot (gk_u + \delta_u)$

$(26a)\ i_a = k_{a(-1)} \cdot (gk_a + \delta_a)$

$(27u)\ DA_u = \delta_u \cdot K_{u(-1)}$

$(27a)\ DA_a = \delta_a \cdot K_{a(-1)}$

$(28u)\ gk_u = \gamma_{0u} + \gamma_{1u} \cdot \left(\Delta y_{u(-1)} \Big/ y_{u(-1)} \right)$

$(28a)\ gk_a = \gamma_{0a} + \gamma_{1a} \cdot \left(\Delta y_{a(-1)} \Big/ y_{a(-1)} \right)$

$(29u)\ z_u = \dfrac{y_u}{k_{u(-1)}}$

$(29a)\ z_a = \dfrac{y_a}{k_{a(-1)}}$

$(30u)\ V_{fu} = K_u - L_{us}^u$

$(30a)\ V_{fa} = K_a - L_{as}^a - L_{as}^u \cdot xra$

$(31u)\ L_{ud}^u = L_{us(-1)}^u \cdot (1 + rl_{u(-1)}) + I_u - DA_u - F_{fu(-1)}$

$(31ai)\ L_{ad} = L_{as(-1)}^a \cdot (1 + rl_{a(-1)}) + L_{as(-1)}^u \cdot (1 + rl_{u(-1)}) \cdot xra + I_a - DA_a - F_{fa(-1)}$

$(31aii)\ L_{ad}^a = v \cdot L_{ad}$

$(31aiii)\ L_{ad}^u = L_{ad} - L_{ad}^a$

$(32u)$ $F_{fu} = Y_u - W_u.N_u - rl_{u(-1)}.L^u_{us(-1)} - DA_u$

$(32a)$ $F_{fa} = Y_a - W_a.N_a - rl_{a(-1)}.L^a_{as(-1)} - rl_{u(-1)}.L^u_{as(-1)}.xra - DA_a$

$(33u)$ $Yr_u = W_u.N_u + r_{mu(-1)}.M_{us(-1)} + rb_{u(-1)}.B^u_{hus(-1)} + rb_{a(-1)}.B^{\$a}_{hus(-1)}.xru + rb_{u(-1)}.B^{\$u}_{hus(-1)}$

$(33a)$ $Yr_a = W_a.N_a + r_{ma(-1)}.M_{as(-1)} + rb_{a(-1)}.B^a_{has(-1)} + rb_{u(-1)}.B^u_{has(-1)}.xra$

$(34u)$ $T_u = \theta_u.Yr_u$

$(34a)$ $T_a = \theta_a.Yr_a$

$(35u)$ $YD_u = Yr_u + \Delta xru.B^{\$a}_{hus(-1)} - T_u$

$(35a)$ $YD_a = Yr_a + \Delta xra.B^u_{has(-1)} - T_a$

$(36u)$ $yd_u = \dfrac{YD_u}{p_{su}}$

$(36a)$ $yd_a = \dfrac{YD_a}{p_{sa}}$

$(37u)$ $yd^e_u = yd_{u(-1)} + \beta_u.(yd_{u(-1)} - yd^e_{u(-1)})$

$(37a)$ $yd^e_a = yd_{a(-1)} + \beta_a.(yd_{a(-1)} - yd^e_{a(-1)})$

$(38u)$ $YD^e_u = yd^e_u.p_{su(-1)}$

$(38a)$ $YD^e_a = yd^e_a.p_{sa(-1)}$

$(39u)$ $V_{hu} = V_{hu(-1)} + YD_u - C_u$

$(39a)$ $V_{ha} = V_{ha(-1)} + YD_a - C_a$

$(40u)$ $v_{hu} = \dfrac{V_{hu}}{p_{su}}$

$(40a)$ $v_{ha} = \dfrac{V_{ha}}{p_{sa}}$

$(41u)$ $V^e_{hu} = V_{hu(-1)} + YD^e_u - C_u$

$(41a)$ $V^e_{ha} = V_{ha(-1)} + YD^e_a - C_a$

$(42u)$ $c_u = \alpha_{1u}.yd^e_u + \alpha_{2u}.v_{hu(-1)}$

$(42a)$ $c_a = \alpha_{1a}.yd^e_a + \alpha_{2a}.v_{ha(-1)}$

$(43ui)$ $M^n_{ud} = V^e_{hu}.(\lambda_{10} + \lambda_{11}.rm_u + \lambda_{12}.rb_u + \lambda_{13}.[rb_a + dxru^e] + \lambda_{14}.[rb_u - \varphi])$

$(43uii)$ $B^u_{hud} = V^e_{hu}.(\lambda_{20} + \lambda_{21}.rm_u + \lambda_{22}.rb_u + \lambda_{23}.[rb_a + dxru^e] + \lambda_{24}.[rb_u - \varphi])$

$(43uiii)$ $B^{\$a}_{hud} = V^e_{hu}.(\lambda_{30} + \lambda_{31}.rm_u + \lambda_{32}.rb_u + \lambda_{33}.[rb_a + dxru^e] + \lambda_{34}.[rb_u - \varphi])$

(43uiv) $B_{hud}^{\$u} = V_{hu}^{e}.(\lambda_{40} + \lambda_{41}.rm_u + \lambda_{42}.rb_u + \lambda_{43}.[rb_a + dxru^e] + \lambda_{44}.[rb_u - \varphi])$

(43uv) $H_{ud}^n = V_{hu} - M_{ud}^n - B_{hud}^u - B_{hud}^{\$a} - B_{hud}^{\$u}$

(43ai) $M_{ad}^n = V_{ha}^e.(\lambda_{50} + \lambda_{51}.rm_a + \lambda_{52}.rb_a + \lambda_{53}.[rb_u + dxra^e])$

(43aii) $B_{had}^a = V_{ha}^e.(\lambda_{60} + \lambda_{61}.rm_a + \lambda_{62}.rb_a + \lambda_{63}.[rb_a + dxru^e])$

(43aiii) $B_{had}^u = V_{ha}^e.(\lambda_{70} + \lambda_{71}.rm_a + \lambda_{72}.rb_a + \lambda_{73}.[rb_a + dxru^e])$

(43aiv) $H_{ad}^n = V_{ha} - M_{ad}^n - B_{had}^u - B_{had}^a$

(44u) $H_{ud} = H_{ud}^n.z_{4u}$

(44a) $H_{ad} = H_{ad}^n.z_{4a}$

(45a) $z_{4u} = 1$ if $H_{ud}^n > 0$

(45u) $z_{4a} = 1$ if $H_{ad}^n > 0$

(46u) $M_{ud} = M_{ud}^n.z_{4u} + (V_{hu} - B_{hud}^u - B_{hud}^{\$a} - B_{hud}^{\$u}).z_{5u}$

(46a) $M_{ad} = M_{ad}^n.z_{4a} + (V_{ha} - B_{had}^u - B_{had}^a).z_{5a}$

(47u) $z_{5u} = 1$ if $H_{ud}^n < 0$

(47a) $z_{5a} = 1$ if $H_{ad}^n < 0$

(48u) $dxru^e = - dxra^e$

(48ai) $dxra^e = \chi^f.dxra^{ef} + \chi^c.dxra^{ec}$

(48aii) $dxra^{ef} = \zeta.\left(\dfrac{xra^{\#} - xra_{(-1)}}{xra_{(-1)}}\right)$

(48aiii) $dxra^{ec} = \xi.\left(\Delta(xra_{(-1)}\Big/ xra_{(-1)})\right)$

(49) $\rho = \left(B_{hud(-1)}^{\$u}\Big/ Y_{a(-1)}.xru_{(-1)}\right)$

(50) $\phi = \kappa.(\Delta(\rho)/\rho)$

(51u) $M_{us} = M_{ud}$

(51a) $M_{as} = M_{ad}$

(52ui) $L_{us}^u = L_{ud}^u$

(52uii) $L_{as}^u = L_{ad}^u.xru$

(52a) $L_{as}^a = L_{ad}^a$

(53u) $B_{bud}^{nu} = M_{us} + V_{bu} - L_{as}^u - L_{us}^u$

$(53a)\ B_{bad}^{na} = M_{as} + V_{ba} - L_{as}^{a}$

$(54u)\ B_{bud}^{u} = B_{bud}^{nu} \cdot z_{6u}$

$(54a)\ B_{bad}^{a} = B_{bad}^{na} \cdot z_{6a}$

$(55u)\ z_{6u} = 1$ if $B_{bud}^{nu} > 0$

$(55a)\ z_{6a} = 1$ if $B_{bad}^{na} > 0$

$(56u)\ A_{ud} = (L_{as}^{u} + L_{us}^{u} - M_{us} - V_{bu}) \cdot z_{7u}$

$(56a)\ A_{ad} = (L_{as}^{a} - M_{as} - V_{ba}) \cdot z_{7a}$

$(57u)\ z_{7u} = 1$ if $B_{bud}^{nu} < 0$

$(57a)\ z_{7a} = 1$ if $B_{bad}^{na} < 0$

$(58u)\ F_{bu} = rl_{u(-1)} \cdot L_{us(-1)}^{u} + rl_{u(-1)} \cdot L_{as(-1)}^{u} + rb_{u(-1)} \cdot B_{bus(-1)}^{u} - rm_{u(-1)} \cdot M_{us(-1)} - ra_{u(-1)} \cdot A_{us(-1)}$

$(58a)\ F_{ba} = rl_{a(-1)} \cdot L_{as(-1)}^{a} + rb_{a(-1)} \cdot B_{has(-1)}^{a} - rm_{a(-1)} \cdot M_{as(-1)} - ra_{a(-1)} \cdot A_{as(-1)}$

$(59u)\ V_{bu} = V_{bu(-1)} + F_{bu}$

$(59a)\ V_{ba} = V_{ba(-1)} + F_{ba}$

$(60u)\ rl_{u} = rb_{u} \cdot (1 + \iota_{u})$

$(60a)\ rl_{a} = rb_{a} \cdot (1 + \iota_{a})$

$(61u)\ r_{mu} = r_{bu}$

$(61a)\ r_{ma} = r_{ba}$

$(62u)\ ra_{u} = rb_{u} \cdot (1 + \sigma_{u})$

$(62a)\ ra_{a} = rb_{a} \cdot (1 + \sigma_{a})$

$(63u)\ g_{u} = g_{u(-1)} \cdot (1 + \upsilon_{u})$

$(63a)\ g_{a} = g_{a(-1)} \cdot (1 + \upsilon_{a})$

$(64u)\ B_{s}^{u} = B_{s(-1)}^{u} + G_{u} - T_{u} + r_{bu(-1)} \cdot B_{s(-1)}^{u} - F_{cbu}$

$(64ai)\ B_{s}^{a} = B_{s(-1)}^{\$a} \cdot (1 + r_{ba(-1)}) + B_{hud(-1)}^{\$u} \cdot (1 + r_{bu(-1)}) \cdot xra + G_{a} - T_{a} - F_{cba}$

$(64aii)\ B_{s}^{\$a} = B_{has}^{a} + B_{hus}^{\$a} + B_{bas}^{a} + B_{cbas}^{\$a}$

$(65u)\ B_{hus}^{u} = B_{hud}^{u}$

$(65a)\ B_{has}^{a} = B_{had}^{a}$

$(66uFX)\ B_{has}^{u} = B_{had}^{u} \cdot xru$

$(66ai)\ B_{hus}^{\$a} = B_{hud}^{\$a} \cdot xra$

$(66aii)$ $B_{hus}^{\$u} = B_{hud}^{\$u}.xra$

$(67u)$ $B_{bus}^{u} = B_{bud}^{u}$

$(67a)$ $B_{bas}^{a} = B_{bad}^{a}$

$(68u)$ $H_{us} = H_{ud}$

$(68a)$ $H_{as} = H_{ad}$

$(69u)$ $A_{us} = A_{ud}$

$(69a)$ $A_{as} = A_{ad}$

$(70u)$ $B_{cbud}^{u} = H_{us} - A_{us}$

$(70a)$ $B_{cbad}^{a} = B_{cbad(-1)}^{a} + \Delta(H_{as}) - \Delta(B_{cbas}^{u}).xra$

$(71u)$ $B_{cbus}^{u} = B_{cbud}^{u}$

$(71a)$ $B_{cbas}^{a} = B_{cbad}^{a}$

$(72uFX)$ $B_{cbas}^{u} = B_{s}^{u} - B_{hus}^{u} - B_{bus}^{u} - B_{cbus}^{u} - B_{has}^{u}$

$(72a)$ $B_{cbad}^{u} = B_{cbas}^{u}.xra$

$(73uFX)$ $xru = constant$

$(73a)$ $xra = xru$

$(74u)$ $F_{cbu} = rb_{u(-1)}.B_{cbus(-1)}^{u} + ra_{u(-1)}.A_{us(-1)}$

$(74a)$ $F_{cba} = r_{ba(-1)}.B_{cbas(-1)}^{a} + ra_{a(-1)}.A_{as(-1)} + rb_{u(-1)}.B_{cbas(-1)}^{u}.xra$

$(66uFL)$ $B_{has}^{u} = B_{s}^{u} - B_{hus}^{u} - B_{bus}^{u} - B_{cbus}^{u} - B_{cbas}^{u}$

$(72uFL)$ $B_{cbas}^{u} = constant$

$(73uFL)$ $xru = B_{has}^{u} \Big/ B_{had}^{u}$

$(75u)$ $CA_{u} = X_{u} - IM_{u} + r_{ba(-1)}.B_{hus(-1)}^{\$a}.xru + r_{bu(-1)}.B_{hud(-1)}^{\$u}$
$\qquad + r_{lu(-1)}.L_{as(-1)}^{u} - r_{bu(-1)}.B_{has(-1)}^{u} - r_{bu(-1)}B_{cbas(-1)}^{u}$

$(75a)$ $CA_{a} = X_{a} - IM_{a} + r_{bu(-1)}.(B_{has(-1)}^{u} + B_{cbas(-1)}^{u}).xra - r_{ba(-1)}.B_{hus(-1)}^{\$a}$
$\qquad - r_{bu(-1)}.B_{hud(-1)}^{\$u}.xra - r_{lu(-1)}.L_{as(-1)}^{u}.xra$

$(76u)$ $KA_{u} = \Delta B_{has}^{u} + \Delta B_{cbas}^{u} - \Delta B_{hus}^{\$a}.xru - \Delta B_{hud}^{\$u} - \Delta L_{as}^{u}$

$(76a)$ $KA_{a} = \Delta B_{hus}^{\$a} + \Delta B_{hud}^{\$u}.xra - \Delta B_{has}^{u}.xra - \Delta B_{cbas}^{u}.xra - \Delta L_{as}^{u}.xra$

APPENDIX B: INITIAL VALUES OF VARIABLES AND PARAMETERS

s_u =	2288.51608	z_{3u} =	0	L_{ud}^u =	5000.00	λ_{23} =	−0.01
s_a =	2288.51608	z_{1a} =	1	L_{ad}^u =	5000.00	λ_{24} =	−0.02
S_u =	4577.03216	z_{2a} =	0	L_{ad}^u =	1000.00	λ_{32} =	−0.01
S_a =	4577.03216	z_{3a} =	0	F_{fu} =	145.631068	λ_{33} =	0.1
y_u =	1830.81286	EMP_u =	0.03	F_{fa} =	145.631068	λ_{34} =	−0.05
y_a =	1830.81286	EMP_a =	0.03	Yr_u =	3125	λ_{40} =	0.125
Y_u =	3661.62573	w_u =	0.5	Yr_a =	3125	λ_{41} =	−0.02
Y_a =	3661.62573	w_a =	0.5	T_u =	625	λ_{42} =	−0.02
p_{yu} =	2	N_u =	2855.800483	T_a =	625	λ_{43} =	−0.05
p_{ya} =	2	N_a =	2855.800483	θ_u =	0.2	λ_{44} =	0.1
p_{mu} =	2	pr_u =	0.641085704	θ_a =	0.2	M_{ad}^n =	1998.381877
p_{ma} =	2	pr_a =	0.641085704	YD_u =	2500	B_{had}^a =	4995.954693
IM_u =	915.406432	g_{pru} =	0.03	YD_a =	2500	B_{had}^u =	2248.179612
IM_a =	915.406432	g_{pra} =	0.03	yd_u =	1250	H_{ad}^n =	757.48
X_u =	915.406432	q_u =	0.3	yd_a =	1250	λ_{50} =	0.2
X_a =	915.406432	q_a =	0.3	yd_u^{te} =	1245.954693	λ_{51} =	0.1
C_u =	2208.73786	im_u =	457.7032158	yd_a^{te} =	1245.954693	λ_{52} =	−0.05
C_a =	2208.73786	im_a =	457.7032158	β_u =	0.2	λ_{53} =	−0.03
I_u =	776.699029	ε_0 =	0.25	β_a =	0.2	λ_{60} =	0.5
I_a =	776.699029	ε_1 =	0.7	YD_u^e =	2491.909385	λ_{61} =	−0.05
G_u =	676.188833	ε_2 =	1	YD_a^e =	2491.909385	λ_{62} =	0.1
G_a =	676.188833	μ_0 =	0.25	V_{hu} =	10000.00	λ_{63} =	−0.03

Variable	Value	Variable	Value	Variable	Value	Variable	Value
P_{su} =	2	μ_1 =	0.7	V_{hu} =	10000.00	λ_{70} =	0.225
P_{sa} =	2	μ_2 =	1	V_{hu} =	5000	λ_{71} =	-0.03
π_u =	0.159927	x_u =	457.7032158	V_{ha} =	5000	λ_{72} =	-0.03
π_a =	0.159927	x_a =	457.7032158	V_{hu}^e =	9991.909385	λ_{73} =	0.07
π_{0u} =	0.159927	K_u =	10000.00	V_{ha}^e =	9991.909385	H_{ud} =	757.48
π_{0a} =	0.159927	K_a =	10000.00	c_u =	1104.368932	H_{ad} =	757.48
π_{1u} =	0.2	K_u =	5000	c_a =	1104.368932	z_{4u} =	1
π_{1a} =	0.2	K_a =	5000	α_{h1u} =	0.75	z_{4a} =	1
W_u =	1	i_u =	388.3495146	α_{2u} =	0.75	M_{ud} =	1998.381877
W_a =	1	i_a =	388.3495146	α_{1a} =	0.035	M_{ad} =	1998.381877
ω_{0u} =	0.2	DA_u =	485.4368932	α_{2a} =	0.035	z_{5u} =	0
ω_{0a} =	0.2	DA_a =	485.4368932	M_{ud}^n =	1998.381877	z_{5a} =	0
w_u^T =	0.5	δ_u =	0.05	B_{hud}^{Su} =	4995.954693	$dxrn^e$ =	0
w_a^T =	0.5	δ_a =	0.05	B_{hud}^a =	999.1909385	$dxra^e$ =	0
ω_{1u} =	0.5	gk_u =	0.03	B_{hud}^u =	1248.988673	χ^f =	0.75
ω_{1a} =	0.5	gk_a =	0.03	H_{ud}^n =	757.48	χ^c =	0.25
ω_{2u} =	0.2	γ_{0u} =	0.02	λ_{10} =	0.2	$dxra^{ef}$ =	0
ω_{2a} =	0.2	γ_{0a} =	0.02	λ_{11} =	0.1	ζ =	0.2
$bandb_u$ =	0.003	γ_{1u} =	0.3	λ_{12} =	-0.05	$dxra^{cc}$ =	0
$bandt_u$ =	0.003	γ_{1a} =	0.3	λ_{13} =	-0.01	η =	0.2
$bandb_a$ =	0.003	z_u =	0.3619304	λ_{14} =	-0.02	ρ =	0.34110224
$bandt_a$ =	0.003	z_a =	0.3619304	λ_{20} =	0.5	ϕ =	-0.00002
z_{1u} =	1	V_{fu} =	5000.00	λ_{21} =	-0.05	M_{us} =	1998.381877

$$
\begin{array}{llll}
z_{2u} = 0 & V_{fa} = 5000.00 & \lambda_{22} = 0.1 & M_{as} = 1998.381877 \\
L_{us}^{u} = 5000.00 & L_{ad}^{a} = 4000 & \lambda_{30} = 0.1 & L_{as}^{a} = 4000 \\
L_{as}^{u} = 1000.00 & \upsilon = 0.8 & \lambda_{31} = -0.01 & B_{bad}^{mu} = 1000 \\
B_{bad}^{ua} = 1000.00 & r_{la} = 0.036 & B_{s}^{a} = 9001.62 & B_{cbad}^{a} = 757.48 \\
B_{bad}^{u} = 1000 & i_{u} = 0.2 & B_{s}^{Sa} = 7752.63 & B_{cbas}^{u} = 757.48 \\
B_{bad}^{a} = 1000.00 & i_{a} = 0.2 & B_{has}^{a} = 4995.954693 & B_{cbas}^{a} = 757.48 \\
z_{6u} = 1 & r_{mu} = 0.03 & B_{has}^{u} = 4995.954693 & B_{chas}^{u} = 904.57 \\
z_{6a} = 1 & r_{ma} = 0.03 & B_{has}^{Sa} = 2248.179612 & B_{cbad}^{u} = 904.57 \\
A_{ad}^{u} = 0 & ra_{u} = 0.033 & B_{has}^{Su} = 999.1909385 & xra = 1 \\
A_{ad}^{a} = 0 & ra_{a} = 0.033 & B_{bas}^{u} = 1248.988673 & xru = 1 \\
z_{7u} = 0 & \upsilon_{u} = 0.1 & B_{bas}^{a} = 1000 & xra^{\#} = 1 \\
z_{7a} = 0 & \upsilon_{a} = 0.1 & B_{bus}^{u} = 1000 & F_{cbu} = 22.06261893 \\
F_{bu} = 172.153357 & g_{u} = 338.0944165 & H_{us}^{u} = 757.48 & F_{cba} = 49.19967755 \\
F_{ba} = 119.203032 & g_{a} = 338.0944165 & H_{as}^{u} = 757.48 & CA_{u} = 0 \\
V_{bu} = 4759.10 & \sigma_{u} = 0.03 & A_{us} = 0 & CA_{a} = 0 \\
V_{ba} = 2244.13 & \sigma_{a} = 0.03 & A_{ad} = 0 & KA_{u} = 0 \\
rI_{u}^{u} = 0.036 & B_{s}^{u} = 9906.19 & B_{cbad}^{u} = 757.48 & KA_{a} = 0 \\
\end{array}
$$

5. Financial flows, distribution and capital controls

5.1 INTRODUCTION: A HUNTED HARE

In 1997, 50 years after its establishment, 15 years after the beginning of the Latin American debt crisis, more than two after the 1994 Mexican crisis, and at the very beginning of the East Asian crisis, the Board of Governors of the International Monetary Fund approved an amendment to its Articles of Agreement, requiring member states to delineate plans aiming at the liberalization of the capital account. Capital controls, which seemed indispensable to Keynes and White (the main figures behind the Bretton Woods negotiation) in order to maintain a stable international financial order, were scrapped. One year later, in a collection of essays reflecting on that landmark change, Dornbusch (1998) titled his article *Capital controls: an idea whose time is past.*

Capital flows were flourishing before the change in the IMF Articles of Agreement was taken, and continued to do so afterwards at exponential growth rates, as will be shown later. Fast forward to 2010, and the same institution published a Staff Position Note saying that, under certain conditions, the use 'of capital controls—in addition to both prudential and macroeconomic policy—is justified as part of the policy toolkit to manage inflows. Such controls, moreover, can retain potency even if investors devise strategies to bypass them, provided such strategies are more costly than the expected return from the transaction' (Ostry et al. 2010, p. 5). That became the 'institutional view' in 2012, when in a display of unprecedented assertiveness the IMF stated that 'in certain circumstances, capital flow management measures can be useful. They should not, however, substitute for warranted macroeconomic adjustment' (IMF 2012, p. 2). More research was forthcoming, analysing possible channels for multilateral cooperation in the 'management of the capital account' (Ostry et al. 2011; Ostry, Ghosh and Korinek 2012). Multilateral controls were precisely what Keynes, and above all White, had proposed to implement, though eventually that instrumentation was not adopted and each country was left to its own devices on how to deal with the issue (De Cecco 1987). The Independent Evaluation Office of the IMF has 'updated' its 2005 evaluation of the 'ambiguities and inconsistencies' in the IMF position and policy advice to individual countries, noting the progress made 'in clarifying, enhancing, and communicating its approach to capital account liberalization' (IMF 2015, p. v). Gallagher (2015) also tells the story of the IMF change of view. What is the explanation for this turnaround, as Dennis Robertson so wonderfully compared, in 'highbrow opinion like a hunted hare', coming round in a circle (Robertson 1963, p. 421)? Has capital account liberalization failed to provide the goods its supporters expected?

The tidal change is clear in other mainstream high-profile outlets. Hélène Rey presented at the 2013 Jackson Hole Symposium of the Federal Reserve a paper saying that 'independent monetary policies are possible if and only if the capital account is managed, directly or indirectly, regardless of the exchange rate regime' (Rey 2013, p. 313). A paper by the Federal Reserve, that will be discussed further below, points towards the increased likelihood of sudden stops and slumps following periods of large capital inflows, with other long-lasting effects on the productive structure (Benigno, Converse and Fornaro 2015). Other international institutions such as UNCTAD had much earlier warnings (UNCTAD 2001, 2006 and, more recently 2014, to name but a few). It is telling, though, that the phrase 'international financial flows have grown at unprecedented rates' is repeated almost year on year. One can find articles in the 1980s stating the same as papers in the late 2000s! And both accounts are correct, which should give the reader a founded impression of the exponential growth in financial flows.

It is already a stylized fact that unrestricted and unregulated global financial flows (such as their state as of now) produce a multiplicity of damages and leave long-lasting consequences and scars, while their alleged 'welfare enhancing' effects have been hard to quantify, if they exist at all (Rey 2013, p. 312). And, more in connection with the argument in this chapter, there are two papers, fresh from the oven at the time of writing this book, that reflect the warnings made repeatedly by different economists (mainly, though not exclusively, from a heterodox orientation) regarding the effects of freely moving global financial flows.

The above-mentioned paper by Benigno, Converse and Fornaro (2015) takes note of 'capital and labour reallocation' away from the manufacturing sector, the one with the faster growth rate of productivity (Timmer, de Vries and de Vries 2014). This shift actually lengthens and sharpens contractions in the bust phase of the cycle (Benigno, Converse and Fornaro 2015, p. 27). Furceri, Jaumotte and Loungani (2015) find, in turn, that capital account liberalization increases income inequality, one important channel being a decreasing level of the wage share, a result not unknown to heterodox authors (Jayadev 2005; Stockhammer 2009).

By this time, it should be clear why a Kaleckian approach can be useful in order to accommodate the interactions between growth and distribution and this new element, which has been given insufficient attention, as we mentioned in the literature review of Kaleckian growth models in Chapter 3. Burkett and Dutt (1991) deal with domestic financial liberalization in a study of the Chilean economy in the late 1970s and early 1980s, but their model still assumes a closed economy. The work of Bhaduri (1987, 2004) analyses the impact of financial flows on aggregate demand, but does not integrate thoroughly the connections between these two factors and income distribution. In this chapter we will develop a model close to La Marca (2005, 2010) and Blecker (2011), but with some important differences regarding the treatment of financial flows and their implications.

The episodes of foreign debt crises in the world in the last three or four decades are far higher than fingers and toes taken together, and nowadays we see in the European Union the problems and consequences of such crises. It still remains the case that, in the last three to four decades, these episodes happened mostly in developing countries; the acuteness of these has already been stated in Chapter 1. In this chapter we will try to fit these factors into an integrated and interactive picture. However, the model to be presented later will focus on one particular channel: private non-financial foreign debt. We have two reasons to choose this focus. First, when dealing with open economy matters the Kaleckian literature has focused so far on the current account (or the trade balance) without incorporating the public sector, and therefore omitting any reference to matters of public debt, for instance. We have mentioned in Chapter 3 works that include the public sector in a closed economy, but we believe it is preferable at this stage to advance step by step, removing assumptions one after another. Since the Kaleckian literature on open economy issues has so far concentrated on the private sector, we decided to continue along that road, leaving the inclusion of public finance considerations for further work. The second reason is that this is a straightforward channel at the core of the three concerns of this thesis: income distribution, growth and foreign debt, the obverse of financial inflows.

The next section will revise the trends in financial flows since the 1980s, while Section 5.3 will include a description of the similarities and differences in the balance of payments crises suffered by two countries, Mexico and South Korea, as example stereotypes of two broader episodes: the Latin American crises of the 1980s and 1990s, and the East Asian crisis of 1997. The main features of a Kaleckian growth model that incorporates foreign private debt will be sketched in Section 5.4, data characteristics will be presented in Section 5.5, and the results of the estimation of that model will be presented in Section 5.6. Section 5.7 will include a summary, discussion and suggestion for a policy framework that attempts to maintain sustainable growth rates with social inclusion, which takes into account the implications of the foreign constraint and foreign indebtedness.

5.2   EBB AND FLOW

We provided a brief summary of net private inflows in the first chapter of this book. There is so much information on international capital flows that a lazy author would just point his or her readers towards some surveys and move on, but in order to reassure the reader of any doubt regarding our commitment with a clear exposition of the facts we are trying to explain, we will indicate some major features of the ebb and flow of international capital and financial movements since the 1990s, and the corresponding changes in assets and liabilities. The focus will be on emerging and developing economies (EDEs).

One such survey, a very thorough one and quite recent at the time of writing this book, is Akyüz (2014). The Institute of International Finance also provides an annual summary of major trends as well. The first thing to notice is that external assets and liabilities of EDEs have grown at a much faster rate than international trade since the late 1990s. On the asset side, official foreign reserves in developing countries have increased substantially, both as a share of GDP and also in other metrics such as short-term external debt (UNCTAD 2015, Chapters 2 and 3). Most of the reserves were held in low-yield assets such as US Treasury bonds.

Generally speaking, sovereign debt has also been reduced relative to GDP in developing countries, though the trend has reversed slightly since the 2008 crisis. There are two other major factors to mention on this topic: the share of sovereign debt denominated in domestic currency, and subject to domestic jurisdiction, has increased substantially (Akyüz 2014, p. 25), but attracting more non-resident investors (Arslanalp and Tsuda 2014; Ebeke and Lu 2014), mostly private investors, not foreign central banks.

However, in our opinion the main stylized fact since the 2000s is the increase in foreign currency-denominated private external debt. Unlike public debt, private external debt did not fall as a share of GDP. And there have also been major changes in its composition. Issuance of debt securities by the private non-banking sector has grown faster than cross-border bank borrowing, though the latter still bears the larger share of total external debt (Chui, Fender and Sushko 2014). And debt denominated in foreign currency has also increased substantially (Akyüz 2014, p. 31), a lot of it being borrowed by overseas affiliates of emerging economy corporations established in off-shore financial centres (Avdjiev, Chui and Shin 2014),

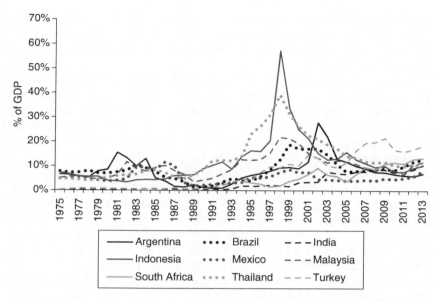

Source: External debt stocks, private non-guaranteed, International Debt Statistics, World Bank.

Figure 5.1   External private debt as percentage of GDP

which makes recording it more difficult. Figure 5.1 shows the evolution of private non-guaranteed external debt in a selected group of developing countries for which there are data available, from the World Development Indicators database (World Bank). Avdjiev, Chui and Shin also highlight the importance of private non-bank *lenders* in providing external financing to EDEs in an important group of countries including Chile, the Czech Republic, India, South Korea, Mexico, Russia, South Africa and Turkey. Their foreign equity liabilities have also seen the increased share of portfolio investment, with a highly pro-cyclical behaviour, though one has to take into account not only the volume of the inflows but also their positive effect on stock prices, inflating their value (Akyüz 2014).

Summing together what we said in the introduction and the picture we have presented in this short section, we can draw the following conclusions. First of all, capital flows to emerging countries have grown at exponential rates in the last 40 years. Their composition varied between equity (FDI and portfolio liabilities) and debt instruments (loans and securities), but there is a noticeable preponderance of volatile flows (portfolios and securities). FDI components in themselves have a high component of volatility, since they include intra-company lending (which can be unrelated to real investment decisions, particularly if driven by financial conditions in capital markets) and retained earnings (which can originate in financial investments).

Secondly, in the 1980s and 1990s external government debt in EDEs, denominated in foreign currencies, grew alongside private external debt, in some cases at a faster rhythm. That trend was reversed in the 2000s, and even more so after the 2008 crisis. Figure 5.1 shows the evolution of private external debt for a number of countries, as a percentage of GDP. One can already identify the waves described by Palma (2001), with the accelerated private indebtedness in Asia during the 1990s as a major highlight. The increase in recent years seems modest compared with that epoch, though measured in current dollars, Brazilian and Indian foreign private debt grew four-fold from 2005 and in Mexico and Turkey it tripled. External sovereign debt has seen an increased share of local currency-denominated debt, issued under local jurisdiction but held by foreign investors. Private debt, instead, has been increasingly denominated in foreign currency, with greater reliance on international bond markets. It can be said that, for the private sector, greater external indebtedness is a sign of financial decisions taken on a highly globalized scale, as illustrated by the higher issuance of debt by off-shore affiliates of EDE corporations (Butzen, Deroose and Ide 2014).

Akyüz (2014) also notes two trends that are important to understanding this picture. First, there is an increasing presence of foreign banks (as subsidiaries or branches) in EDEs. Indeed, these seem to be major holders of government debt. Secondly, in recent years stock markets and credit markets in EDEs have reversed a sustained trend of the 2000s. Namely, during the first decade of the 21st century those markets lowered the loans and stocks denominated in hard currency. That trend has reversed since the 2008 global crisis, though the levels are still far from the peaks of the 1990s.

There is a country which replicates almost every single feature mentioned above. Kaltenbrunner and Painceira (2015) describe the developments in the financial integration of the Brazilian economy to world financial markets. They highlight the increased exposure of foreign investors in domestic currency markets, mainly in short-term assets including government bonds, financed by borrowing in international markets. In that sense, variables like the exchange rate and the portfolio decisions of investors in the domestic market become de-linked from the economic fundamentals of Brazil. They strengthen their case by noting the very tight correlation, for instance in exchange rate movements, between countries that also observed major inflows, even though they had different macroeconomic fundamentals, such as South Korea, South Africa and Turkey. In the next section we will further explore the experience of two countries after liberalization processes, both of which ended in financial and exchange rate crises.

5.3 SOME CRISIS EXPERIENCES

Crises in Latin America have been characterized by the sustained presence of current account deficits (Kregel 1998, p. 46; López G. 2004, p. 202). In the Bretton Woods era, these deficits were occasioned by trade imbalances, since imports reacted more strongly than exports to economic activity both domestically and globally, added to the importance of foreign technology as a component of domestic investment. In the post-Bretton Woods era, these deficits were severely aggravated from the late 1970s by the openness of the capital and financial account, together with the international liquidity created by the oil shock in 1973 (Maes and Clement 2013, pp. 6–10). Latin American foreign debt doubled between 1978 and 1981 (Correa and Vidal 2006, p. 166). It can be said that both government and private debt rose to levels not known previously, though the particular circumstances of each country can obviously differ. In the Chilean experience during the late 1970s and early 1980s, a balanced public budget coexisted with a huge build-up of foreign private indebtedness. As Diaz-Alejandro so clearly stated, in a classic that still resonates today, 'recent Chilean experience shows that a balanced budget by itself will prevent neither a serious financial crisis nor acute macroeconomic turbulence' (Diaz-Alejandro 1985, p. 23). During the first years of the last Argentinean dictatorship, the budget deficit fell substantially. However, when the inflows stopped and the private sector (where the distinction between a banking and a private non-financial corporation was blurred) was unable to honour its debts, governments stepped in and nationalized their debts (Calcagno 1984). The Brazilian crisis was due, on the contrary, mainly to borrowing by the government sector in order to fund public investment problems, with a current account deficit aggravated by the oil crisis in 1979.

The composition and pace of these foreign inflows did not remain the same throughout the period. In the 1970s, there was an increasing short-term profile of debt, and lenders were mainly international banks. The ensuing debt crisis in the 1980s crippled American banks, which were on the brink of collapse and retracted from these markets. And balance of payments shortages caused high levels of inflation and even hyperinflation in a number of countries. The next wave was different, with money coming in the form of portfolio investment and FDI (mainly in concept of purchases of firms and privatizations). These inflows helped to build up foreign reserves, to fund an expansion in bank credit and to stabilize the exchange rate (for instance, regarding Argentina see De Lucchi (2013)), but did not help to increase investment substantially. But even if debt were not at ostensibly high levels by today's standards (Argentina in the 1990s, for one, would have met the Maastricht Criteria every single year), countries were severely dependent on the continuous inflow of foreign financial flows to sustain the current account deficit and debt servicing, particularly as most of these were denominated in a foreign currency (the dollar, usually). Sudden stops of financial flows left governments on the brink of default, and in many cases the jump was unavoidable.

The underlying dynamics in East Asian countries was different (Kregel 1998; Palma 2001). These countries did not have unsustainable current account deficits. In South Korea for instance, even though there was a pervasive state 'interference' in the development process, investment was being carried out mainly by chaebols, private conglomerates that diversified into unrelated lines of business. Government savings were structurally higher than public investment (Storm and Naastepad 2005, p. 1075). The significant inflow of foreign savings was mainly composed of long-term loans from private lenders and public institutions (including multilateral development banks) subject to the regulatory supervision of a non-independent Bank of Korea, while FDI and portfolio inflows were negligible (Noland 2007, p. 486). The banking system was under government control (Chang, Park and Yoo 2001, p. 141), and together with capital controls it decoupled domestic from international financial markets. Loans were the main source of funding for firms, while on the external front the Korean won combined periods of overvaluation with undervaluation from the 1960s until the 1990s without facing wide fluctuations in the current account, and government usually ran surpluses even during the 1990s. The Korean government had a fiscal surplus of 0.5 per cent in 1995 and a deficit of 0.3 per cent in 1996, hardly unsustainable figures.

In the Korean case, there starts a process of financial deregulation in the early 1990s, with interest rate deregulation, stock market openness, foreign exchange liberalization and a reduction of policy-oriented loans. A summary of the measures instrumented in those years can be found in Chang, Park and Yoo (2001, pp. 141–142), Griffith-Jones, Gottschalk and Cirera (2003, pp. 93–96, a paper that also describes the process of capital account liberalization in other OECD countries) and Noland (2007, pp. 510–521). The financial fragility induced by this liberalization process is striking. Foreign assets diminished and foreign borrowing increased, short-term external debt exploded (reaching around 250 per cent of foreign reserves, according to Noland 2007, p. 501). In fact, short-term debt was over 60 per cent of all debt during the 1990s up until the crisis (Crotty and Dymski 2001, p. 69). Even though the exchange rate market was liberalized, inflows kept it at a very stable level up to the crisis (Crotty and Dymski 2001, p. 63). Foreign lending to the stock market, the development of derivatives (Neftci 1998 provides a picture of the developments on this front), a deterioration in the terms of trade (the price of semiconductors, one of its main exports, fell 90 per cent in two years (Kregel 1998, p. 54)) and the fragilities of lenders themselves (Japanese banks in particular) all led to a fast and deep contagion of outflows as the rest of East Asia was suffering (Thailand, Taiwan, Hong Kong, Indonesia, Philippines).

Even though both South Korea and Mexico 'enjoyed' a flood of short-term and FDI capital inflows, in the latter case it was directed towards acquisition of public companies and public expenditures, as well as to finance a structural trade deficit. In the Korean case, it was mainly destined towards financial corporations and chaebols, and investment. The deterioration in private non-financial corporations' balance sheets was acute (chaebols were leveraged in excess of 500 per cent) and the 'cure', the IMF programme, killed the patient, with a debt-deflation process following suit (Kregel 1998, pp. 58–59).

Other experiences also illustrate the dangers posed by massive waves of financial inflows. We have already mentioned the case of Brazil, which replicates most of the features financial flows had since the 1990s. Turkey and South Africa are other examples, with financial inflows reaching more than 10 per cent of GDP. The Turkish case is remarkable for the widening in financial inflows in the last 20 years (Bedirhanoglu et al. 2013, p. 152).

We believe that the differences between the Mexican (particularly the Tequila crisis) and the South Korean episodes help us to understand in a clear way different types of balance of payments crises, and are very relevant to understanding the Eurozone crisis, where countries face huge housing and commercial property booms, and firms, households and banks are heavily indebted in spite of (or causing, one may say) a not 'reckless' fiscal behaviour prior to 2008. The next section will present a Kaleckian growth model that integrates some of these features, focusing mainly on private external debt, for the reasons mentioned in the introduction.

5.4   A KALECKIAN MODEL WITH PRIVATE FOREIGN DEBT

We present first the asset structure of this simulated economy and the flows that happen within one period. However, when presenting the dynamics and assumptions, we will not be describing the movement of each and every variable, that is, we will not be making in this case an SFC

Table 5.1   Balance sheet

Households		Firms		Central bank		Rest of world	
Assets	Liabilities/ Net wealth	Assets	Liabilities/ Net wealth	Assets	Liabilities/ Net wealth	Assets	Liabilities/ Net wealth
p_eQ	NW_h	K	ED	R	H	D	R
		H	p_eQ				
			NW_f				

model. Instead, our formulation will make the model more amenable for econometric purposes.

In this model, we have four sectors. Households, firms, the central bank (no government activity, its pertinence will be clear later) and the rest of the world. Households hold equities p_eQ, which are their sole asset, and since they do not have any liability in this model, this is also their net wealth NW_h. Firms, in turn, have real capital as an asset K plus the cash H they get from the central bank in exchange for the foreign currency they sell, foreign loans ED (adjusted by the exchange rate), equity p_eQ as liabilities, and net wealth NW_f as a residual. If there are sustained periods of current account surplus they might be net creditors to the rest of the world, but we rule out that possibility in the model. When financial inflows from abroad destined to firms exceed the current account deficit, or coexist with a current account surplus, then foreign reserves R owned by the central bank increase. Table 5.1 presents what we have just said.

In Table 5.2, we present a matrix tracking all the flows allowed in this model. A plus is a source of money; a minus represents uses of money. There is one good apt for consumption C, investment gK and export purposes X. Subtracting imports IM (which are assumed to be used only as an input, and not for consumption), we get GDP Y. Firms pay the wage bill ψY (equal to the wage share ψ times GDP), interest services on previous loans iED_{-1} and dividends Div. Households invest all their savings S_h in acquiring equities, which is one out of three sources of funds for funding investment in this model. The other two are retained profits F_f and foreign loans D, which are also lent for speculative purposes (more on this later, when we explain the determinants of financial flows in the model). As we mentioned above, the central bank buys the foreign currency with high-powered money. Repeating the convention of the previous chapter, uses of funds have a negative sign, and sources of funds have a positive sign. The price of equities is fixed, and we will also refrain from making assumptions about the borrowing behaviour of firms. It will be assumed that foreign lending is both demand and supply

Table 5.2   Transaction matrix

	Households	Firms		Central Bank	Rest of world
		Current	Capital		
Consumption	$-C$	$+C$			
Investment		$+gK$	$-gK$		
Exports		$+X$			$-X$
Imports		$-IM$			$+IM$
GDP		Y			
Wage bill	$+\psi Y$	$-\psi Y$			
Interest		$-iED_{-1}$			$+iD_{-1}$
Dividends	$+Div$	$-Div$			
Savings	S_h	S_f			$-B$
Profits		$-F_f$	$+F_f$		
Equities	$-p_eQ$		$+p_eQ$		
Borrowing			$\Delta(ED)$		$-\Delta(D)$
Cash			$-\Delta(H)$	$+\Delta(H)$	
Reserves				$-\Delta(R)$	$+\Delta(R)$

driven, or governed by pull and push factors, epitomized by the phrase 'when it rains, it pours'.

Following the example set in Chapter 4, we will present the equations that convey the logic and main characteristics of the model, leaving a whole enunciation of the equations and stability analysis for the appendix. Many issues are dealt with in a similar fashion to Chapter 4, so there will inevitably be some repetition.

5.4.1   Prices, Wages and Shares

Prices are set on a mark-up over costs basis. Inputs are labour and imports. Productivity growth is assumed to be exogenous, and the production function has fixed coefficients. Every input that enters into the price function has an income share, but interest payments will be treated slightly differently from the model in Chapter 4.

The mark-up is constant in the short run, but it is not fixed in the long run, being the result of price and wage bargaining in the economy. We had an introduction in Chapter 4 to the post-Keynesian approach to wage determination, when we described workers' wage demand. In that model, workers targeted a specific real wage, influenced by a non-linear Phillips curve. We will explore the issue a little further, analysing not only workers' targets but also firms' ambitions.

To start with, in the medium to long run, the wage share moves according to the evolution of nominal wages, prices and productivity, so we can write the following equation, with a $\wedge$ denoting growth rates:

$$\hat{\psi} = \hat{W} + \hat{a}_0 - \hat{p} \qquad (5.1)$$

ψ represents the wage share; $\hat{W}$ represents the growth rate of nominal wages; $\hat{a}_0$ represents the growth rate of labour productivity, which will be assumed to be exogenous and constant, so that $\hat{a}_0 = -\alpha$; and $\hat{p}$ represents inflation.

The conflicting claims approach to income distribution, the one we adopt here, states that different income earner groups have aspirations which may not be compatible, leading to distributive conflict which can be expressed in inflationary movements, and possible repercussions in economic activity. Rowthorn (1977) provides the first modern formulation of a Kaleckian approach to conflicting claims analysis, though several concepts were already present in the work of Joan Robinson (1965 [1956]), for instance. Lavoie (2014, Chapter 8) gives a thorough account of its developments. Other articles worth noting are Dutt (1992), Lavoie (2002), Cassetti (2003), Arestis and Sawyer (2005), the aforementioned work of Dallery and Van Treeck (2011), Sasaki (2011) and Rochon and Setterfield (2012), among many others.

Workers have a target wage share, and they try to achieve it by adjusting their nominal wage. We will not dwell on explanations of the target wage share, but we will add another factor influencing nominal wage increases: the movement in the real exchange rate. Formally:

$$\hat{W} = \phi(\psi_w - \psi) + \gamma e \qquad (5.2)$$

If the wage share is below the target, workers will demand higher nominal wages. But they also try to recover from real devaluations. Why is that? It is due to the fact that the price of many goods that comprise a typical consumption basket, particularly foodstuffs, is determined (or influenced, to say the least) by prices set in international markets, denominated in a foreign currency. This problem does not apply to the United States of course, since that 'foreign currency' is precisely the dollar, but it is certainly an issue in emerging and developing economies. But wait, we said that pass-through from devaluations to prices has notoriously fallen; how is that compatible with our model?

There are two channels for that to happen. The first is shown in the above equation: the parameter γ captures workers' bargaining position in order to successfully counteract real depreciations. Taken as exogenous in this model, we do not argue for its constancy in the real world, being affected by the level of employment, wage-bargaining conditions (at a firm level or a centralized level), and so on.

The other channel has to do with the other player at the bargaining table, firms. Firms also target a certain wage share, implicitly a profit share. And whenever the actual wage share is above their target, they increase prices:

$$\hat{p} = \rho(\psi - \psi_f) \tag{5.3}$$

with ψ_f being the wage share targeted by firms. That concept is made to depend on a couple of factors. First, exchange rate depreciations. As we said in the previous chapter, firms usually raise their mark-up in case of devaluation, lowering the real wage and the wage share. The second factor has to do with foreign borrowing. The equation is as follows:

$$\psi_f = \tau - \delta e - \omega d \tag{5.4}$$

τ is an exogenous constant, which can represent a maximum level that the capitalist class tolerates. Before dismissing this assertion as a 'baseless conspiracy theory', we beg the reader to remember the chorus of business voices rising in despair and pointing to inflationary fears that threaten the very heart of capitalism awakened by 'populist politicians', whenever there is a mild recovery in workers' living standards. Coming back to Chapter 3, it is worth mentioning that there are reasons of this sort behind the fact that the wage share of income in Argentina has barely touched 50 per cent.

Now, focusing again on equation (5.4), why would higher indebtedness by firms lead them to try to lower the wage share? There are arguments to support this assertion. The first one is that higher borrowing implies (given the interest rate) higher interest payments and margin compressions, leading firms to pass on interest costs and lower other types of costs, such as labour. Financially troubled firms face more difficult terms when accessing finance, and have to make up by increasing internal sources of funding.

The other main reason is that, as shown in the data presented above, higher indebtedness has come along with the liberalization of the capital and financial account, increased movement of capital across the globe, and pressures over labour market institutions. The above-mentioned paper by Furceri, Jaumotte and Loungani (2015), plus many heterodox works before the IMF 'recantation', support this view, and this is a channel by which to incorporate the detrimental effect of foreign private indebtedness on income distribution.

If we put equations (5.2), (5.3) and (5.4) into (5.1) and rearrange, we have the following expression:

$$\hat{\psi} = \psi(-\phi - \rho) - \rho\omega d + \phi\psi_w + e(\gamma - \rho\delta) - \alpha + \rho\tau \qquad (5.5)$$

Let's see what each term represents. ϕ and ρ represent the speed of adjustment in nominal wages and prices towards the target levels. ϕ influences as well how capable trade unions are in achieving their goal ($\phi\psi_w$), while $\rho\tau$ influences the same for firms (a higher τ implies that firms accept a higher wage share, or lower profit share). In turn, ($\gamma - \rho\delta$) captures the relative strength of both sides on fighting or sustaining real devaluations. Faster rates of productivity growth decrease the wage share, the same effect as higher foreign indebtedness.

The stability analysis is detailed in the appendix to this chapter, but a few lines can be written here. Stability, in this differential equation, requires that $\frac{\partial\hat{\psi}}{\partial\psi}$ be negative. For that to happen, ($\gamma - \rho\delta$) should be positive, or if negative, it should have a very small absolute value. It is usually the case, especially in developing countries, that devaluations lower the wage share, which would imply that the term in parentheses is negative. However, keeping this in mind, it will be assumed that the difference is small.

Before moving on to the effective demand aspect of the model, it should be expressed that we abstracted from possible direct influences of the state of demand on income distribution. As we mentioned above, the relative bargaining strength of firms and workers is considered exogenous, so that capacity utilization (the preferred proxy in Kaleckian models for the state of aggregate demand) does not enter in (5.5).

5.4.2 Effective Demand and Balance Sheets

As was presented in Chapter 3, when dealing with effective demand in a Kaleckian model, one tackles savings decisions, investment decisions and the current account (in the open economy case). Let's move in that order.

Savings propensities depend on the source of income. As Table 5.2 shows, households have wage income and dividend income. Retained earnings by firms (their savings) are the residual after distributing dividends. As for the magnitude of these three saving propensities, we can safely assume that $s_w < s_d < s_f$, with s_w representing the saving propensity out of wage income, s_d representing the same for dividend income, and s_f being firms' retention ratio. Normalizing by the capital stock, making the proper substitutions, with u being the capacity utilization rate and π being the profit share, we have the savings rate for the whole economy as:

$$\sigma = S/K = [\pi(s_f + s_d - s_f s_d) + s_w\psi]\,Y/K = [\pi(s_f + s_d - s_f s_d) + s_w\psi]u \qquad (5.6)$$

As we reviewed in Chapter 3, the investment function is the source of much controversy among Kaleckian authors. In the present formulation, we will respect a linearized version of the Bhaduri and Marglin (1990) specification, but with one more element. Our specification of the investment function is as follows:

$$g = I/K = g_o + \beta u + \theta \pi - vid \qquad (5.7)$$

We allow for an exogenous parameter, representing 'animal spirits', or a secular trend of growth. We include capacity utilization and the profit share. The last element is foreign indebtedness; Ndikumana (1999) stressed the role of debt servicing as a constraining factor in the evolution of investment. Juselius and Drehmann (2015) state, strangely surprised, that 'we find that the debt service burden also plays an important role at the aggregate level that has generally been overlooked: it has a strong negative impact on consumption and investment' (p. 4). Giroud and Mueller (2015) found, for the US, that heavily leveraged firms laid off more workers than low-leveraged firms. It also helps to capture the sensitivity of investment to cash flows, pioneered in the work of Fazzari, Hubbard and Petersen (1988). Deeper implications of the role of the interest rate in Kaleckian models can be found in the work of Lavoie (1992, 1993, 1995a) and Hein (2006, 2012), among others mentioned in Chapter 3.

Turning to the current account balance, it is the result of the difference between exports, imports and interest payments, expressed in national currency:

$$B = X - IM - iED \qquad (5.8)$$

When normalized by the capital stock, and expressed in linear functional form, the current account depends, as usual, on the real exchange rate, on domestic economic activity (represented by capacity utilization), on foreign economic activity and on debt servicing. This is summed up in equation (5.9):

$$b = B/K = \varepsilon e - \zeta u + \chi u^f - oid \qquad (5.9)$$

Following La Marca (2010), we state that capacity utilization moves according to:

$$\hat{u} = \lambda(g + b - \sigma) \qquad (5.10)$$

Or, after all the substitutions,

$$\hat{u} = \lambda \{u(\beta - \zeta - [\pi(s_f + s_d - s_f s_d) + s_w \psi]) - id(v + o) + \theta\pi +$$

$$\varepsilon e + g_0 + \chi u^f\} \qquad (5.10')$$

There are three endogenous variables: capacity utilization, the wage share and foreign indebtedness. When thinking about the stability of the equation, the terms that represent the effect on aggregate savings $(\pi(s_f + s_d - s_f s_d) + s_w \psi)$ plus income elasticity of imports (ζ) should be higher than the response of investment to changes in aggregate demand, measured by β. This is the usual Keynesian stability condition that was discussed in Chapter 3, and it will be assumed that it holds, so that the partial derivative $\frac{\partial \hat{u}}{\partial u}$ is negative. As is clear by the term $id(v + o)$, capacity utilization reacts negatively to debt increases. The last issue, the response of capacity utilization to changes in income distribution, captures the typical Kaleckian characteristic of the model. A priori, it is not possible to assume a profit-led behaviour of the economy. The exact conditions are shown in the appendix.

5.4.3 Foreign Capital Flows

So far, the model has been very similar to the work of La Marca (2005, 2010) and Blecker (2011). The main difference concerns the role of debt servicing in the price equation, and a slightly different investment function. However, La Marca deals with foreign flows by focusing on the sustainability of the current account of the balance of payments. But there is no logical need for which private capital and financial flows should exactly compensate any surplus or deficit in the current account, since foreign reserves are free to accommodate any difference, in accounting terms. Even if the inflow of FDI and portfolio flows more than compensate a current account deficit and increase foreign reserves, the argument developed in this chapter is that their effect is not innocuous. This section deals with the drivers of such flows, and how to integrate them into a Kaleckian model.

The literature since Calvo, Leiderman and Reinhart (1996) has separated 'pull' and 'push' factors. The former concerns the demand for foreign capital, while the latter deals with the supply. Other separation, which overlaps to some extent with the previous one, is to analyse global and domestic factors that propel these flows, whether they reflect 'fundamentals' of the recipient country (the 'pull' factor) or are mainly driven by the 'global financial cycle' (related to the sources of flows, or 'push' factors). And the evidence seems to attach greater weight to the second factor, particularly in what refers to global financial risks, risk perception and volatility, in a list including Forbes and Warnock (2012), Claessens and Ghosh (2013), Rey

(2013), Ahmed and Zlate (2013), Butzen, Deroose and Ide (2014) and IMF (2014), to name just a few. Bruno and Shin (2014) stress global factors for cross-border bank lending.

Nier, Sedik and Mondino (2014) defend the non-linearity of global capital flows, in which domestic fundamentals gain relevance in the context of low global volatility (measured by an index called VIX), but that in difficult times global conditions rule the roost. The above-mentioned work of Kaltenbrunner and Painceira (2015) highlights that, even in the context of an almost ever-enduring interest rate differential between Brazil and the US, short-term capital flows to Brazil intensified in 2006 relative to 2005, together with other risky assets, in agreement with Rey (2013). Ahmed and Zlate (2013), besides noting the role of global factors already mentioned, found a significant role for growth and interest rate differentials.

That is why we adopt the following equation to capture the determinants of foreign private flows:

$$\hat{d} = \eta u + \mu(i - i^f) + (1 - \mu)(d^f - d) \qquad (5.11)$$

The first term, u, captures the influence of domestic factors through the rate of capacity utilization. As we mentioned, a higher u is associated with higher imports, therefore demanding more external financing to cover the trade deficit. It also encourages firms to look for funds to fund their investment decisions, both at home and abroad.

The other two terms capture as well the distinction made in previous chapters between 'fundamentalist' and 'chartist' traders. The former base their expectations according to some rule regarding what they perceive to be some 'fundamental' indicators of debt sustainability and economic pace. The latter follow recent market movements and trends, and derive investment strategies based on that analysis. Assuming the (not unreasonable) assumption that exchange rate movements are driven by financial flows, the second term captures precisely that: the difference between domestic and foreign interest rate as an explanatory factor of foreign borrowing. In this interpretation, it would be capturing the behaviour of 'chartist' traders.[1] But before the reader thinks that this is an endorsement of the Uncovered Interest Rate Parity (UIP), according to which 'the interest rate differential between two countries should be an unbiased predictor of the change in the exchange rate between them' (Chinn and Quayyum 2012, p. 1), our formulation states that this effect might be counteracted (or reinforced) by the excess (or shortage) of borrowing over some 'critical' value as judged by fundamentalist traders, therefore the upperscript f. Note that this value is mainly conventional, varying from country to country, not specifically related to any actual fundamental. In the line of the literature mentioned some paragraphs above, this term stands for the importance of the global financial cycle in driving financial flows. UIP is rejected not only by post-Keynesian authors as Lavoie (2000; Harvey 2004) but also mainstream authors such as Engel (2015) and Rey (2013).

It may well be asked why would firms in emerging markets borrow even if surges of financial flows increase credit availability? The answer can be found in two factors. First, the financial system in emerging markets is generally underdeveloped, without sufficient depth, with few financing instruments at expensive interest rates, though there are exceptions to this description. On top of that, and noting the increased relevance of foreign financial institutions in domestic markets (Akyüz 2014; IMF 2014), these foreign institutions are great when it comes to engineering new financial products for underdeveloped financial systems, facilitating at the same time channels for inflows and outflows. An interesting study by Brown, Kirschenmann and Ongena (2011) found using a Bulgarian dataset of over a hundred thousand loans denominated in euros to over sixty thousand firms, a third of these loans were requested in *domestic* currency. The authors argue that these might reflect the desire of banks to match their liabilities (euro funding) to their assets, an argument also valid for the Argentinean experience during the currency board. The missing link in the banks' strategy refers to the mismatch in the balance sheet of borrowers: they have foreign currency liabilities, but they do not necessarily have foreign currency assets.

5.4.4 A Graphic Description

A graphic depiction might be useful to understand the dynamics in the model. Figure 5.2 shows the curves related to the wage share (equation (5.5)), capacity utilization (equation (5.10)) and foreign private debt (equation (5.11)), when they are all in equilibrium, that is, when their rate of change is zero. Remember that, from equation (5.5), we have that $\hat{\psi}$ is a vertical line in the plane (d, u), since u does not appear in that equation. Given the stability conditions (which are mentioned in the appendix together with the list of equations), under a very reasonable constellation of parameters (which are more likely to hold in a wage-led regime) the existence of a point such as (d^*, u^*, ψ^*) is very likely. The slope of the curve $\hat{u}$ is due to the fact that $\frac{\partial \hat{u}}{\partial d}$ is negative, while the slope of $\hat{d}$ reflects the positive $\frac{\partial \hat{d}}{\partial u}$. Finally, the slope of the curve $\hat{\psi}$ is negative: a higher indebtedness leads to a lower wage share.

Almost all the studies we surveyed stressed the role of global factors as drivers of financial flows. Investors tend to misperceive risk when they flow, underestimating them when they flow in and overestimating them

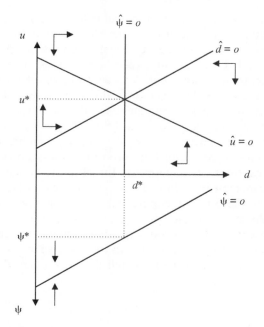

Source: Author's elaboration.

Figure 5.2 Stability in the model

when they flow out, though in the latter case episodes of self-fulfilling prophecies are rather the norm. How can we capture that in our model? We admit that we have presented an equilibrium-type model, and that modifications would need to be adopted in order to reflect cycles of the Kindlebergerian sort of 'mania, panics and crash'. But our model still captures important real world dynamics, and can account for the findings of Jayadev (2005), Stockhammer (2009), Furceri, Jaumotte and Loungani (2015) and Benigno, Converse and Fornaro (2015), which we take to be representative given the coincidence between such diversely oriented economists.

This chapter puts the emphasis on a foreign-driven contraction with a deterioration in the wage share, though we are certainly aware that the effects to be described might take some time to build up, more than this schematic presentation may assume. Suppose for instance, that fundamentalist traders have a more positive view of the country, or are more willing to lend to it, or that the capital account has been opened and therefore they are willing to tolerate more leveraged borrowers, so that d^f goes up. It can also be associated with a change in global risk perception, perhaps influenced by US monetary policy (McCauley, McGuire and Sushko (2015)). One cannot stress enough the conventional nature of this parameter, but, running the risk of repeating ourselves, it is not necessarily related to any actual fundamental indicator, and can vary from country to country. As risk assessment becomes looser, money flows into the country. As debt starts to pile up, firms pass their higher costs to prices, and start to reduce their investment in an attempt to control their borrowing. Though income distribution might be turning in their favour, they might not be able to recover all the interest payments that flow out of the country.

Figure 5.3 captures what happens. Initially, the economy is still at (d^*, u^*, ψ^*). The increase in d^f shifts the $\hat{d}$ towards the right, to d'. With time, the restrictions on investment, coping with the worsening in income distribution, bring the economy towards (d'', u'', ψ''). If the economy is of a wage-led nature, the initial fall in investment (due to higher interest payments) might be exacerbated by the downfall in the wage share. Alternatively, in a profit-led case there might be some relief to investment due to a fall in

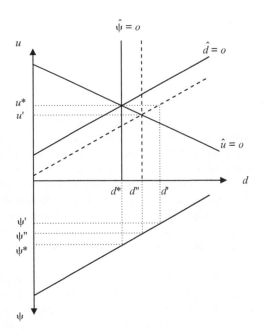

Source: Author's elaboration.

Figure 5.3 Shock to 'fundamental' debt levels

relative costs, though not enough to offset the burden of debt servicing. The deterioration in the wage share does not happen at once, however. It is quite likely that initially the exchange rate appreciates, but this is a short-lived effect. It is assumed here that a certain deleveraging process (of the private sector) takes place. The deterioration in the exchange rate might have opposing effects, enhancing profitability but hurting consumption and the burden of foreign-denominated debt. Overall, the model does conclude that output will eventually contract, in the new equilibrium state.

5.5   THE DATA

Having explained in Section 5.3 why we chose the economies of South Korea and Mexico to illustrate the points captured so far in our model, let's present a brief description of the data we used and the picture it gives about the performance of these two countries since the 1970s.

The South Korean data were taken from the website of the Bank of Korea. The wage share was constructed as the ratio of compensation of employees to GDP, both registered in Korean won at current prices. The private debt ratio includes in its numerator the Corporate Non-financial External Debt, and in the denominator the GDP, also in Korean won at current prices. As a proxy of capacity utilization, we used the logarithm of GDP in won at *constant* prices, data taken from the OECD (2013). Figures 5.4 to 5.6 present their evolution during the period 1970–2011.

It can be seen that the wage share, starting from low levels (the bottom occurred in 1974), increased in a more or less sustained fashion up until the early 1990s. It had some peaks right up to the 1997 crisis, it decreased later and it only recovered in the mid 2000s, when it stabilized at around 46 per cent. Private debt in turn had a rather stable level in the 1970s, and after 1980 it started a steadily decreasing trend, until the early 1990s. At that time, there was a fast build-up of private debt that reached its peak in 1997, and after a deleveraging process returned to its normal low levels. In the case of GDP, South Korea enjoyed growth rates of around 10 per cent up until the early 1990s as well, with some shocks such as 1980 and other cyclical fluctuations of a rather small amplitude. The average growth rate during the 1990s was around 6.60 per cent, never reaching the 10 per cent threshold except in 1999, as the recovery from the crisis took speed. In the 2000s, the South Korean economy grew at an average rate of 4.2 per cent, substantially lower than its previous records, but never suffered a recession, not even in the 2008/9 crisis.

In the case of Mexico, data were taken from the OECD and the World Bank. We use the Labour Income Share of the Total Economy for the wage share; the logarithm of GDP at constant pesos for the utilization rate; and

Source: Bank of Korea.

Figure 5.4   Wage share in South Korea

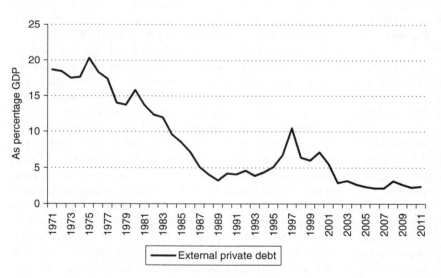

Source: Bank of Korea.

Figure 5.5   Foreign private debt in South Korea

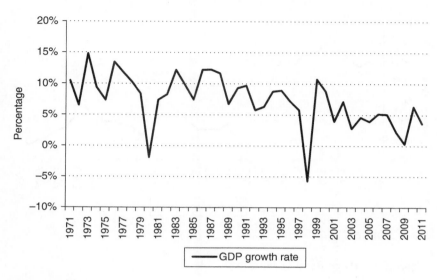

Source: OECD.

Figure 5.6 GDP growth rate in South Korea

the private debt ratio includes in the denominator the GDP at current dollars, and in the numerator the private nonguaranteed external debt stocks from the World Bank (http://datos.bancomundial.org/indicador/DT.DOD.DPNG.CD). Figures 5.7 to 5.9 show their evolution for the period 1971–2009.

The charts show that, after the debt crisis in 1982, GDP growth became more volatile; the wage share diminished substantially and failed to recover to previous levels; and private debt peaked twice as a share of GDP. The average rate of growth was 2.21 per cent during the 1980s, but only 0.10 per cent from 1982 to 1988. There was a recovery after the liberalization of the trade and financial account of the balance of payments, which coincided in time with another build-up of private debt. The fluctuations after the Tequila crisis in 1995 were closely linked to the evolution of the US economy. Mexico suffered from the explosion of the dotcom bubble, and even more severely from the bursting of the housing bubble in the US.

5.6 RESULTS

Each variable, for both countries, was shown to have a unit root. When analysing the presence of a cointegration relationship between the variables,

Source: OECD.

Figure 5.7   Wage share in Mexico

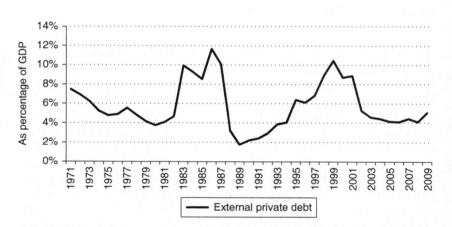

Source: Author's calculations based on International Debt Statistics, World Bank.

Figure 5.8   Foreign private debt in Mexico

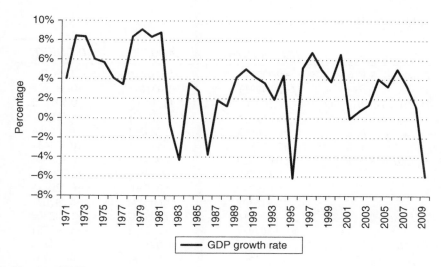

Source: OECD.

Figure 5.9   GDP growth rate in Mexico

and taking care of potential econometric anomalies (such as the non-normality of residuals) we chose the following specification: for Mexico, we will test one cointegrating relation (with an intercept in both the cointegration equation and in the VAR), and with two dummies to control for outliers, in the years 1988 and 2009. The year 1988 was the aftermath of a restructuring of public and private debt, while the full impact of the global financial crisis was felt in 2009. In the case of South Korea, we will test for two cointegrating relations (with an intercept only in the cointegration equation) with two dummies, for the years 1974 and 1980, in the aftermath of the first and second oil shock, and in the latter case it was also the year of the assassination of President Park Chung-Hee.

Since we have evidence of a cointegrating relation in the case of the Mexican economy, the Granger causality test showed us that this relation holds between the logarithm of GDP and the logarithm of the wage share. The results are presented in Table 5.3. We have therefore chosen the order wage share–GDP–debt for the specification of the test. We report first the cointegrating equation for Mexico normalized by the wage share, with the t-values in parentheses:

$$L(Wagesh) = -7.273765 + 0.377506*L(GDP) + 0.092530*L(Debt)$$

$$(4.88699) \qquad (1.55725) \qquad (5.12)$$

Table 5.3   Vector Error Correction Model in Mexico

	D(LWAGESH)	D(LGDP)	D(LDEBT)
Equation (5.13)	−0.232213	−0.062410	−0.256407
	(−2.84931)	(−1.03162)	(−0.59382)
D(LWAGESH(−1))	0.10976	−0.214107	0.501512
	(0.61292)	(−1.61065)	(0.52858)
D(LGDP(−1))	0.546653	0.486361	1.288884
	(2.07285)	(2.48442)	(0.92245)
D(LDEBT(−1))	0.018829	0.004487	0.330604
	(0.67868)	(0.21788)	(2.24914)
C	−0.029749	0.015306	−0.020215
	(−2.31630)	(1.60547)	(−0.29707)
DUM88	−0.017316	−0.029982	−1.082308
	(−0.36796)	(−0.82856)	(−4.34078)
DUM09	0.077435	−0.091827	0.242190
	(1.67150)	(−2.67024)	(0.98673)
R^2	0.347938	0.342269	0.490725
F	2.667979	2.601895	4.817874

Source: Author's calculations.

The cointegration analysis shows the existence of a stable long-run relation between output and the wage share, and according to the Granger
causality test we have evidence to support the view that the former affects
more the latter than vice versa. The coefficients corresponding to foreign
private debt are not significant, though they present a positive sign.
We are more interested in the sign of the coefficient than in its magnitude,
though in the case of private debt it seems to be rather small.

What results do we get for South Korea? The Block exogeneity test
shows us that private debt causes in the Granger sense both GDP and
the wage share, but it is not caused by either of them, so it can be called a
'weakly exogenous variable'. The chosen order is the same as in Mexico.
The results show that GDP causes in a Granger sense the wage share, and
that private debt does the same with GDP. We show therefore the first
cointegrating equation normalized for the wage share and the second
normalized for the GDP, assigning a zero coefficient. Again, we put in
parentheses the t-values.

The first cointegrating equation is as follows:

$$L(Wagesh) = -2.16164 - 0.213194*L(GDP) + 0.066576* L(Debt)$$

$$(-3.03479) \qquad (0.844659) \qquad (5.13)$$

The second equation reads:

$$L(GDP) = -8.173034 + 0.137012*L(Debt)$$

$$(0.672056) \qquad\qquad (5.14)$$

It might seem that there is a significant negative relationship between the wage share and GDP, as well as the relation between debt and GDP, though the latter is not significant at all. The first finding (the negative relation between GDP and the wage share) might be explained by the substantial increase in productivity during the period observed. If real wage growth does not keep up with productivity growth, the wage share might fall (Storm and Naastepad 2005, p. 1080). However, the short-run impact might not be the same, and as we mentioned we will perform impulse–response simulations which will sum up the short- and long-run interactions between the variables.

We now turn to the short-run interactions, which are summed up in the Error Correction Model (ECM) for each variable. Table 5.3 shows the results of the ECM for Mexico, which includes two dummy variables, for the years 1988 and 2009. We include in parentheses the t-values.

Even though the equations are not very conclusive (the F-value is very low), we can draw some results from them. GDP seems to be path dependent, in the sense that it is self-reinforcing: higher GDP (or GDP growth) yesterday seems to cause higher GDP today, giving a warning against contractionary policies. The economy seems to be profit led in the short term, though the result is not significant. Foreign private debt does not seem to affect GDP negatively, but again, the significance level is very low. To sum up with Mexico, Figure 5.10 shows the impulse–response simulations performed with the results, showing the response to a generalized one standard deviation innovation, avoiding then any discussion about the ordering of the variables.

Based on these graphs, but keeping in mind the little confidence one can attach to the results, the following conclusions come to mind:

- The wage share is positively affected by GDP, especially in the short run, while in the long run the impact is smaller. There is also a negative impact of higher private debt.
- GDP does not seem to move with changes in income distribution, though one can say that the positive impact of the innovations is very short lived, reflecting perhaps the negative coefficient in the ECM. The path-dependent behaviour of GDP that we saw in those results is present, and we have a negative impact of foreign private debt on GDP, though a warning should be made regarding its low significance level.

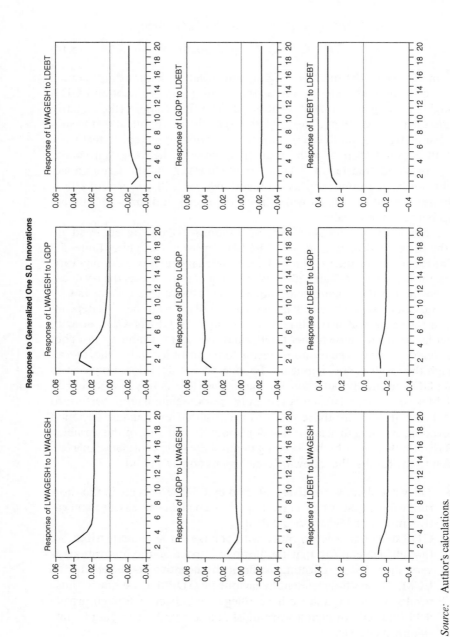

Source: Author's calculations.

Figure 5.10 Impulse–response functions in Mexico

156

Table 5.4   Vector Error Correction Model in South Korea

	D(LWAGESH)	D(LGDP)	D(LDEBT)
Equation (5.13)	−0.169357	0.026165	−0.084755
	(−4.44928)	(0.36993)	(−0.14284)
Equation (5.14)	0.009079	−0.033313	0.042911
	(3.50105)	(−6.91304)	(1.06151)
D(LWAGESH(−1))	0.332966	0.148656	−0.051109
	(3.40522)	(0.81814)	(0.03353)
D(LGDP(−1))	0.273172	−0.009272	0.493647
	(3.98904)	(−0.07286)	(0.46244)
D(LDEBT(−1))	−0.010498	−0.060136	0.046220
	(−0.95195)	(−2.93450)	(0.26886)
DUM74	−0.092116	−0.021061	0.071374
	(−5.94201)	(−0.73109)	(0.29535)
DUM80	0.011777	−0.117865	0.218270
	(0.77252)	(−4.16075)	(0.91851)
R^2	0.711792	0.595820	0.031268
F	13.58344	8.107803	0.177523

Source: Author's calculations.

It must be mentioned that these results are in agreement with Onaran and Galanis (2012), who found Mexico to be profit led overall, but do not match those of López G. (2012b), who found that Mexico is a case of a strongly wage-led economy, also using a cointegrated VAR approach although with different specification and time-span. López G., Sánchez and Spanos (2011) also found a positive relation between trade protection and output, and a negative one between the latter and the real exchange rate. This last result is compatible and even complementary with the wage-led characteristic of the Mexican economy.

What about South Korea? Table 5.4 shows the ECM results for that country. Again, t-values are in the parentheses.

The ECM equation of debt has very low significance and hardly any strong conclusion can be based on it. Our results show us that GDP impacts positively in the short run on the wage share, contradicting some-what the long-run cointegrating coefficients that we found earlier. Foreign private debt also seems to affect GDP negatively. Both results are signifi-cant. And even though the economy seems to be wage led, the significance level is too low to say anything about it. Keeping this in mind, the impulse–response simulations are shown in Figure 5.11.

We can see in these simulations how the positive initial effect of GDP on

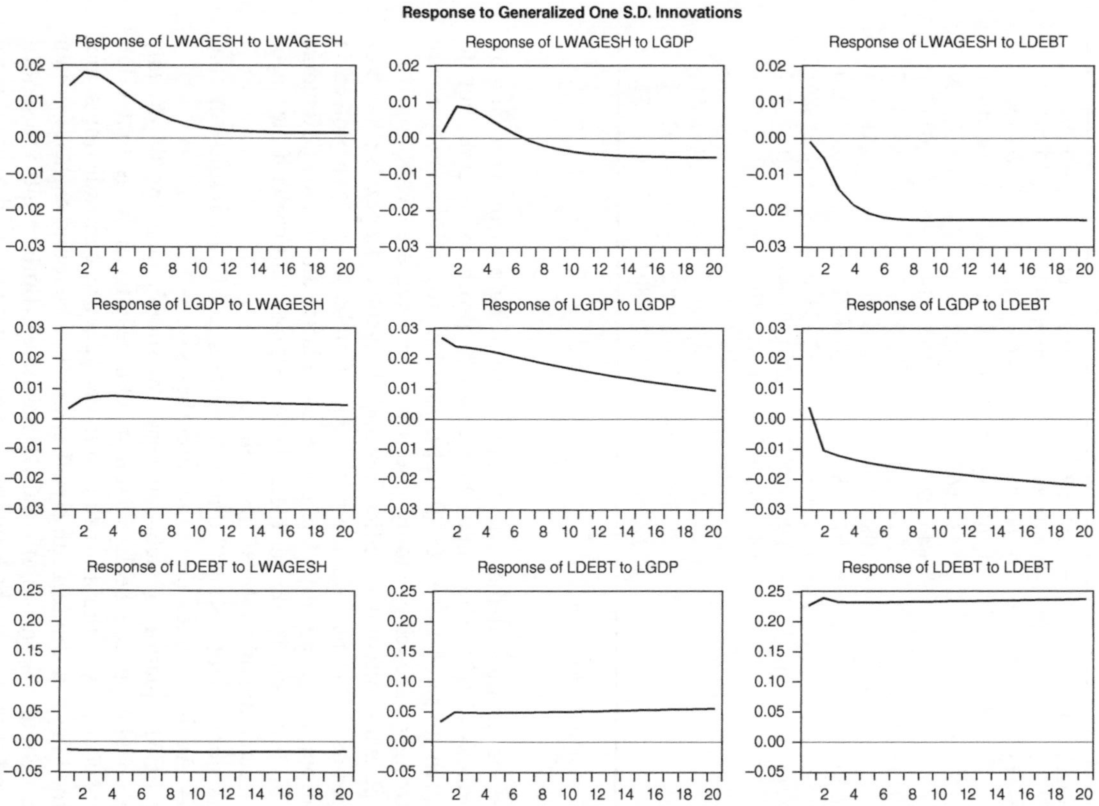

Response to Generalized One S.D. Innovations

Response of LWAGESH to LWAGESH

Response of LWAGESH to LGDP

Response of LWAGESH to LDEBT

Response of LGDP to LWAGESH

Response of LGDP to LGDP

Response of LGDP to LDEBT

Response of LDEBT to LWAGESH

Response of LDEBT to LGDP

Response of LDEBT to LDEBT

Source: Author's calculations.

Figure 5.11   Impulse–response functions in South Korea

158

the wage share disappears in time, and we can see the substantive impact of private debt on GDP; the effect on the wage share was also negative, but not significant. This finding is consistent with Storm and Naastepad (2005), in the sense that GDP growth (and particularly manufacturing growth) was the main driver of productivity growth in East Asian countries, and therefore it tends to lower the wage share, for a given real wage. It is certainly the case that the Korean state did not only aim at 'disciplining capital' but also labour (Seguino 1999, p. 321; Storm and Naastepad 2005, p. 1086). We can also see the short-run wage-led characteristics of the Korean economy.

These results are compatible with the channels we emphasized in the model presented above and provide some evidence for the existence of a negative impact of foreign private borrowing on GDP and distribution, however one must remain cautious in taking them at face value. Our findings also stand in line with Kregel's description, in the sense that even though foreign indebtedness has been the trigger of too many crises, financial flows enter through different channels. Our model captures one of those (private borrowing), and our findings (Korea with private debt, but not Mexico) are in close agreement with that argument: South Korea (taken as an example of the East Asian countries) was severely harmed by a wave of capital inflows to the private sector, while in the Mexican case we could not establish a close relationship between private debt and GDP growth. It is the case, therefore, that other factors should be included in the model to account for its trajectory. However, we do not believe the South Korean case to be a one-off episode of balance of payments crisis driven by speculative inflows and their interaction with the balance sheet of the private sector. Many European countries provide more recent examples, and are witness to the relevance of these types of models.

Stylized as it is, the model is open to further expansions, adding additional features and feedbacks. In particular, the introduction of government (foreign) debt is a must. However, proponents of Modern Monetary Theory, such as Wray (2012), would argue that what is important is the currency in which debt is denominated. If public debt is denominated in domestic currency, there is no possibility of default, since a government can always print the currency in which debt is denominated. And as we said earlier, it is certainly true that since the 2000s an increasing proportion of public debt in developing countries has been denominated in domestic currency. Undoubtedly, if Greece had a central bank catering to its needs, it would have avoided many of the difficulties it went through after 2009. The policy of the European Central Bank is actually quite indicative of this: since the mere announcement of the Outright Monetary Transaction programme in 2012, yields on sovereign debt have fallen substantially, because investors expect that the ECB will stand behind the debt of its country members.

Unfortunately, this is not the end of the story. Going back to the discussion in Chapter 4, if there is a sudden capital outflow investors will most likely demand hard foreign currency, forcing a devaluation or putting pressure on foreign exchange reserves. If there is a flexible exchange rate regime, there will be a devaluation, and investors will face a capital loss on their holdings if they are denominated in domestic currency; otherwise the loss will be burdened on the public sector. With a fixed exchange rate regime, there will be pressure on the foreign exchange reserves.

We would like to emphasize in the strongest possible terms that it is certainly better to have public (and private) debt denominated in the domestic currency. However, in many emerging countries, that does not relieve them of the problem: as long as there is a dollarization threat, sudden outflows will present an enduring threat, particularly with open capital and financial accounts, and with economies more integrated to the global financial system.

The reader may ask, what is the problem if devaluation happens? Besides the danger of accelerating inflation at home (though, as we reviewed in Chapter 4, the pass-through from exchange rate movements to prices has fallen since the 1990s), one has to consider the balance sheet of firms. In an important study, Mantey (2013) shows the negative effect of devaluations on exporting firms (yes, exporting) in a number of emerging countries because most of their liabilities were denominated in foreign currency, so that the possible gains in competitiveness following a devaluation were eroded through its impact on the financial fragility of firms. And that is one of the main messages of the models presented in this chapter and in the previous one, even if details may differ: the balance sheet structure of the different sectors has an importance of its own.

Coming back to possible ways to expand the model to include government debt, as reviewed in the literature in Chapter 3, with exogenous government expenditure and tax receipts adjusting according to the state of aggregate demand, plus taking into account the interest payments on public debt, a stable steady state exists (Serrano 1995; Allain 2015). However, when dealing with foreign debt (and assuming for simplicity that it is all denominated in foreign currency) further complications arise. First, interest payments do not add to domestic demand, but to a current account deficit. This issue has already been reflected in equation (5.9), when dealing with private debt. But in the context of public debt, this feature eliminates the effect of interest payments in fostering some portion of domestic demand, probably through pension funds. Secondly, lack of foreign currency (for instance, if there is a sudden decrease in d^f

in equation (5.11) and governments find it harder to fund themselves) may force a reduction in government spending, bringing down domestic demand, as in the typical IMF austerity solution for balance of payments crises. A steady state could still be found if (as is likely) imports diminish, so the modified model would deploy a behaviour similar to ours, but growth rates would be smaller.

When there is a lack of currency, governments are not alone with funding problems regarding their external debt: firms usually face the same problem at the same time, so that the trouble is compounded. It is not so uncommon for foreign private debt to be nationalized and put on the shoulders of the state, which in turn puts harsher constraints on 'pure' government expenditure, but cleans the balance sheet of those firms. But default episodes happen as well, accompanied by debt restructuring processes that lower debt levels.

A final issue to consider refers to foreign investors' decisions regarding the allocation of their investment between public and private debt. If a strong investment sentiment arises (say, reflected in a higher g_o coefficient), then public borrowing requirements will fall for a given growth rate of public expenditure, because tax receipts will increase. In this sense, it is the composition of the demand side that determines the allocation of debt, while investors may decide the maturity and the type of claim (loans or portfolio) they acquire.

5.7   HOT MONEY: TAMING THE FIRE

Several developing countries face a dilemma, on two different fronts. Given their productive structure, whenever they embark on a growth process, they are faced with a scarcity of foreign exchange and hit the limits set by the current account. The literature on balance of payments constraints (McCombie and Thirlwall 2004; Thirlwall 2011) has extensively addressed the issue. Even if they attempt a development strategy oriented towards exports, they may well initially go through a period of trade deficits until they reorient their productive capabilities, and the same goes for an import substitution strategy. Higher commodity prices may at times (like during the late 2000s–early 2010s) provide a sort of relief for primary-products exporters, but the impact is not the same for all developing countries. Higher wheat and soya prices (such as in Argentina or Brazil), though benefiting producers with better terms of trade, can have inflationary pressures on basic necessities. The effect on non-oil-producers in the Middle East and North Africa was mentioned as a cause of the Arab Revolutions! It must be emphasized that this is not a problem of lack of savings. It is a problem of lack of hard foreign currency, usually dollars. We may speak of foreign 'capital', but it should be clear to the reader that domestic resources, domestic 'capital', can be mobilized through credit policies oriented for that purpose, as the experience of development banks shows.

But even if a country has a balanced current account, those dollars may come anyhow, because of global financial conditions outside the control of developing countries, and at times of stress they can be forced to keep foreign investment in, due to negative effects of exchange rate volatility or private sector exposure to external conditions. Moreover, channels may develop by which domestic investors flee their money out of the country, in spite of capital controls. Having no other option but to lure investors, that is usually done by raising domestic interest rates in relation to international rates. What are the dangers? And what are the policy responses to mitigate those dangers?

From the previous discussion, it should be clear by now that, even if you want to attract foreign capital, say in order to develop domestic credit markets or to foster investment (such incentives mentioned in the early literature by McKinnon (1973) and Shaw (1973)), foreign investors usually do not invest in the most beneficial sectors for the host economies. They tend to invest in real estate assets, to increase stock prices beyond any reasonable level, to foster non-tradable sectors. As we mentioned at the beginning of the chapter, one very interesting finding by Benigno, Converse and Fornaro (2015) is the damaging impact of large capital inflows on productivity, because they tend to raise the share of services, including construction and finances, to the detriment of manufactures. The effects may well be dubbed a 'financial Dutch disease' (Botta, Godin and Missaglia 2014). Equally important, most emerging countries' financial markets are just too small and underdeveloped to absorb and recycle the huge tidal waves of inflows without excessively distorting asset prices. Haldane (2011) has aptly named this the 'big fish, small pond problem'.

And the effect on income distribution is not neutral. The impact on manufactures tends to reduce wages; households become more indebted; the business sector has a playing field inclined in its favour, so that labour protection is eroded, or trade unions are coerced into wage restriction agreements; firms find it more profitable to invest in buoyant financial markets and speculative projects than in productive investment, and the productive capabilities are even worsened, with lower productivity levels. And huge inflows are followed by huge outflows, which leave enduring scars, in terms of bankruptcy, unemployment and wasted resources.

So, emerging markets may be caught in a dilemma: they may have to attract foreign inflows, but these have unwelcome effects. And even when they do not need those inflows, they come anyway and the host country is left to deal with the aftermath. What is to be done? What is the role of capital controls in all this? Our focus will not be on what the world can do for developing countries (for that matter, see Kregel (2004) or UNCTAD (2015), for instance) but what developing countries can do for themselves.

The reader may have the impression, after reading what we have written above, that we are advising passivism/defeatism as the only reasonable economic policy. Keep rates high so that money keeps flowing in. The reader would be wrong, though. Governments have a whole range of alternatives, some complementary to others, to use as much policy space as they have in order to push for a development strategy that accommodates, or even better, that is based on a more egalitarian income distribution pattern, all the while avoiding lack of hard currency and the ever-present threat of external asphyxiation.

The first thing to note is that the domestic credit policy need not be restricted to the mere determination of the interest rate (Studart 1995). Notwithstanding the predominant practice among central bankers, credit policy concerns much more than setting the base interest rate to fine tune the economy. A government can make use of public banks, development banks, direct credit orientation (such as establishing a minimum quota of credit to certain sectors, or facilitating direct lines of credit, or easing norms for credit standards), and so on. One need not even point towards 'heterodox' and 'unconventional' developing countries' experiences with public banks: Mazzucato (2013) tells a story about how governments actually fostered innovation, with research funding (another type of financial assistance). Even in austerity-driven Europe, the experience of the Krediet für Weideraufbau (KfW), a public development bank, should be recalled every time 'experts' dismiss an activist credit policy as contrary to 'successful experience of advanced countries'. Nor is public development banking inextricably linked to corruption and obscurity. It could well be argued that the most transparent financial institution in the world is the BNDES, the Brazilian development bank, which publishes on its website every granted credit line. Though episodes of corruption may occur, this type of transparency makes it easier for them to be detected. As a final reflection on this issue, a big battle in public speech will be won when people (and policy makers) realize that the control of price variables (in this case, the base interest rate) does not prevent nor necessarily conflict with quantity interventions in the sense of direct or indirect credit orientation. And credit orientation provides its finest results when it is linked to sustainable development models, which are mostly related to manufacturing development, as has been a central tenet of post-Keynesian economics since the work of Kaldor (1967) and as corroborated lately by Timmer, de Vries and de Vries (2014). The manufacturing sector usually provides the larger gains in productivity, not only directly but also indirectly by fostering the development of services linked to technologically intensive services with high wage levels.

A typical preventive measure to protect the economy from the unwanted damage from financial capital flows is to accumulate foreign exchange reserves, as has been mentioned previously. These reserves act as an 'insurance policy', given the lack of a more global approach to steam capital inflows (UNCTAD 2015). Motivations may also relate to a 'mercantilist' economic policy by which governments try to keep their exchange rate at a certain level. However, foreign exchange reserves were accumulated even by countries that experienced substantial appreciation in their exchange rates, such as Brazil. Some authors, including heterodox economists such as Patnaik (2007) and Bibow (2008, 2011), emphasize the costly side of reserve accumulation, namely the 'need' to sterilize the increased money supply by issuing other types of liabilities, usually paying a higher interest rate than that earned on the reserves themselves. As an alternative policy, Bibow (2011) recommends capital account management which, as we mentioned earlier, has recently been acknowledged even by the IMF. We do support this as well, and more on that will be said a few paragraphs below. There are countless summaries of experiences with capital management measures, from a more orthodox perspective, as Edwards (2007), to less mainstream views such as those found in UNCTAD (2003), Epstein (2005), Gallagher, Ocampo and Griffith-Jones (2012) and Gallagher (2014), among many others.

However, there is no 'incompatibility' between reserve accumulation and capital account management. Reserve accumulation works, as recently exemplified by Bussière et al. (2015). It may not be a costless measure, but its effectiveness is almost beyond doubt. In addition, capital controls can help reduce the necessary amount of reserves, if they succeed in diminishing the inflow and sudden reversal of financial flows. That would be one role of capital controls.

But capital controls cannot fully isolate a country from the global financial cycle. Does it mean that they are useless? On the contrary, they have a very important role to play. As expressed by UNCTAD: 'Capital account management should be used to try to influence the composition and maturity of flows' (2014, p. 133). Tong and Wei (2011) found that, even though the volume of capital flows does not have a significant influence on liquidity crunches in crisis periods, their composition does have a significant effect, with greater reliance on non-FDI flows previous to crises having a worsening effect on credit crunches. Athukorala and Rajapatirana (2003) concluded for the period 1985–2000 that, even though Asian countries had experienced larger capital inflows than Latin American economies, the real exchange rate in the former countries had appreciated less than in the latter, because Latin American countries received a larger proportion of non-FDI flows.

As can be inferred from the above, emerging economies should discourage certain types of flows, such as short-term debt or portfolio flows, and encourage (or tolerate) others, such as long-term funds aimed at productive sectors. Instead of allowing them to inflate the construction sector, commercial and housing bubbles, or stock exchange bubbles, they can be allowed or encouraged to finance productive investment, though caution should prevail. As mentioned above, Avdjiev, Chui and Shin (2014) highlight the increased relevance of borrowing by foreign affiliates of emerging market companies, one of many typical ways (including problems with transfer prices) to move capital out of a country. It was common for multinational companies to 'lend' to their affiliates, and call back that loan in times of need, even though it may have been totally fictitious. To counteract such practice, one could implement a kind of refundable tax on foreign loans between affiliated companies, which would be rebated upon proof of productive investment.

Though there is no 'one-measure-fits-all' instrument, neither in space (countries involved) nor time (different conjuncture) there are some widely used varieties of capital controls, such as unremunerated reserve requirements (for instance, forcing an investor buying stocks or bonds to also allocate a determinate amount in an unremunerated term account), minimum stay periods, or outright prohibition of certain types of investment, in (commercial or residential) real estate, financial derivatives, and so on. Even more important is to have a 'dynamic' perspective, as Grabel (2012) emphasized, in the sense that the measures should be periodically revised and updated based on results.

With the previous caveat in mind, that is, to look not only at the total volume but also at the composition of financial flows, it should be stressed that capital account management measures are very effective. Ahmed and Zlate (2013) found that capital control measures discouraged portfolio flows; Baumann and Gallagher (2012) found that capital controls in Brazil helped to shift foreign inflows towards longer-term investment outlets; Jara and Olaberría (2013) found some evidence that capital controls help to reduce the association between large capital inflows and booms in house prices. The literature mentioned above also surveys many other articles.

One natural issue to take into account when designing policies to curb speculative inflows has to do with the issue of currency mismatches that may arise in the balance sheet of the private sector, both financial and non-financial. As discussed in Section 5.1, there is a noticeable increase in private foreign borrowing. Banks are also a transmission channel for problems related to debt denominated in a foreign currency, which has given rise to too many financial crises, ultimately burdening the state when it chooses to rescue its financial system. The experience of the Argentinean banking system in the 1990s should not be forgotten, in this respect. Banks had a huge proportion of dollar-denominated deposits, but also had significant amounts of dollar-denominated loans. In other words, they did not have currency mismatch, but their borrowers did. The lesson we draw from this is that an integrated, economy-thorough approach should be adopted when analysing possible interactions. The drawback is that this may require or demand a lot of knowledge, skills and willingness from authorities/regulators, knowledge that may be scarce in emerging markets. Finally, the hardest part in terms of political skill refers to the conciliation of (or prioritization between) aspirations and fragilities of the different social groups and institutions of the society.

NOTE

1.   Higher domestic interest rates also encourage firms to borrow in less expensive international markets, increasing foreign inflows.

APPENDIX: LIST OF EQUATIONS OF THE MODEL

A. Distribution

Short-run, fixed mark-up pricing function:

$$p = (1 + z)(Wa_0 + E\overline{P}m) \tag{1}$$

Where z is the mark-up, W is the nominal wage, a_0 is the inverse of the labour productivity, E is the nominal exchange rate, $\overline{P}$ is the foreign price level and m represents the volume of imports. From here, we deduct the profit share and the wage share, and we present the real exchange rate:

$$\pi = \frac{z}{1 + z} \tag{2}$$

$$\psi = \frac{Wa_0}{p} \tag{3}$$

$$e = \frac{E\overline{P}}{p} \tag{4}$$

$$\pi + \psi + em = 1 \tag{5}$$

In the long-run, the mark-up is not fixed. The wage share moves according to:

$$\hat{\psi} = \hat{W} + \hat{a}_0 - \hat{p} \tag{6}$$

Wage claims by workers are given by:

$$\hat{W} = \phi(\psi_w - \psi) + \gamma e \tag{7}$$

Prices increase according to:

$$\hat{p} = \rho(\psi - \psi_f) \tag{8}$$

The wage share targeted by firms moves according to:

$$\psi_f = \tau - \delta e - \omega d \tag{9}$$

Putting equations (7), (8) and (9) into (6) and rearranging, we get:

$$\hat{\psi} = \psi(-\phi - \rho) - \rho\omega d + \phi\psi_w + e(\gamma - \rho\delta) - \alpha + \rho\tau \quad (10)$$

Differentiating (10) with respect to the two endogenous variables that appear on the right-hand side of the equation, ψ and d, are:

$$\frac{\partial\hat{\psi}}{\partial\psi} = \left(-\phi - \rho + \frac{\partial e}{\partial\psi}(\gamma - \rho\delta)\right) \quad (11)$$

$$\frac{\partial\hat{\psi}}{\partial d} = -\rho\omega \quad (12)$$

Equation (12) is straight out negative. $\frac{\partial e}{\partial\psi}$ is negative as well, since a higher real wage entails a real appreciation. If $\gamma > \rho\delta$ or slightly less, equation (11) is negative and its stability is assured. We will assume just that.

B. Effective Demand

Retained earnings are a fraction s_f of total profits. The rest of profits are distributed as dividends.

$$F_f = s_f \pi Y \quad (13)$$

Households' propensity to save out of wage income is different (and lower) than savings out of dividends income.

$$S_h = s_w \psi Y + s_d(1 - s_f)\pi Y \quad (14)$$

Normalizing by the capital stock, the savings rate for the whole economy is:

$$\sigma = S/K = [\pi(s_f + s_d - s_f s_d) + s_w\psi] Y/K = [\pi(s_f + s_d - s_f s_d) + s_w\psi]u \quad (15)$$

The investment function is:

$$g = I/K = g_o + \beta u + \theta\pi - \nu id \quad (16)$$

We reproduce the determinants of the trade balance as presented above:

$$b = B/K = \varepsilon e - \zeta u + \chi u^f - oid \quad (17)$$

Capacity utilization moves according to:

$$\hat{u} = \lambda(g + b - \sigma) \tag{18}$$

Putting (15), (16) and (17) into (18), we get:

$$\hat{u} = \lambda\{u(\beta - \zeta - [\pi(s_f + s_d - s_f s_d) + s_w \psi]) - id(v + o) + \theta\pi + \varepsilon e$$

$$+ g_0 + \chi u^f\} \tag{19}$$

Differentiating (19) with respect to the endogenous variables results in:

$$\frac{\partial \hat{u}}{\partial u} = -\lambda\{[\pi(s_f + s_d - s_f s_d) + s_w \psi] - \beta + \zeta\} \tag{20}$$

$$\frac{\partial \hat{u}}{\partial d} = -i\lambda(v + o) \tag{21}$$

$$\frac{\partial \hat{u}}{\partial \psi} = \lambda\left\{(-u)\left[\frac{\partial\pi}{\partial\psi}(s_f + s_d - s_f s_d) + s_w\right] + \theta\frac{\partial\pi}{\partial\psi} + \varepsilon\frac{\partial e}{\partial\psi}\right\} \tag{22}$$

In equation (20), the term in brackets (which represents the effect of the change in savings) plus the income elasticity of imports need to be stronger than the response of investment to changes in capacity utilization. This is the usual Keynesian stability condition mentioned in Chapter 3, and we will assume it holds good here. Therefore, (20) is negative. The same sign is valid for (21). As for (22), it represents the wage-led or profit-led nature of the economy. The term in parentheses represents the decrease in savings given a higher wage share (remember that $\frac{\partial\pi}{\partial\psi}$ is negative); the second and third terms capture the effect on investment and the trade balance. If $(-u)[\frac{\partial\pi}{\partial\psi}(s_f + s_d - s_f s_d) + s_w]$ is greater than the sum of $\theta\frac{\partial\pi}{\partial\psi}$ and $\varepsilon\frac{\partial e}{\partial\psi}$, the economy is wage-led. If not, it is profit-led.

C. Foreign Financial Flows

Foreign flows in the model are governed by the following equation:

$$\hat{d} = \eta u + \mu(i - i^f) + (1 - \mu)(d^f - d) \tag{23}$$

The partial derivatives are:

$$\frac{\partial\hat{d}}{\partial d} = -(1 - \mu) \tag{24}$$

$$\frac{\partial \hat{d}}{\partial u} = \eta \tag{25}$$

D. The System and its Stability

We have a three-variables linear system, represented by:

$$\begin{pmatrix} \hat{\Psi} \\ \hat{u} \\ \hat{d} \end{pmatrix} = \begin{pmatrix} \dfrac{\partial \hat{\Psi}}{\partial \psi} & 0 & \dfrac{\partial \hat{\Psi}}{\partial d} \\[2mm] \dfrac{\partial \hat{u}}{\partial \psi} & \dfrac{\partial \hat{u}}{\partial u} & \dfrac{\partial \hat{u}}{\partial d} \\[2mm] 0 & \dfrac{\partial \hat{d}}{\partial u} & \dfrac{\partial \hat{d}}{\partial d} \end{pmatrix} \begin{pmatrix} \psi \\ u \\ d \end{pmatrix}$$

In matters of signs, the Jacobin matrix is as follows:

$$J = \begin{pmatrix} - & 0 & - \\ ? & - & - \\ 0 & + & - \end{pmatrix}$$

The Routh-Horwitz conditions for stability of a 3 × 3 system are such that:

i. $\mathrm{Tr}(J) < 0$
ii. $\mathrm{Det}\,|J| < 0$
iii. $\mathrm{Det}\,|1| + \mathrm{Det}\,|2| + \mathrm{Det}\,|3| > 0$
iv. $\mathrm{Tr}(J)(\mathrm{Det}\,|1| + \mathrm{Det}\,|2| + \mathrm{Det}\,|3|) + \mathrm{Det}\,|J| > 0$

The trace must be negative (and that condition is fulfilled already at plain sight); the determinant of the Jacobin must be negative; the sum of the determinants of the diagonal elements (the 1, 2 and 3, in condition (iii)) must be positive, and that sum times the negativity of the trace, plus the determinant, must also be positive. Denoting the elements of the Jacobin matrix as a_{ij}, with i representing the row and j the column as usual, the determinant of the Jacobin is:

$$\mathrm{Det}|J| = a_{11}\begin{vmatrix} a_{22} & a_{23} \\ a_{32} & a_{33} \end{vmatrix} - a_{12}\begin{vmatrix} a_{21} & a_{23} \\ a_{31} & a_{33} \end{vmatrix} + a_{13}\begin{vmatrix} a_{21} & a_{22} \\ a_{31} & a_{32} \end{vmatrix}$$

$$\mathrm{Det}|J| = (-)\begin{vmatrix} - & - \\ + & - \end{vmatrix} - 0\begin{vmatrix} ? & - \\ 0 & - \end{vmatrix} + (-)\begin{vmatrix} ? & - \\ 0 & + \end{vmatrix}$$

If the economy is wage-led (which implies a positive a_{21}), this determinant is necessarily negative. If aggregate-demand is profit-led, there are still some parameter constellations under which it would fulfil the condition.

The determinants of the elements of the diagonal are:

$$\text{Det}|1| = \begin{pmatrix} a_{22} & a_{23} \\ a_{32} & a_{33} \end{pmatrix} = \begin{pmatrix} - & - \\ + & - \end{pmatrix} > 0$$

$$\text{Det}|2| = \begin{pmatrix} a_{11} & a_{13} \\ a_{31} & a_{33} \end{pmatrix} = \begin{pmatrix} - & - \\ 0 & - \end{pmatrix} > 0$$

$$\text{Det}|3| = \begin{pmatrix} a_{11} & a_{12} \\ a_{21} & a_{22} \end{pmatrix} = \begin{pmatrix} - & 0 \\ ? & - \end{pmatrix} > 0$$

Therefore, condition (iii) is also satisfied. For a sufficiently large trace in absolute value, and for a small value of the determinant, the fulfilment of condition (iv) is satisfied.

6. Epilogue: challenges and possibilities

6.1 A COMPLEX PICTURE

Developing countries do not have it easy. The deregulating trend in the capital account since the end of the Bretton Woods regime has left them exposed to wide fluctuations of financial flows, seemingly out of their control. The ideological mantra of laissez-faire disseminated by international organizations, business interests and some central powers chastises those countries that try to have some sort of influence on the determination and behaviour of the capitals that flood them.

This condemnation of policy intervention has not been confined to emerging countries. The most obvious example is to be found in the Eurozone. All the features described in Chapter 5, and throughout the book, can be easily identified: widening disparity in income distribution; a depressing influence on economic activity which was compensated in some countries by the build-up of private indebtedness (while others chose to free ride on the external demand of these countries); massive surges of financial capital coming from the more developed financial centres in the region. The build-up of private indebtedness was not restricted solely to households: firms and banks also borrowed heavily, with a misappreciation of the underlying developments in the repayment capability of borrowers, in many cases to speculate on real estate prices (or other asset prices) or to develop financial services. In sum, a whole downgrade of the productive structure is noticeable in most of the Eurozone members.

These patterns are all too well known for developing economies. And the panorama for the coming years presents similar challenges. This last period saw an increase in the financial flows to these countries, many of which experienced accelerated private indebtedness, such as Brazil, South Korea, Malaysia, Turkey, Mexico and many others, as we described in the previous chapter. The expected reversal in these flows, which had already started by the time this book was being written (September 2015), will not only show how well prepared emerging markets are to withstand a more illiquid financial environment, but will also reveal the transformation in their productive structures, partly caused by the previous inflows.

The higher level of terms of trade many developing countries enjoyed between 2000 and 2014 was used by some governments (particularly in, but not limited to, Latin America) to capture rents from primary and extractive sectors and transfer them to lower-income sectors, even reducing income inequality in several cases. The rise of China as a global economic superpower had severe implications for the productive orientation of both emerging and developed economies. For instance, Germany sharpened its pattern as a global producer of high-value technological goods, mainly capital and luxury goods. In the case of emerging economies not integrated into the value chain of Chinese manufacturing goods (as many Asian countries are), the main effect came through higher commodity prices and higher infrastructure investment sponsored by the Chinese government.

Higher financial inflows and higher commodity prices are a perfect combination to build up vulnerabilities to external shocks, though there are obvious exceptions.[1] These fragilities reveal themselves when the foreign financing stops or reverses course, as has been the case in 2014 and 2015. Devaluations are happening across the board; many countries are losing foreign reserves; investment projects (many financed with foreign credit or foreign direct investment) in extractive industries or even infrastructure have been postponed; pressures on the balance of payments are diminishing the will of governments to deepen or maintain in some cases progressive income policies; and signs of financial stress are mounting, particularly in middle-income countries. The picture seems complex.

6.2 CHALLENGES AND POSSIBILITIES

It looks like the task of combining a more egalitarian income distribution with steady and decent growth rates, in the midst of financial outflows, will be a more daunting enterprise in the near future, for developing economies. Export demand does not seem to be a powerful growth engine, with trade growth barely matching world output growth, and showing reconfiguration patterns with a higher preponderance of 'North–North' trade, that is, trade between developed economies (UNCTAD 2015, Chapter 1). The source of growth will have to be found at home.

And the insertion of emerging economies in the international financial markets has created new fragilities, as the 2008 financial crisis has shown. Greater presence of foreign banks, for instance, can multiply the negative effects of financial outflows, by suctioning out capital (and precious foreign exchange reserves) and drying the credit supply. Multinational enterprises also accelerate the remittance of profits from subsidiaries to their home companies when the situation turns for the worse.

But the previous discussion has shown us that countries are not devoid of possibilities and instruments to tame this adverse scenario.

As an example, from a financial point of view, countries have different alternatives within the international regulatory framework for banking activities (known as the Basel III rules) to impose higher capital requirements to subsidiaries of foreign banks, preventing profit distribution to home quarters. But these same rules restrict the lending capabilities of big banks (which are usually state owned in many developing countries) to orient their lending to small and medium-sized enterprises.

The unconventional monetary policy instrumented in developed countries also provides lessons for less financially developed economies. Central banks have implemented measures that come very close to redirecting the credit supply, such as the targeted refinancing of banks' liabilities if they increase their lending to the real economy (Targeted Longer Term Refinancing Operations, by the European Central Bank) or outright corporate bonds purchases.

Unavoidably, a more engaging role in credit allocation seems to be the call of the day. Interventions in the credit spreads (the difference between passive and active interest rates), lower requirements for creditworthiness, and a more active role in the search for funding of infrastructure projects, all require the abandonment of policy inactivity. But this activism, which faces the opposition of business interests at home and financial (and political) centres abroad, needs not to be restricted merely to financial considerations. The resilience shown by developing countries to the 2008 financial crisis has been due to an approach that favours domestic employment and income growth as opposed to the widespread desire for 'sound finance', that is, austerity measures. The mitigation of foreign exchange scarcity, a typical and recurrent illness of emerging economies, cannot be pursued by appeals to the restoration of 'business confidence' by cuts in public expenditure, the cancellation of investment projects and a reduction of the 'size of the state'. On the contrary, the identification and promotion of strategic sectors, combined with protections that minimize the impact of the volatility of the international financial cycle on the domestic economy, need an engaging public sector with clear priorities and political willingness and strength to undertake these challenging enterprises. The disparaging effects of different 'pure' exchange rate regimes in different contexts, as reviewed in Chapter 4, is just another example.

And the solution to certain fragilities can arise as a by-product of seemingly unrelated policies. Keeping employment and incomes at high levels reduces financial fragility and provides the conditions for faster recoveries. It helps to overcome funding shortages of pension funds and public revenues, should that be a concern. It helps to develop a more skilled labour force and to increase labour productivity. It creates a more stable environment for investment activities, reducing uncertainties regarding revenues expectations.

It is my expectation that this book has contributed to the realization that a more egalitarian income distribution, high employment levels and sustained income growth are all requirements for a sustained, stable, robust and inclusive growth process. I acknowledge that the political discourse is mostly against this message. But social scientists would lose their raison d'être if they gave up the hope of contributing at least a grain of sand to the construction of a more enlightened, aware and engaging society.

NOTE

1. To make a simple point: not all emerging economies are net commodity-producers. Therefore, the recent fall in commodity prices will have a different impact on different countries. Some may even have a balanced impact, such as Gambia, which saw a reduction in both its export (minerals) and import (oil) goods. East African countries such as Kenya, some Middle Eastern economies like Egypt or countries like Turkey and India are likely to enjoy better terms of trade.

References

Ahmed, S. and Zlate, A. (2013): *Capital flows to emerging market economies: a brave new world?*, International Finance Discussion Papers No. 1081, Board of Governors of the Federal Reserve, Washington, DC.

Akyüz, Y. (2014): *Internationalization of finance and changing vulnerabilities in emerging and developing economies*, Discussion Paper No. 217, United Nations Conference on Trade and Development, Geneva.

Alesina, A. and Perotti, R. (1996): *Income distribution, political instability and investment*, European Economic Review, Vol. 40 (2), pp. 1203–1228.

Alesina, A. and Rodrik, D. (1994): *Distributive politics and economic growth*, Quarterly Journal of Economics, Vol. 109 (2), pp. 465–490.

Allain, O. (2015): *Tackling the instability of growth: a Kaleckian–Harrodian model with an autonomous expenditure component*, Cambridge Journal of Economics, Vol. 39 (5), pp. 351–371.

Amiti, M., Itskhoki, O. and Konings, J. (2014): *Importers, exporters, and exchange rate disconnect*, American Economic Review, Vol. 104 (7), pp. 1942–1978.

Ampudia Márquez, N.A. (2011): *Política monetaria no convencional, traspaso inflacionario e impactos en la distribución factorial del ingreso*, Economía UNAM, Vol. 8 (22), pp. 37–54.

Arestis, P. (2006): *Financial liberalization and the relationship between finance and growth*, in P. Arestis and M. Sawyer (eds): A Handbook of Alternative Monetary Economics, Edward Elgar Publishing, Cheltenham and Northampton, MA.

Arestis, P. and Milberg, W. (1993–1994): *Degree of monopoly, pricing, and flexible exchange rate*, Journal of Post Keynesian Economics, Vol. 16 (2), pp. 167–188.

Arestis, P. and Sawyer, M. (2005): *Aggregate demand, conflict and capacity in the inflationary process*, Cambridge Journal of Economics, Vol. 29 (6), pp. 959–974.

Arslanalp, S. and Tsuda, T. (2014): *Tracking global demand for emerging market sovereign debt*, Working Paper No. 14/39, International Monetary Fund, Washington, DC.

Asimakopulos, A. (1975): *A Kaleckian theory of income distribution*, Canadian Journal of Economics, Vol. 8 (3), pp. 313–333.

Asimakopulos, A. (1991): Keynes's General Theory and Accumulation, Cambridge University Press, Cambridge.

Aspromourgos, T. (2009): The Science of Wealth: Adam Smith and the Framing of Political Economy, Routledge, London.

Athukorala, P.C. and Rajapatirana, S. (2003): *Capital inflows and the real exchange rate: comparative study of Asia and Latin America*, World Economy, Vol. 26 (4), pp. 613–637.

Atkinson, A.B. (2015): Inequality, Harvard University Press, Cambridge, MA.

Atkinson, A.B., Piketty, T. and Saez, E. (2011): *Top incomes in the long run of history*, Journal of Economic Literature, Vol. 49 (1), pp. 3–71.

Auerbach, P. and Skott, P. (1988): *Concentration, competition and distribution – a critique of theories of monopoly capital*, International Review of Applied Economics, Vol. 2 (1), pp. 42–61.

Avdjiev, S., Chui, M. and Shin, H.S. (2014): *Non-financial corporations from emerging market economies and capital flows*, BIS Quarterly Review 2014, December, pp. 67–77.

Azpiazu, D. (ed.) (1999): La Desregulación de los Mercados. Paradigma e Inequidades de las Políticas del Neoliberalismo, Grupo Editorial Norma, Buenos Aires.

Backhouse, R.E. and Boianovsky, M. (2015): *Secular stagnation: the history of a macroeconomic heresy*, Blanqui Lecture, 19th Annual Conference of the European Society for the History of Economic Thought, Rome, 14–16 May.

Backus, D., Brainard, W., Smith, G. and Tobin, J. (1980): *A model of U.S. financial and nonfinancial economic behaviour*, Journal of Money, Credit and Banking, Vol. 12 (2), pp. 259–293.

Bank for International Settlements (2006): 76th Annual Report, Bank for International Settlements, Basel.

Baran, P. and Sweezy, P. (1966): Monopoly Capital, Monthly Review, New York.

Barba, A. and Pivetti, M. (2012): *Distribution and accumulation in post-1980 advanced capitalism*, Review of Keynesian Economics, Vol. 0 (1), Inaugural issue, pp. 126–142.

Barnes, M. and Olivei, G. (2003): *Inside and outside the bounds: threshold estimates of the Phillips curve*, Federal Reserve Bank of Boston, New England Economic Review, pp. 3–18.

Basualdo, E. (2006): Estudios de Historia Económica Argentina. Desde mediados del siglo XX a la actualidad, Siglo XXI-FLACSO, Buenos Aires.

Baumann, B. and Gallagher, K. (2012): *Navigating capital flows in Brazil and Chile*, Initiative for Policy Dialogue Working Paper Series, Columbia University, New York.

Bedirhanoglu, P., Cömert, H., Eren, I., Erol, I., Demiroz, D., Erdem, N., Gungen, A., Marois, T., Topal, A., Türel, O., Yalman, G., Yeldan, E. and Voyoda, E. (2013): *Comparative perspectives on financial systems in the EU: country report on Turkey*, Studies in Financial Systems No. 11, FESSUD, Leeds.

Belabed, C., Theobald, T. and Van Treeck, T. (2013): *Income distribution and current account imbalances*, IMK Working Paper No. 126-2013, IMK at the Hans Boeckler Foundation, Düsseldorf.

Bellamy Foster, J. (2013): *Marx, Kalecki and socialist strategy*, Monthly Review, Vol. 64 (11), available at http://monthlyreview.org/2013/04/01/marx-kalecki-and-socialist-strategy (accessed 15 January 2015).

Benigno, G., Converse, N. and Fornaro, L. (2015): *Large capital inflows, sectoral allocation, and economic performance*, International Financial Discussion Paper No. 1132, Board of Governors of the Federal Reserve, Washington, DC.

Bentolila, S. and Saint-Paul, G. (2003): *Explaining movements in the labour share*, Journal of Macroeconomics, Vol. 3 (1), pp. 1–33.

Bernanke, B. (2002): *On Milton Friedman's ninetieth birthday*, remarks at the conference to honour Milton Friedman, University of Chicago, Chicago, Illinois, available at http://www.federalreserve.gov/boarddocs/Speeches/2002/20021108/default.htm (accessed 15 August 2015).

Bernanke, B. (2004): *The great moderation*, speech at the meeting of the Eastern Economic Association, Washington, DC, available at http://www.federalreserve.gov/BOARDDOCS/speechES/2004/20040220/default.htm (accessed 15 August 2015).

Bezemer, D. (2011): *Causes of financial instability: don't forget finance*, Working Paper No. 665, Levy Economics Institute of Bard College, Annandale-on-Hudson.

Bhaduri, A. (1987): *Dependent and self-reliant growth with foreign borrowing*, Cambridge Journal of Economics, Vol. 11 (3), pp. 269–273.

Bhaduri, A. (2004): *The opportunities and dangers of international capital inflows for developing countries from an effective demand perspective*, in Z. Sadowski and A. Szeworski (eds): Kalecki's Economics Today, Routledge, London.

Bhaduri, A. and Marglin, S. (1990): *Unemployment and the real wage*, Cambridge Journal of Economics, Vol. 14 (4), pp. 375–393.

Bibow, J. (2008): *Insuring against private capital flows: is it worth the premium? What are the alternatives?*, Working Paper No. 553, Levy Economics Institute of Bard College, Annandale-on-Hudson.

Bibow, J. (2011): *Permanent and selective capital account management regimes as an alternative to self-insurance strategies in emerging-market economies*, Working Paper No. 683, Levy Economics Institute of Bard College, Annandale-on-Hudson.

Bindseil, U. (2004): *The operational target of monetary policy and the rise and fall of Reserve Position Doctrine*, Working Paper Series, No. 372, European Central Bank, Frankfurt am Main.

Blecker, R. (1999): *Kaleckian macro models for open economies*, in J. Deprez and J.T. Harvey (eds): Foundations of International Economics, Routledge, London.

Blecker, R. (2002): *Distribution, demand and growth in neo-Kaleckian macro models*, in M. Setterfield (ed.): The Economics of Demand-Led Growth: Challenging the Supply-Side Vision of the Long Run, Edward Elgar Publishing, Cheltenham and Northampton, MA.

Blecker, R. (2011): *Open economy models of distribution and growth*, in E. Hein and E. Stockhammer (eds): A Modern Guide to Keynesian Macroeconomics and Economic Policies, Edward Elgar Publishing, Cheltenham and Northampton, MA.

Boianovsky, M. (1995): *Wicksell's business cycle*, European Journal of the History of Economic Thought, Vol. 2 (2), pp. 375–411.

Borio, C. and Disyatat, P. (2009): *Unconventional monetary policy: an appraisal*, BIS Working Papers No. 292, Bank for International Settlements, Basel.

Borrill, P. and Tesfatsion, L. (2010): *Agent-based modelling: the right mathematics for the social sciences?*, Working Paper No. 10023, Department of Economics, Iowa State University.

Bortz, P. (2014): *Foreign debt, distribution, inflation and growth in an SFC model*, European Journal of Economics and Economic Policies: Intervention, Vol. 11 (3), pp. 269–299.

Botta, A., Godin, A. and Missaglia, M. (2014): *Finance, foreign (direct) investment and Dutch Disease: the case of Colombia*, DEM Working Paper Series No. 90 (09-14), Universitá di Pavia.

Bowles, S. and Boyer, R. (1995): *Wages, aggregate demand, and employment in an open economy: an empirical investigation*, in G. Epstein and H. Gintis (eds): Macroeconomic Policy After the Conservative Era. Studies in Investment, Saving and Finance, Cambridge University Press, Cambridge.

Brainard, W. and Tobin, J. (1968): *Pitfalls in financial model building*, American Economic Review, Vol. 58 (2), pp. 99–122.

Brown, M., Kirschenmann, K. and Ongena, S. (2011): *Foreign currency loans – demand or supply driven?*, Working Paper No. 2011-2, Swiss National Bank, Zurich.

Bruno, V. and Shin, H.S. (2014): *Cross-border banking and global liquidity*, BIS Working Papers No. 458, Bank for International Settlements, Basel.

Burgess, S. (2011): *Measuring financial sector output and its contribution to UK GDP*, Bank of England Quarterly Bulletin, 2011 (3), pp. 234–245.

Burkett, P. and Dutt, A.K. (1991): *Interest rate policy, effective demand, and growth in LDCs*, International Review of Applied Economics, Vol. 5 (2), pp. 127–153.

Bussière, M., Cheng, G., Chinn, M. and Lisack, N. (2015): *For a few dollars more: reserves and growth in times of crises*, Document de Travail No. 550, Banque de France, Paris.

Butzen, P., Deroose, M. and Ide, S. (2014): *Global imbalances and gross capital flows*, National Bank of Belgium Economic Review 2014, September, pp. 41–60.

Caiani, A., Caverzasi, E., Godin, A., Riccetti, L., Russo, A., Gallegati, M., Kinsella, S. and Stiglitz, J.E. (2014): *Innovation, demand and finance in an agent based-stock flow consistent model*, in F. Miguel, F. Amblard, J. Barceló and M. Madella (eds): Proceedings of the Social Simulation Conference, Universidad Autónoma de Barcelona, Barcelona.

Caiani, A., Godin, A., Caverzasi, E., Gallegati, M., Kinsella, S. and Stiglitz, J.E. (2015): *Agent based-stock flow consistent macroeconomics*, Working Paper S120, University of Limerick.

Caiani, A., Godin, A. and Lucarelli, S. (2012): *Schumpeter in a matrix: a stock flow consistent analysis of technological change*, Quaderni di Dipartimento No. 175, Dipartimento di economia politica e metodi quantitative, Università degli studi di Pavia.

Calcagno, A.F. (1984): *Politiques monetaristes et dynamiques financières, les experiences de l'Argentine et du Chili*, Ph.D. dissertation, Université Paris 1.

Calvo, G., Leiderman, R. and Reinhart, C. (1996): *Inflows of capital to developing countries in the 1990s*, Journal of Economic Perspectives, Vol. 10 (2), pp. 123–139.

Canitrot, A. (1981): *Teoría y práctica del liberalism. Política antiinflacionaria y apertura económica en la Argentina, 1976–1981*, Desarrollo Económico, Vol. 21 (3), pp. 131–189.

Carrión Alvarez, M. and Ehnts, D. (2014): *The roads not taken: graph theory and macroeconomic regimes in stock-flow consistent modelling*, available at http://papers.ssrn.com/sol3/papers.cfm?abstract_id=2518204 (accessed 25 May 2015).

Carter, S. (2007): *Real wage productivity elasticity across advanced economies, 1963–1999*, Journal of Post Keynesian Economics, Vol. 29 (4), pp. 573–600.

Carvalho, L. and Rezai, A. (2015): *Personal income inequality and aggregate demand*, Cambridge Journal of Economics, available at doi: 10.1093/cje/beu085.

Cassetti, M. (2003): *Bargaining power, effective demand and technical progress: a Kaleckian model of growth*, Cambridge Journal of Economics, Vol. 27 (3), pp. 449–464.

Cassetti, M. (2012): *Macroeconomic outcomes of changing social bargains. The feasibility of a wage-led open economy reconsidered*, Metroeconomica, Vol. 63 (1), pp. 64–91.

Caverzasi, E. and Godin, A. (2013): *Stock-flow consistent modelling through the ages*, Working Paper No. 745, Levy Economics Institute of Bard College, Annandale-on-Hudson.

Cecchetti, S.G. and Kharroubi, E. (2012): *Reassessing the impact of finance on growth*, BIS Working Papers No. 381, Bank for International Settlements, Basel.

Chandrasekhar, C.P. (2008): *Global liquidity and financial flows to developing countries: new trends in emerging markets and their implications*, G-24 Discussion Paper No. 52, United Nations.

Chang, H.J., Palma, J.G. and Whittaker, D.G. (eds) (2001): Financial Liberalization and the Asian Crisis, Palgrave, Basingstoke.

Chang, H.J., Park, H.J. and Yoo, C.G. (2001): *Interpreting the Korean crisis: financial liberalization, industrial policy and corporate governance*, in H.J. Chang, J.G. Palma and D.G. Whittaker (eds): Financial Liberalization and the Asian Crisis, Palgrave, Basingstoke.

Checchi, D. and García-Peñalosa, C. (2005): *Labour market institutions and the personal distribution of income in the OECD*, CESifo Working Paper No. 1608. Munich.

Chick, V. and Caserta, M. (1997): *Provisional equilibrium in macroeconomic theory*, in P. Arestis, J.G. Palma and M. Sawyer (eds): Capital Controversy, Post-Keynesian Economics and the History of Economic Thought: Essays in Honour of Geoff Harcourt, Vol. 2, Routledge, London.

Chinn, M. and Quayyum, S. (2012): *Long horizon uncovered interest rate parity re-assessed*, Working Paper No. 18482, National Bureau of Economic Research, Cambridge, MA.

Chirinko, R. (1993): *Business fixed investment spending: modelling strategies, empirical results, and policy implications*, Journal of Economic Literature, Vol. 31 (4), pp. 1875–1911.

Chui, M., Fender, I. and Sushko, V. (2014): *Risks related to EME corporate balance sheets: the role of leverage and currency mismatch*, BIS Quarterly Review 2014, September, pp. 35–47.

Chutasripanich, N. and Yetman, J. (2015): *Foreign exchange intervention: strategies and effectiveness*, BIS Working Papers No. 499, Bank for International Settlements, Basel.

Cibils, A. and Allami, C. (2008): *La financiarización en la Argentina*

1990–2007: un estudio de caso, presented at the 2nd Jornadas de Economía Política, San Miguel, 10–11 November.

Cincotti, S., Roberto, M. and Teglio, A. (2010): *Credit money and macroeconomic instability in the agent-based model and simulator Eurace*, Economics: The Open-Access, Open-Assessment E-Journal, Vol. 4, 2010-26, available at http://dx.doi.org/10.5018/economics-ejournal.ja.2010-26 (accessed 25 May 2015).

Cingano, F. (2014): *Trends in income inequality and its impact on economic growth*, OECD Social, Employment and Migration Working Papers, No. 163, OECD, Paris.

Claessens, S. and Ghosh, S. (2013): *Capital flows volatility and systemic risk in emerging markets: the policy toolkit*, in O. Canuto and S. Ghosh (eds): Dealing with the Challenges of Macro Financial Linkages in Emerging Markets, World Bank, Washington, DC.

Clark, J.B. (1899): The Distribution of Wealth, Macmillan, London.

Copeland, M.A. (1949): *Social accounting for money flows*, Accounting Review, Vol. 24 (3), pp. 254–264.

Coremberg, A., Marotte, B., Rubini, H. and Tisocco, D. (2007): *La inversión privada en la Argentina (1950–2000)*, Temas Grupo Editorial: UADE–ANCE, Buenos Aires.

Correa, E. and Vidal, G. (2006): *Financial deregulation and capital flows in Latin American countries*, in P. Arestis, J. Ferreiro and F. Serrano (eds): Financial Developments in National and International Markets, Palgrave Macmillan, Basingstoke.

Cripps, F. and Godley, W. (1976): *A formal analysis of the Cambridge economic policy group model*, Economica, 43 (November), pp. 335–348.

Crotty, J. and Dymski, G. (2001): *Can the global neoliberal regime survive victory in Asia?*, in P. Arestis and M. Sawyer (eds): Money, Finance and Capitalist Development, Edward Elgar Publishing, Cheltenham and Northampton, MA.

Cutler, D.M., Poterba, J.M. and Summers, L.H. (1990): *Speculative dynamics and the role of feedback traders*, American Economic Review, Vol. 80 (2), pp. 63–68.

Da Silva, C.E.S. and Vernengo, M. (2008): *The decline of the exchange rate pass-through in Brazil: explaining the 'fear of floating'*, International Journal of Political Economy, Vol. 37 (4), pp. 64–79.

Dabla-Norris, E., Kochhar, K., Suphaphiphat, N., Ricka, F. and Tsounta, E. (2015): *Causes and consequences of income inequality: a global perspective*, Staff Discussion Note 15/13, International Monetary Fund.

Dafermos, Y. (2012): *Liquidity preference, uncertainty, and recession in a stock-flow consistent model*, Journal of Post Keynesian Economics, Vol. 34 (4), pp. 749–776.

Dafermos, Y. and Papatheodorou, C. (2011): *Functional and personal income distribution in a stock-flow consistent model*, presented at the 15th conference of the Research Network Macroeconomic Policies, Berlin, 28–29 October.

Dallery, T. (2007): *Kaleckian models of growth and distribution revisited: evaluating their relevance through simulations*, presented at the 11th conference of the Research Network Macroeconomic Policies, Berlin, 26–27 October.

Dallery, T. and Van Treeck, T. (2011): *Conflicting claims and equilibrium adjustment processes in a stock-flow consistent macro model*, Review of Political Economy, Vol. 23 (2), pp. 189–211.

Damill, M. and Keifman, S. (1992): *Liberalización de comercio en una economía de alta inflación: Argentina 1989–1991*, Documentos CEDES No. 72, Buenos Aires.

Davidson, P. (1982): International Money and the Real World, Macmillan, London.

De Cecco, M. (1987): *Inflation and structural change in the euro-dollar market*, in M. de Cecco and J.P. Fitoussi (eds): Monetary Theory and Economic Institutions, Macmillan, Basingstoke.

De Grauwe, P. and Grimaldi, M. (2006): The Exchange Rate in a Behavioural Finance Framework, Princeton University Press, Woodstock (England).

De Lucchi, J.M. (2013): *Endogenous money and foreign debt sustainability during Argentinean convertibility*, Review of Keynesian Economics, Vol. 1 (3), pp. 322–346.

Diaz-Alejandro, C. (1985): *Good-bye financial repression, hello financial crash*, Journal of Development Economics, Vol. 19 (1–2), pp. 1–24.

Dobb, M. (1973): Theories of Value and Distribution Since Adam Smith, Cambridge University Press, Cambridge.

Dornbusch, R. (1998): *Capital controls: an idea whose time is past*, Essays in International Finance No. 207, Princeton University, Princeton, NJ.

Dos Santos, C.H. (2002): *Three essays in stock-flow consistent macroeconomic modelling*, Ph.D. Dissertation, New School for Social Research, New York.

Dos Santos, C.H. (2005): *A stock-flow consistent general framework for formal Minskyan analyses of closed economies*, Journal of Post Keynesian Economics, Vol. 27 (4), pp. 712–735.

Dos Santos, C.H. and Zezza, G. (2008): *A simplified, benchmark, stock-flow consistent Post Keynesian growth model*, Metroeconomica, Vol. 63 (1), pp. 170–199.

Downward, P. and Lee, F. (2001): *Post Keynesian pricing theory 'reconfirmed'? A critical review of Asking About Prices*, Journal of Post Keynesian Economics, Vol. 23 (3), pp. 465–483.

Downward, P. and Reynolds, P. (1996): *Alternative perspectives on Post-Keynesian price theory*, Review of Political Economy, Vol. 8 (1), pp. 67–78.

Duménil, G. and Lévy, D. (1999): *Being Keynesian in the short term and classical in the long term: the traverse to classical long-term equilibrium*, The Manchester School, Vol. 67 (6), pp. 684–716.

Duménil, G. and Lévy, D. (2012): *Being Post-Keynesian in the medium term and Classical-Marxian in the long term?*, available at http://www.jourdan.ens.fr/levy/dle2012o.pdf (accessed 10 February 2015).

Dünhaupt, P. (2012): *Financialization and the rentier income share – evidence from the USA and Germany*, International Review of Applied Economics, Vol. 26 (4), pp. 465–487.

Dutt, A.K. (1984): *Stagnation, income distribution and monopoly power*, Cambridge Journal of Economics, Vol. 8 (1), pp. 25–40.

Dutt, A.K. (1990): Growth, Distribution and Uneven Development, Cambridge University Press, Cambridge.

Dutt, A.K. (1992): *Conflict inflation, distribution, cyclical accumulation and crises*, European Journal of Political Economy, Vol. 8 (4), pp. 579–597.

Dutt, A.K. (2003): *New growth theory, effective demand, and Post-Keynesian dynamics*, in N. Salvadori (ed.): Old and New Growth Theories – An Assessment, Edward Elgar Publishing, Cheltenham and Northampton, MA.

Eatwell, J., Mouakil, T. and Taylor, L. (2008): *Liquidity, leverage and the impact of sub-prime turbulence*, Centre for Financial Analysis and Policy, Judge Business School, University of Cambridge.

Ebeke, C. and Lu, Y. (2014): *Emerging market local currency bond yields and foreign holdings in the post-Lehman period – a fortune or misfortune?*, IMF Working Paper No. 14/29, International Monetary Fund, Washington, DC.

Ederer, S. and Stockhammer, E. (2008): *Demand effects of the falling wage share in Austria*, Empirica, Vol. 35 (5), pp. 481–502.

Ederer, S., Onaran, O. and Stockhammer, E. (2009): *Functional income distribution and aggregate demand in the Euro-area*, Cambridge Journal of Economics, Vol. 33 (1), pp. 139–159.

Edwards, S. (ed.) (2007): Capital Controls and Capital Flows in Emerging Economies, University of Chicago Press, Chicago.

Enders, W. (2010): Applied Econometric Time-Series, 3rd edition, John Wiley & Sons, New York.

Engel, C. (2015): *Exchange rates, interest rates, and the risk premium*, Working Paper No. 21042, National Bureau of Economic Research, Cambridge, MA.

Epstein, G.A. (ed.) (2005): Financialization and the World Economy, Edward Elgar Publishing, Cheltenham and Northampton, MA.

Epstein, G.A. and Jayadev, A. (2005): *The rise of rentier incomes in OECD countries: financialization, central bank policy and labor solidarity*, in G.A. Epstein (ed.): Financialization and the World Economy, Edward Elgar Publishing, Cheltenham and Northampton, MA.

Epstein, G.A. and Power, D. (2003): *Rentier incomes and financial crises: an empirical examination of trends and cycles in some OECD countries*, Canadian Journal of Development Studies, Vol. 24 (2), pp. 229–248.

European Commission (2007): Employment in Europe, European Commission, Brussels.

European Commission (2013): *AMECO Database*, European Commission, Brussels.

Fazzari, S., Hubbard, R.G. and Petersen, B. (1988): *Financing constraints and corporate investment*, Brookings Papers on Economic Activity, Vol. 1988 (1), pp. 141–195.

Feiwel, G.R. (1975): The Intellectual Legacy of Michal Kalecki, University of Tennessee Press, Knoxville.

Feldman, E. and Sommer, J. (1986): Crisis Financiera y Endeudamiento Externo en la Argentina, Centro Editor de América Latina, Buenos Aires.

Felipe, J. and Kumar, U. (2011): *Unit labour costs in the Eurozone*, Working Paper No. 651, Levy Economics Institute of Bard College, Annandale-on-Hudson.

Ferreres, O. (2005): Dos Siglos de Economía Argentina (1810–2004): Historia Argentina en Cifras, El Ateneo, Buenos Aires.

Foley, D. (2008): Adam's Fallacy: A Guide to Economic Theology, Harvard University Press, Cambridge, MA.

Fontana, O. and Godin, A. (2013): *Securitization, housing market and banking sector behaviour in a stock-flow consistent model*, Economics Discussion Paper No. 2013-13, Kiel Institute for the World Economy.

Forbes, K.J. and Warnock, F.E. (2012): *Capital flow waves: surges, stops, flight and retrenchment*, Journal of International Economics, Vol. 88 (2), pp. 235–251.

Frankel, J. and Froot, K. (1990): *Chartists, fundamentalists and trading in the foreign exchange market*, American Economic Review, Vol. 80 (2), pp. 181–185.

Fry, M. (1980): *Saving, investment, growth and the cost of financial repression*, World Development, Vol. 8 (4), pp. 317–327.

Furceri, D., Jaumotte, F. and Loungani, P. (2015): *The distributional effects of capital account liberalization*, IMF Working Paper, forthcoming, International Monetary Fund, Washington, DC.

Galbraith, J.K. (2012): Inequality and Instability, Oxford University Press, Oxford.

Gallagher, K. (2014): Ruling Capital: Emerging Markets and the Re-regulation of Cross-Border Finance, Cornell University Press, Ithaca, NY.

Gallagher, K. (2015): *Contesting the governance of capital flows at the IMF*, Governance, Vol. 28 (2), pp. 185–198.

Gallagher, K., Ocampo, J.A. and Griffith-Jones, S. (2012): Regulating Capital Flows for Long-Run Development, Frederick S. Pardee Center for the Study of Longer Range Development, Boston University, Boston.

Galor, O. and Zeira, J. (1993): *Income distribution and macroeconomics*, Review of Economic Studies, Vol. 60 (1), pp. 35–52.

Gasparini, L. (2005): *El fracaso distributivo de Argentina: el papel de la integración y las políticas públicas*, in G. Marquez (ed.): ¿Para Bien o Para Mal?: Debate sobre el Impacto de la Globalización en los Mercados de Trabajo de América Latina, Interamerican Development Bank, Washington, DC.

Gaulier, G. and Vicard, V. (2013): *The signatures of Euro area imbalances*, COMPNet Policy Brief No. 02/2013, European Central Bank, Frankfurt am Main.

Gerchunoff, P. and Llach, L. (2000): El Ciclo de la Ilusión y el Desencanto, Ariel, Buenos Aires.

Giroud, X. and Mueller, H. (2015): *Firm leverage and unemployment during the Great Recession*, Working Paper No. 21076, National Bureau of Economic Research, Cambridge, MA.

Godin, A. (2012): *Guaranteed green jobs: sustainable full employment*, Working Paper No. 722, Levy Economics Institute of Bard College, Annandale-on-Hudson.

Godley, W. (1996): *Money, finance and national income determination: an integrated approach*, Working Paper No. 167, Levy Economics Institute of Bard College, Annandale-on-Hudson.

Godley, W. (1999a): *Money and credit in a Keynesian model of income determination*, Cambridge Journal of Economics, 23 (4), pp. 393–411.

Godley, W. (1999b): *Seven unsustainable processes: medium-term prospects and policies for the United States and the world*, Strategic Analysis, Levy Economics Institute of Bard College, Annandale-on-Hudson.

Godley, W. (1999c): *Open economy macroeconomics using models of closed systems*, Working Paper No. 285, Levy Economics Institute of Bard College, Annandale-on-Hudson.

Godley, W. and Cripps, F. (1978): *Control of imports as a means to full employment and the expansion of world trade*, Cambridge Journal of Economics, Vol. 2 (2), pp. 327–334.

Godley, W. and Cripps, F. (1983): Macroeconomics, Fontana, London.

Godley, W. and Izurieta, A. (2004): *The US economy: weaknesses of the 'strong' recovery*, Banca Nazionale del Lavoro Quarterly Review, Vol. 57 (2), pp. 131–139.

Godley, W. and Lavoie, M. (2005): *Comprehensive accounting in simple open economy macroeconomics with endogenous sterilization or flexible exchange rates*, Journal of Post Keynesian Economics, Vol. 28 (2), pp. 241–276.

Godley, W. and Lavoie, M. (2007a): Monetary Economics: An Integrated Approach to Credit, Money, Income, Production and Wealth, Palgrave Macmillan, New York.

Godley, W. and Lavoie, M. (2007b): *Fiscal policy in a stock-flow consistent (SFC) model*, Journal of Post Keynesian Economics, Vol. 30 (1), pp. 79–100.

Godley, W. and Lavoie, M. (2007c): *A simple model of three economies with two currencies: the Eurozone and the USA*, Cambridge Journal of Economics, Vol. 31 (1), pp. 1–23.

Godley, W. and Zezza, G. (2006): *Debt and lending: a cri de coeur*, Policy Note 2006/04, Levy Economics Institute of Bard College, Annandale-on-Hudson.

Goldberg, P.K. and Pavcnik, N. (2007): *Distributional effects of globalization in developing countries*, Journal of Economic Literature, Vol. 45 (1), pp. 39–82.

Gordon, D. (1995): *Growth, distribution, and the rules of the game: social structuralist macrofoundations for a democratic economic policy*, in G. Epstein and H. Gintis (eds): Macroeconomic Policy After the Conservative Era. Studies in Investment, Saving and Finance, Cambridge University Press, Cambridge.

Grabel, I. (2012): *Dynamic capital regulations, IMF irrelevance and the crisis*, in K.P. Gallagher, S. Griffith-Jones and J.A. Ocampo (eds): Regulating Capital Flows for Long-Run Development, Frederick S. Pardee Center for the Study of Longer Range Development, Boston University, Boston.

Graña, J.M. (2007): *Distribución funcional del ingreso en la Argentina 1935–2005*, Documento de Trabajo No. 8, CEPED, University of Buenos Aires.

Graña, J. and Kennedy, D. (2008): *Salario real, costo laboral y productividad. Argentina 1947–2006*, Documento de Trabajo No. 12, CEPED, University of Buenos Aires.

Greene, W.H. (2011): Econometric Analysis, 7th edition, Prentice Hall, New York.

Greenspan, A. (1997): Hearing before the Subcommittee on Domestic and International Monetary Policy, House of Representatives, available at http://commdocs.house.gov/committees/bank/hba38677. 000/hba38677_0f.htm (accessed 15 August 2015).

Griffith-Jones, S., Gottschalk, R. and Cirera, X. (2003): *The OECD experience with capital account liberalization*, in UNCTAD (ed.): Management of Capital Flows: Comparative Experiences and Implications for Africa, UNCTAD, Geneva.

Hagemann, H. (1999): *The development of business-cycle theory in the German language area 1900–1930*, Storia del Pensiero Economico, Vol. 37 (1), pp. 87–122.

Hagemann, H. (2001): *Wicksell's 'new theory of crises': an introduction*, Structural Change and Economic Dynamics, Vol. 12 (3), pp. 331–334.

Haldane, A. (2011): *The big fish small pond problem*, speech at the Institute for New Economic Thinking Annual Conference, Bretton Woods, NH.

Harcourt, G.C. (2006): The Structure of Post-Keynesian Economics. The Core Contributions of the Pioneers, Cambridge University Press, Cambridge.

Harrod, R.F. (1939): *An essay in dynamic theory*, Economic Journal, Vol. 49 (2), pp. 14–33.

Harvey, J. (1993): *The institution of foreign exchange trading*, Journal of Economic Issues, Vol. 27 (3), pp. 679–698.

Harvey, J. (2004): *Deviations from uncovered interest rate parity: a Post Keynesian explanation*, Journal of Post Keynesian Economics, Vol. 29 (1), pp. 19–35.

Harvey, J. (2009): Currencies, Capital Flows and Crises. A Post Keynesian Analysis of Exchange Rate Determination, Routledge, London.

Hein, E. (2006): *Interest, debt and capital accumulation – a Kaleckian approach*, International Review of Applied Economics - Vol. 20 (3), pp. 337–352.

Hein, E. (2009): *'Financialisation' in a comparative static, stock-flow consistent post-Kaleckian distribution and growth model*, Ekonomiaz, Vol. 72 (3), pp. 120–139.

Hein, E. (2011): *Distribution, 'financialisation' and the financial and economic crisis – implications for post-crisis economic policies*, MPRA Paper No. 31.180.

Hein, E. (2012): The Macroeconomics of Finance-Dominated Capitalism – and Its Crisis, Edward Elgar Publishing, Cheltenham and Northampton, MA.

Hein, E. (2015): *Finance-dominated capitalism and redistribution of income: a Kaleckian perspective*, Cambridge Journal of Economics, Vol. 39 (3), pp. 907–934.

Hein, E. and Ochsen, C. (2003): *Regimes of interest rates, income shares, savings and investment: a Kaleckian model and empirical estimations for some advanced OECD economies*, Metroeconomica, Vol. 54 (4), pp. 404–433.

Hein, E. and Schoder, C. (2011): *Interest rates, distribution and capital accumulation – a post-Kaleckian perspective on the U.S. and Germany*, International Review of Applied Economics, Vol. 25 (6), pp. 693–723.

Hein, E. and Stockhammer, E. (2011): *A post-Keynesian macroeconomic model of inflation, distribution and employment*, in E. Hein and E. Stockhammer (eds): A Modern Guide to Keynesian Macroeconomics and Economics Policies, Edward Elgar Publishing, Cheltenham and Northampton, MA.

Hein, E. and Tarassow, A. (2010): *Distribution, aggregate demand and productivity growth – theory and empirical results for six OECD countries based on a post-Kaleckian model*, Cambridge Journal of Economics, Vol. 34 (4), pp. 727–754.

Hein, E. and Van Treeck, T. (2010): *'Financialisation' in post-Keynesian models of distribution and growth: a systematic review*, in M. Setterfield (ed.): Handbook of Alternative Theories of Economic Growth, Edward Elgar Publishing, Cheltenham and Northampton, MA.

Hein, E. and Vogel, L. (2008): *Distribution and growth reconsidered – empirical results for six OECD countries*, Cambridge Journal of Economics, Vol. 32 (3), pp. 479–511.

Hein, E., Lavoie, M. and Van Treeck, T. (2011): *Some instability puzzles in Kaleckian models of growth and distribution*, Cambridge Journal of Economics, Vol. 35 (3), pp. 587–612.

Hein, E., Lavoie, M. and Van Treeck, T. (2012): *Harrodian instability and the 'normal rate' of capacity utilization in Kaleckian models of distribution and growth – a survey*, Metroeconomica, Vol. 63 (1), pp. 39–69.

Helleiner, E. (1994): States and the Reemergence of Global Finance: From Bretton Woods to the 1990s, Cornell University Press, Ithaca, NY.

Hicks, J. (1966): The Theory of Wages, 2nd edition, Macmillan, London.

Hicks, J. (1974): The Crisis in Keynesian Economics, Basil Blackwell, Oxford.

Hodgson, G. (2007): *Meanings of methodological individualism*, Journal of Economic Methodology, Vol. 14 (2), pp. 211–226.

Humphrey, T. (1985): *The early history of the Phillips curve*, Economic Review, Vol. 71 (5), pp. 17–24.

International Labour Office (2011): World of Work Report: Making Markets Work for Jobs, ILO, Geneva.

International Monetary Fund (2007): World Economic Outlook, IMF, Washington, DC.

International Monetary Fund (2012): The liberalization and management of capital flows: an institutional view, IMF, Washington, DC.

International Monetary Fund (2013): World Economic Outlook, IMF, Washington, DC.

International Monetary Fund (2014): Global Financial Stability Report, IMF, Washington, DC.

International Monetary Fund (2015): The IMF Approach to Capital Account Liberalization. Revisiting the 2005 IEO Evaluation, Independent Evaluation Office of the International Monetary Fund, Washington, DC.

Jara, A. and Olaberría, E. (2013): *Are all capital inflows associated with booms in house prices? An empirical evaluation*, Documentos de Trabajo No. 696, Banco Central de Chile, Santiago.

Jaumotte, F. and Tytell, I. (2007): *How has the globalization of labor affected the labor income share in advanced countries?*, IMF Working Papers 07/298, IMF, Washington, DC.

Jayadev, A. (2005): *Financial liberalization and its distributional consequences: an empirical exploration*, Ph.D. dissertation, University of Massachusetts Amherst.

Juselius, K. (2006): The Cointegrated VAR Model: Methodology and Applications, Oxford University Press, Oxford.

Juselius, M. and Drehmann, M. (2015): *Leverage dynamics and the real burden of debt*, BIS Working Papers No. 501, Bank for International Settlements, Basel.

Kaldor, N. (1955): *Alternative theories of distribution*, Review of Economic Studies, Vol. 23 (2), pp. 83–100.

Kaldor, N. (1957): *A model of economic growth*, Economic Journal, Vol. 67 (4), pp. 591–624.

Kaldor, N. (1961): *Capital accumulation and economic growth*, in F.A. Lutz and D.C. Hague (eds): The Theory of Capital, St. Martin's Press, London.

Kaldor, N. (1966): *Marginal productivity and the macro-economic theories of distribution: comment on Samuelson and Modigliani*, Review of Economic Studies, Vol. 33 (4), pp. 309–319.

Kaldor, N. (1967): Strategic Factors in Economic Development, Cornell University Press, Ithaca, NY.

Kaldor, N. (1982): The Scourge of Monetarism, Oxford University Press, Oxford.

Kaldor, N. and Mirrlees, J. (1962): *A new model of economic growth*, Review of Economic Studies, Vol. 29 (3), pp. 174–192.

Kalecki, M. (1943): *Political aspects of full employment*, Political Quarterly, Vol. 14 (4), pp. 322–330.

Kalecki, M. (1971): Selected Essays in the Dynamics of the Capitalist Economy, Cambridge University Press, Cambridge.

Kaltenbrunner, A. and Painceira, J.P. (2015): *Developing countries' changing nature of financial integration and new forms of external vulnerability: the Brazilian experience*, Cambridge Journal of Economics, Vol. 39 (5), pp. 1281–1306.

Keynes, J.M. (1971–1989): The Collected Writings of John Maynard Keynes, Macmillan/Cambridge University Press for Royal Economic Society, London:

   Vol. V: Treatise on Money (Volume I) [1930];
   Vol. VI: Treatise on Money (Volume II) [1930];
   Vol. VII: The General Theory of Employment, Interest and Money [1936];
   Vol. XIII: The General Theory and After: Preparation;
   Vol. XIV: The General Theory and After: Defence and Development.
   Vol. XXV: Activities 1940–44: Shaping the Post-War World: The Clearing Union.

Kim, J.H. (2006): *A two-sector model with target-return pricing in a stock-flow consistent framework*, ROBINSON Working Paper No. 06-01, University of Ottawa.

King, J.E. (2012): The Microfoundations Delusion: Metaphor and Dogma in the History of Macroeconomics, Edward Elgar Publishing, Cheltenham and Northampton, MA.

Kinsella, S. (2011): *Words to the wise: stock flow consistent modelling of financial instability*, Geary Working Paper 2011/30, UCD Geary Institute.

Kinsella, S. and O'Shea, T. (2010): *Solution and simulation of large stock flow consistent monetary production models via the Gauss Seidel Algorithm*, available at http://papers.ssrn.com/sol3/papers.cfm?abstract_id=1729205 (accessed 25 May 2015).

Kinsella, S. and Tiou Tagba-Aliti, G. (2012): *Simulating the impact of austerity on the Irish economy using a stock-flow consistent model*, presented at the 16th conference of the Research Network Macroeconomics and Macroeconomic Policies (FMM), Berlin, 25–27 October.

Kinsella, S., Godin, A. and Tiou Tagba-Aliti, G. (2012): *Method to simultaneously determine stock, flow and parameter values in large stock flow consistent models*, Research Note No. 20, Institute for New Economic Thinking, New York.

Kinsella, S., Greiff, M. and Nell, E.J. (2011): *Income distribution in a stock-flow consistent model with education and technological change*, Eastern Economic Journal, Vol. 37 (1), pp. 134–149.

Kregel, J.A. (1989): *Savings, investment and finance in Kalecki's theory*, in M. Sebastiani (ed.): Kalecki's Relevance Today, Macmillan, London.

Kregel, J.A. (1998): *East Asia is not Mexico: the difference between balance of payments crises and debt deflation*, in K.S. Jomo (ed.): Tigers in Trouble: Financial Governance, Liberalisation and Crises in East Asia, Zed Press, London.

Kregel, J.A. (2004): *Can we create a stable international financial environment that ensures net resource transfers to developing countries?*, Journal of Post Keynesian Economics, Vol. 26 (4), pp. 573–590.

Kurz, H. (1990): *Technical change, growth and distribution: a steady-state approach to 'unsteady' growth*, in H. Kurz: Capital, Distribution and Effective Demand, Polity Press, Cambridge.

Kurz, H. (1990 [1986]): *Normal positions and capital utilization*, Political Economy, Vol. 2 (1), pp. 37–54. Reprinted in H. Kurz: Capital, Distribution and Effective Demand, Polity Press, Cambridge.

Kurz, H. and Salvadori, N. (2003): *Theories of economic growth – old and new*, in N. Salvadori (ed.): Old and New Growth Theories – An Assessment, Edward Elgar Publishing, Cheltenham and Northampton, MA.

La Marca, M. (2005): *Foreign debt, growth and distribution in an investment-constrained system*, in N. Salvadori and R. Balducci (eds): Innovation, Unemployment and Policy in the Theories of Growth and Distribution, Edward Elgar Publishing, Cheltenham and Northampton, MA.

La Marca, M. (2010): *Real exchange rate, distribution and macro fluctuations in export-oriented economies*, Metroeconomica, Vol. 61 (1), pp. 124–151.

Lanata Briones, C. and Lo Vuolo, R. (2008): *El proceso de ahorro-inversión en la Argentina. Una aproximación a las relaciones causales de los procesos de crecimiento y distribución*, Working Paper No. 63, Centro Interdisciplinario para el Estudio de Políticas Públicas, Buenos Aires.

Lanata Briones, C. and Lo Vuolo, R. (2011): *Regímenes de acumulación, cambios estructurales y límites al crecimiento económico en la Argentina de la post-Convertibilidad*, Working Paper No. 81, Centro Interdisciplinario para el Estudio de Políticas Públicas, Buenos Aires.

Lavagna, R. (1978a): *Aldo Ferrer y la política económica en la Argentina de posguerra*, Desarrollo Económico, Vol. 17 (4), pp. 654–664.

Lavagna, R. (1978b): *Distribución del ingreso e inversión*, Desarrollo Económico, Vol. 18 (1), pp. 138–144.

Lavoie, M. (1992): Foundations of Post-Keynesian Economic Analysis, Edward Elgar Publishing, Aldershot.

Lavoie, M. (1993): *A post-classical view of money, interest, growth and distribution*, in G. Mongiovi and C. Rühl (eds): Macroeconomic Theory: Diversity and Convergence, Cambridge University Press, Cambridge.

Lavoie, M. (1995a): *Interest rates in post-Keynesian models of growth and distribution*, Metroeconomica, Vol. 46 (2), pp. 146–177.

Lavoie, M. (1995b): *The Kaleckian model of growth and distribution and its neo-Ricardian and neo-Marxian critiques*, Cambridge Journal of Economics, Vol. 19 (6), pp. 789–818.

Lavoie, M. (1996): *Traverse, hysteresis, and normal rates of capacity utilization in Kaleckian models of growth and distribution*, Review of Radical Political Economics, Vol. 28 (4), pp. 113–147.

Lavoie, M. (2000): *A post Keynesian view of interest parity theorems*, Journal of Post Keynesian Economics, Vol. 23 (1), pp. 163–179.

Lavoie, M. (2001): *The reflux mechanism in the open economy*, in L.P. Rochon and M. Vernengo (eds): Credit, Interest Rates and the Open Economy, Edward Elgar Publishing, Cheltenham and Northampton, MA.

Lavoie, M. (2002): *The Kaleckian growth model with target return pricing and conflict inflation*, in M. Setterfield (ed.): The Economics of Demand-Led Growth: Challenging the Supply-Side Vision of the Long Run, Edward Elgar Publishing, Cheltenham and Northampton, MA.

Lavoie, M. (2006a): *A fully coherent post-Keynesian model of currency boards*, in C. Gnos and L.P. Rochon (eds): Post Keynesian Principles of Economic Policy, Edward Elgar Publishing, Cheltenham and Northampton, MA.

Lavoie, M. (2006b): *Endogenous money: accommodationist*, in P. Arestis and M. Sawyer (eds): Handbook of Alternative Monetary Economics, Edward Elgar Publishing, Cheltenham and Northampton, MA.

Lavoie, M. (2008): *Financialisation issues in a post-Keynesian stock-flow consistent model*, Intervention: European Journal of Economics and Economic Policies, Vol. 5 (2), pp. 331–356.

Lavoie, M. (2009): *Cadrisme within a post-Keynesian model of growth and distribution*, Review of Political Economy, Vol. 21 (3), pp. 369–391.

Lavoie, M. (2010a): *Surveying short run and long run stability issues with the Kaleckian model of growth*, in M. Setterfield (ed.): Handbook of Alternative Theories of Economic Growth, Edward Elgar Publishing, Cheltenham and Northampton, MA.

Lavoie, M. (2010b): *Changes in central bank procedures during the subprime crisis and their repercussions on monetary theory*, International Journal of Political Economy, Vol. 39 (3), pp. 3–23.

Lavoie, M. (2014): Post Keynesian Economics, Edward Elgar Publishing, Cheltenham and Northampton, MA.

Lavoie, M. and Daigle, G. (2011): *A behavioural finance model of exchange rate expectations within a stock-flow consistent framework*, Metroeconomica, Vol. 62 (3), pp. 434–458.

Lavoie, M. and Ramírez-Gastón, P. (1997): *Traverse in a two-sector Kaleckian model of growth with target-return pricing*, Manchester School of Economic and Social Studies, Vol. 65 (2), pp. 145–169.

Lavoie, M. and Zhao, J. (2010): *A study of the diversification of China's foreign reserves within a three-country stock-flow consistent model*, Metroeconomica, Vol. 61 (3), pp. 558–592.

Lawson, T. (2007): *An orientation for a green economics?*, International Journal of Green Economics, Vol. 1 (3), pp. 250–267.

Lazonick, W. (2011): *Reforming the financialized business corporation*, Employment Policy and Research Network, available at http://www.employmentpolicy.org/topic/21/research/reformingfinancialized-corporation (accessed 15 August 2015).

Lazonick, W. (2012): *Financialization of the U.S. corporation: what has been lost, and how it can be regained*, MPRA Paper No. 42307.

Lazonick, W. and O'Sullivan, M. (2000): *Maximizing shareholder value: a new ideology for corporate governance*, Economy and Society, Vol. 29 (1), pp. 13–35.

Le Heron, E. (2009): *Fiscal and monetary policies in a Keynesian stock-flow consistent model*, Estudos do GEMF 2009-01, Faculdade de Economia, University of Coimbra.

Le Heron, E. (2012): *Confidence, increasing risks, income distribution and crisis in a post Kaleckian stock flow consistent model*, presented at the conference Political Economy and the Outlook for Capitalism, Paris, 5–7 July.

Lee, F. (1998): Post Keynesian Price Theory, Cambridge University Press, Cambridge.

Lindenboim, J., Kennedy, D. and Graña, J.M. (2005): *Distribución funcional del ingreso en Argentina. Ayer y hoy*, Documentos de Trabajo No. 4, CEPED, UBA.

Lindenboim, J., Kennedy, D. and Graña, J.M. (2006): *Distribución, consumo e inversión en la Argentina a comienzos del siglo XXI*, Realidad Económica, No. 218, pp. 65–92.

Lindenboim, J., Kennedy, D. and Graña, J.M. (2011): *Wage share and aggregate demand: contributions for labour and macroeconomic policy*, presented at the 2nd conference on Regulating for Decent Work: Regulating for a Fair Recovery, International Labour Organization, Geneva.

López G., J. (2004): *Economic crises in Latin America: some considerations in the light of Kalecki's theory*, in Z. Sadowski and A. Szeworski (eds): Kalecki's Economics Today, Routledge, London.

López G., J. (2012a): *Keynes, Kalecki and the real world*, presented at the workshop Cambridge Approach to Economics – History and Legacy, Florence, 20–22 March.

López G., J. (2012b): *Effective demand and income distribution in the recent evolution of the Mexican Economy*, presented at the 4th GREThA/

GRES International Conference on Economic Development, Bordeaux, 13–15 June.

López G., J. and Assous, M. (2012): Michal Kalecki, Palgrave Macmillan, Basingstoke.

López G., J., Sánchez, A. and Spanos, A. (2011): *Macroeconomic linkages in Mexico*, Metroeconomica, Vol. 62 (2), pp. 356–385.

López-Pérez, V. (2015): *Do professional forecasters behave as if they believe in the new Keynesian Phillips Curve for the euro area?*, Working Paper No. 1763, European Central Bank, Frankfurt am Main.

Lucas Jr., R. (2003): *Macroeconomic priorities*, American Economic Review, Vol. 93 (1), pp. 1–14.

Luxemburg, R. (1951 [1913]): The Accumulation of Capital, Routledge, London.

Lye, J. and McDonald, I. (2008): *The Eisner puzzle, the unemployment threshold and the range of equilibria*, International Advances in Economic Research, Vol. 14 (2), pp. 125–141.

Maes, I. and Clement, P. (2013): *The Latin American debt crisis: at the origins of the BIS macro-prudential approach to financial stability*, Working Paper No. 247, National Bank of Belgium, Brussels.

Mantey, C. (2013): *¿Conviene flexibilizar el tipo de cambio para mejorar la competitividad?*, Problemas del Desarrollo, Vol. 44 (3), pp. 9–32.

Marcuzzo, M.C. (2010): *Whose welfare state: Beveridge versus Keynes*, in R. Backhouse and T. Nishizawa (eds): No Wealth but Life: Welfare Economics and the Welfare State in Britain, 1880–1945, Cambridge University Press, Cambridge.

Martin, B. (2008): *Fiscal policy in a stock-flow consistent model: a comment*, Journal of Post Keynesian Economics, Vol. 30 (4), pp. 649–667.

Marx, K. (1865): *Value, price and profit*, available at https://www.marxists.org/archive/marx/works/1865/value-price-profit/ (accessed 15 January 2015).

Marx, K. (1867, 1885, 1894): *Das Kapital*, Vol. I, II and III, available at http://www.marxists.org/archive/marx/works/ (accessed 15 January 2015).

Mazier, J. and Tiou Tagba-Aliti, G. (2012): *World imbalances and macroeconomic adjustments: a three-country stock-flow consistent model with fixed or flexible prices*, Metroeconomica, Vol. 63 (2), pp. 358–388.

Mazzucato, M. (2013): The Entrepreneurial State: Debunking Public versus Private Sector Myths, Anthem Press, London.

McCarthy, J. (2007): *Pass-through of exchange rates and import prices to domestic inflation in some industrialized economies*, Eastern Economic Journal, Vol. 33 (4), pp. 511–537.

McCauley, R., McGuire, P. and Sushko, V. (2015): *Global dollar credit:*

links to US monetary policy and leverage, BIS Working Papers No. 483, Bank for International Settlements, Basel.

McCombie, J. and Thirlwall, A. (eds) (2004): Economic Growth and the Balance of Payments Constraint, Palgrave Macmillan, Basingstoke.

McCombie, J., Pugno, M. and Soro, B. (eds) (2002): Productivity Growth and Economic Performance, Palgrave Macmillan, Basingstoke.

McKinnon, R. (1973): Money and Capital in Economic Development, Brookings Institution, Washington, DC.

McLeay, M., Radia, A. and Thomas, R. (2014): *Money creation in the modern economy*, Bank of England Quarterly Bulletin, First Quarter, pp. 14–27.

Mendieta-Muñoz, I. (2013): *El modelo de objetivos de inflación y el efecto pass-through en America Latina*, Revista de Economía Crítica, Vol. 15 (1), pp. 5–30.

Michelena, G. (2014): *La liberalización comercial en el marco de las Cadenas Globales de Valor*, Revista Argentina de Economía Internacional, No. 3, pp. 47–59.

Mirowski, P. (1984): *Physics and the 'marginalist revolution'*, Cambridge Journal of Economics, Vol. 8 (4), pp. 361–379.

Missaglia, M. (2007): *Demand policies for long run growth: being Keynesian both in the short and in the long run?*, Metroeconomica, Vol. 58 (1), pp. 54–74.

Moosa, I. (2003): International Financial Operations, Palgrave Macmillan, Basingstoke.

Mott, T. and Slattery, E. (1994): *The influence of changes in income distribution on aggregate demand in a Kaleckian model: stagnation vs. exhilaration reconsidered*, in P. Davidson and J. Kregel (eds): Employment, Growth and Finance, Edward Elgar Publishing, Aldershot.

Naastepad, C.W.M. (2006): *Technology, demand and distribution: a cumulative growth model with an application to the Dutch productivity growth slowdown*, Cambridge Journal of Economics, Vol. 30 (3), pp. 403–434.

Naastepad, C.W.M. and Storm, S. (2006): *OECD demand regimes (1960–2000)*, Journal of Post Keynesian Economics, Vol. 29 (2), pp. 211–246.

Ndikumana, L. (1999): *Debt service, financing constraints, and fixed investment: evidence from panel data*, Journal of Post Keynesian Economics, Vol. 21 (3), pp. 455–478.

Neftci, S.N. (1998): *FX short positions, balance sheets and financial turbulence: an interpretation of the Asian financial crisis*, Working Paper No. 11, Center for Economic Policy Analysis, New School for Social Research, New York.

Nersisyan, Y. and Wray, L.R. (2010): *Does excessive sovereign debt really hurt growth?*, Working Paper No. 603, Levy Economics Institute of Bard College, Annandale-on-Hudson.

Nier, E., Sedik, T.S. and Mondino, T. (2014): *Gross private capital flows to emerging markets: can the global financial cycle be tamed?*, IMF Working Paper No. 14/29, International Monetary Fund, Washington, DC.

Nikiforos, M. (2012): *On the 'utilization controversy': a theoretical and empirical discussion of the Kaleckian model of growth and distribution*, Working Paper No. 739, Levy Economics Institute of Bard College, Annandale-on-Hudson.

Nogueira Junior, R. and León-Ledesma, M.A. (2010): *Is low inflation really causing the decline in exchange rate pass-through?*, Studies in Economics No. 1002, School of Economics, University of Kent.

Noland, M. (2007): *South Korea's experience with international capital flows*, in S. Edwards (ed.): Capital Controls and Capital Flows in Emerging Economies, University of Chicago Press, Chicago.

OECD (2007): OECD Employment Outlook, OECD, Paris.

OECD (2008): Growing Unequal? Income Distribution and Poverty in OECD Countries, OECD, Paris.

OECD (2013): *OECD.StatExtracts*, OECD, Paris.

Onaran, Ö. and Galanis, G. (2012): *Is aggregate demand wage-led or profit-led?*, Conditions of Work and Employment Series No. 40, International Labour Office, Geneva.

Onaran, Ö. and Stockhammer, E. (2004): *Accumulation, distribution and employment: a structural VAR approach to a post-Keynesian macro model*, Structural Change and Economic Dynamics, Vol. 15 (3), pp. 421–447.

Onaran, Ö. and Stockhammer, E. (2006): *Do profits affect investment and employment? An empirical test based on the Bhaduri–Marglin model*, in E. Hein, A. Heise and A. Truger (eds): Wages, Employment, Distribution and Growth. International Perspectives, Macmillan, Basingstoke.

Ono, F.H. and Oreiro, J.L. (2006): *Technological progress, income distribution and capacity utilization*, in N. Salvadori (ed.): Economic Growth and Distribution: On the Nature and Causes of the Wealth of Nations, Edward Elgar Publishing, Cheltenham and Northampton, MA.

Orhangazi, Ö. (2008): Financialization and the US Economy, Edward Elgar Publishing, Cheltenham and Northampton, MA.

Ostry, J., Berg, A. and Tsangarides, C. (2014): *Redistribution, inequality and growth*, Staff Discussion Note No. 14/02, International Monetary Fund, Washington, DC.

Ostry, J.D., Ghosh, A.R., Habermeier, K., Chamon, M., Qureshi, M.S. and Reinhardt, D.B.S. (2010): *Capital inflows: the role of controls*, Staff Position Note 10/04, International Monetary Fund, Washington, DC.

Ostry, J.D., Ghosh, A.R., Habermeier, K., Laeven, L., Chamon, M.,

Qureshi, M.S. and Kokenine, A. (2011): *Managing capital flows: what tools to use?*, Staff Discussion Note No. 11/06, International Monetary Fund, Washington, DC.

Ostry, J.D., Ghosh, A.R. and Korinek, A. (2012): *Multilateral aspects of managing the capital account*, Staff Discussion Note No. 12/10, International Monetary Fund, Washington, DC.

Palley, T. (1996): *Inside debt, aggregate demand and the Cambridge theory of distribution*, Cambridge Journal of Economics, Vol. 20 (4), pp. 465–474.

Palley, T. (2003): *The economics of exchange rates and the dollarization debate: the case against extremes*, International Journal of Political Economy, Vol. 33 (1), pp. 61–82.

Palley, T. (2008): *Financialisation: what it is and why it matters*, in E. Hein, T. Niechoj, P. Spahn and A. Truger (eds): Finance-Led Capitalism? Macroeconomic Effects of Changes in the Financial Sector, Metropolis-Verlag, Magburg.

Palley, T. (2010): *Inside debt and economic growth: a neo-Kaleckian analysis*, in M. Setterfield (ed.): Handbook of Alternative Theories of Economic Growth, Edward Elgar Publishing, Cheltenham and Northampton, MA.

Palley, T. (2012): *From Financial Crisis to Stagnation*, Cambridge University Press, Cambridge.

Palley, T. (2013): Financialization, Palgrave Macmillan, Basingstoke.

Palma, J.G. (2001): *Three-and-a-half cycles of 'mania, panic, and (asymmetric) crash': East Asia and Latin America compared*, in H.J. Chang, J.G. Palma and D.G. Whittaker (eds): Financial Liberalization and the Asian Crisis, Palgrave, Basingstoke.

Palumbo, A. and Trezzini, A. (2003): *Growth without normal capacity utilization*, European Journal of the History of Economic Thought, Vol. 10 (1), pp. 109–135.

Panigo, D., Depetris-Chauvín, E., Pasquini, R. and Pussetto, L. (2007): *Evolución y determinantes de la inversión privada en Argentina*, Documento de Trabajo, Centro para la Estabilidad Financiera.

Panigo, D., Herrero, D., López, E., Montagu, H. and Toledo, F. (2009): *Modelo macroeconométrico estructural para Argentina*, Documento de Trabajo, Dirección Nacional de Programación Macroeconómica, Ministerio de Economía y Producción.

Panigo, D., Toledo, F. and Agis, E. (2008): *Poder de mercado, crecimiento y distribución funcional del ingreso en Argentina*, Working Paper, Dirección Nacional de Programación Macroeconómica, Ministerio de Economía y Finanzas Públicas.

Papadimitriou, D. (2008): *Promoting equality through an employment of last resort policy*, Working Paper No. 545, Levy Economics Institute of Bard College, Annandale-on-Hudson.

Papadimitriou, D., Zezza, G. and Nikiforos, M. (2013): *A Levy Institute model for Greece*, Research Project Reports, Levy Economics Institute of Bard College, Annandale-on-Hudson.

Papadimitriou, D., Zezza, G. and Nikiforos, M. (2014): *Prospects and policies for the Greek economy*, Economics Strategic Analysis, Levy Economics Institute of Bard College, Annandale-on-Hudson.

Pasinetti, L.L. (1962): *Rate of profit and income distribution in relation to the rate of economic growth*, Review of Economic Studies, Vol. 29 (4), pp. 267–279.

Passarella, M. (2012): *A simplified stock-flow consistent dynamic model of the systemic financial fragility in the 'New Capitalism'*, Journal of Economic Behavior and Organization, Vol. 83 (3), pp. 570–582.

Patnaik, P. (2007): *Financial crisis, reserve accumulation and capital flows*, Economic and Political Weekly, Vol. 42 (50), pp. 45–51.

Peach, R., Rich, R. and Cororaton, A. (2011): *How does slack influence inflation?*, Current Issues in Economics and Finance, Vol. 18 (3), pp. 1–7.

Pérez Caldentey, E. (2007): *Balance of payments constrained growth within a consistent stock-flow framework: an application to the economies of CARICOM*, in Economic Commission for Latin America and the Caribbean (ed.): Caribbean Development Report, Vol. 1, Economic Commission for Latin America and the Caribbean, Santiago.

Perotti, R. (1992): *Income distribution, politics, and growth*, American Economic Review, Vol. 82 (2), pp. 311–316.

Philippon, T. (2012): *Has the US finance industry become less efficient? On the theory and measurement of financial intermediation*, Working Paper No. 18077, National Bureau of Economic Research, Cambridge, MA.

Phillips, A.W. (1958): *The relationship between unemployment and the rate of change of money wages in the United Kingdom 1861–1957*, Economica, Vol. 25 (100), pp. 283–299.

Piketty, T. (2014): Capital in the 21st Century, Harvard University Press, Cambridge, MA.

Pilkington, M. (2008): *Conceptualizing the shadow financial system in a stock-flow consistent framework*, Global Business and Economic Anthology, Vol. 2, pp. 268–279.

Pivetti, M. (1991): An Essay on Money and Distribution, Palgrave Macmillan, London.

Pyatt, G. and Round, J.I. (1985): Social Accounting Matrix. A Basis for Planning, World Bank, Washington, DC.

Quantitative Micro Software (2004): *Eviews 5 User's Guide*.

Rajan, R. (2010): Fault Lines, Princeton University Press, Princeton, NJ.

Reinhart, C. and Rogoff, K. (2010): *Growth in a time of debt*, Working Paper No. 15639, National Bureau of Economic Research, Cambridge, MA.

Rey, H. (2013): *Dilemma not trilemma: the global financial cycle and monetary policy independence*, Proceedings of the Economic Symposium of the Federal Reserve Bank of Kansas City, Jackson Hole, WY.

Ricardo, D. (1951 [1821]): Principles of Political Economy and Taxation, 3rd edition, Vol. I of The Works and Correspondence of David Ricardo, ed.: Piero Sraffa, Cambridge University Press, Cambridge.

Robertson, D.H. (1963): Lectures on Economic Principles, Fontana Library, London.

Robinson, J. (1962): Essays on the Theory of Economic Growth, Macmillan, London.

Robinson, J. (1965 [1956]): The Accumulation of Capital, Macmillan, London.

Robinson, S. (1989): *Multisectoral models*, in H. Chenery and T.N. Srinivasan (eds): Handbook of Development Economics, Vol. 2, North Holland, Amsterdam.

Robinson, S. (2006): *Macro models and multipliers: Leontief, Stone, Keynes and CGE models*, in A. de Janvry and R. Kanbur (eds): Poverty, Inequality and Development: Essays in Honor of Erik Thorbecke, Springer, New York.

Rochon, L.P. (1999): Credit, Money and Production: An Alternative Post-Keynesian Analysis, Edward Elgar Publishing, Cheltenham and Northampton, MA.

Rochon, L.P. and Setterfield, M. (2012): *A Kaleckian model of growth and distribution with conflict inflation and Post Keynesian nominal interest rate rules*, Journal of Post Keynesian Economics, Vol. 34 (3), pp. 497–520.

Rodriguez, F. and Jayadev, A. (2010): *The declining labor share of income*, Human Development Research Paper 2010/36, United Nations Development Programme.

Romer, P. (1986): *Increasing returns and long-run growth*, Journal of Political Economy, Vol. 94 (5), pp. 1003–1037.

Rossi, P. (2010): *Currency speculation and exchange rates*, presented at the 14th conference of the Research Network Macroeconomics and Macroeconomic Policies, Berlin, 29–30 October.

Rowthorn, R. (1977): *Conflict, inflation and money*, Cambridge Journal of Economics, Vol. 1 (3), pp. 215–239.

Rowthorn, R. (1989 [1981]): *Demand, real wages and economic growth*, Thames Papers in Political Economy, Autumn, pp. 1–39. Reprinted in M. Sawyer (ed.): Post Keynesian Economics, Edward Elgar Publishing, Aldershot.

Ryoo, S. and Skott, P. (2013): *Public debt and full employment in a stock-flow consistent model of a corporate economy*, Journal of Post Keynesian Economics, Vol. 35 (4), pp. 511–528.

Sadowski, Z. and Szeworski, A. (eds) (2004): Kalecki's Economics Today, Routledge, London.

Sasaki, H. (2011): *Conflict, growth, distribution, and employment: a long-run Kaleckian model*, International Review of Applied Economics, Vol. 25 (5), pp. 539–557.

Sawyer, M. (1985): The Economics of Michal Kalecki, Macmillan, London.

Schoder, C. (2011): *Kaleckian vs Marxian specifications of the investment function: some empirical evidence for the US*, MPRA Paper No. 29584.

Schroeder, E. (2015): *Eurozone imbalances: measuring the contribution of expenditure switch and expenditure volume 1990–2013*, Working Paper No. 1508, Department of Economics, New School for Social Research, New York.

Schumpeter, J.A. (1934): The Theory of Economic Development, Harvard University Press, Cambridge, MA.

Schumpeter, J.A. (1954): History of Economic Analysis, Oxford University Press, New York.

Seguino, S. (1999): *The investment function revisited: disciplining capital in South Korea*, Journal of Post Keynesian Economics, Vol. 22 (2), pp. 313–338.

Seppecher, P. (2012a): *Monnaie endogene et agents heterogenes dans un model stock-flux coherent*, presented at the conference Political Economy and the Outlook for Capitalism, Paris, 5–7 July.

Seppecher, P. (2012b): *Flexibility of wages and macroeconomic instability in an agent-based computational model with endogenous money*, Macroeconomic Dynamics, Vol. 16 (2), pp. 284–297.

Serrano, F. (1995): *The Sraffian supermultiplier*, Ph.D. Dissertation, Faculty of Economics and Politics, University of Cambridge.

Serrano, F. and Summa, R. (2015): *Mundell–Fleming without the LM curve: the exogenous interest rate in an open economy*, Review of Keynesian Economics, Vol. 3 (2), pp. 248–268.

Setterfield, M. and Cornwall, J. (2002): *A neo-Kaldorian perspective on the rise and decline of the Golden Age*, in M. Setterfield (ed.): The Economics of Demand-Led Growth: Challenging the Supply-Side Vision of the Long Run, Edward Elgar Publishing, Cheltenham and Northampton, MA.

Shaikh, A. (2007): *A proposed synthesis of classical and Keynesian growth*, SCEPA Working Papers 2007-1, Schwartz Center for Economic Policy Analysis (SCEPA), The New School, New York.

Inequality, growth and 'hot' money

Shaikh, A. (2009): *Economic policy in a growth context: a classical synthesis of Keynes and Harrod*, Metroeconomica, Vol. 60 (3), pp. 347–364.

Sharpe, S. and Suarez, G. (2014): *The insensitivity of investment to interest rates: evidence from a survey of CFOs*, Finance and Economics Discussion Series No. 2014-02, Federal Reserve Board, Washington, DC.

Shaw, E. (1973): Financial Deepening in Economic Development, Oxford University Press, New York.

Shin, H.S. (2009): *Securitisation and financial stability*, Economic Journal, Vol. 119 (1), pp. 309–332.

Skidelsky, R. (2003): John Maynard Keynes 1883–1946. Economist, Philosopher, Statesman, Macmillan, London.

Skott, P. (2010): *Growth, instability and cycles: Harrodian and Kaleckian models of accumulation and income distribution*, in M. Setterfield (ed.): Handbook of Alternative Theories of Economic Growth, Edward Elgar Publishing, Cheltenham and Northampton, MA.

Skott, P. (2012): *Theoretical and empirical shortcomings of the Kaleckian investment function*, Metroeconomica, Vol. 63 (1), pp. 109–138.

Solow, R. (1956): *A contribution to the theory of economic growth*, Quarterly Journal of Economics, Vol. 70 (1), pp. 65–94.

Spronk, R., Verschoor, W. and Zwinkels, R. (2013): *Carry trade and foreign exchange rate puzzles*, European Economic Review, Vol. 60, pp. 17–31.

Steindl, J. (1976 [1952]): Maturity and Stagnation in American Capitalism, Monthly Review, New York.

Stirati, A. (2010a): *Interpretation of the classics: the theory of wages*, Departmental Working Papers of Economics No. 116, University Roma Tre.

Stirati, A. (2010b): *Changes in functional income distribution in Italy and Europe*, Departmental Working Papers of Economics No. 119, University Roma Tre.

Stock, J. and Watson, M. (2002): *Has the business cycle changed and why?*, in M. Gertler and K. Rogoff (eds): NBER Macroeconomics Annual, Vol. 17, MIT Press, Cambridge, MA.

Stock, J. and Watson, M. (2010): *Modelling inflation after the crisis*, Working Paper No. 16488, National Bureau of Economic Research, Cambridge, MA.

Stockhammer, E. (2004): The Rise of Unemployment in Europe, Edward Elgar Publishing, Cheltenham and Northampton, MA.

Stockhammer, E. (2005): *Shareholder value orientation and the investment–profit puzzle*, Journal of Post Keynesian Economics, Vol. 28 (2), pp. 193–215.

Stockhammer, E. (2009): *Determinants of functional income distribution in OECD countries*, IMK Studies No. 05/2009, Hans Böckler Stiftung, Düsseldorf.

Stockhammer, E. (2013): *Why have wage shares fallen? A panel analysis of the determinants of functional income distribution*, Conditions of Work and Employment Series No. 35, International Labour Office, Geneva.

Stockhammer, E. and Stehrer, R. (2011): *Goodwin or Kalecki on demand? Functional income distribution and aggregate demand in the short run*, Review of Radical Political Economy, Vol. 43 (4), pp. 506–522.

Storm, S. and Naastepad, C.W.M. (2005): *Strategic factors in economic development: East Asian industrialization 1950–2003*, Development and Change, Vol. 36 (6), pp. 1059–1094.

Storm, S. and Naastepad, C.W.M. (2009): *Labour market regulation and labour productivity growth: evidence for 20 OECD countries 1984–2004*, Industrial Relations, Vol. 48 (4), pp. 629–654.

Storm, S. and Naastepad, C.W.M. (2012): Macroeconomics Beyond the NAIRU, Harvard University Press, Cambridge, MA.

Storm, S. and Naastepad, C.W.M. (2015): *Europe's Hunger Games: income distribution, cost competitiveness and crisis*, Cambridge Journal of Economics, Vol. 39 (3), pp. 959–986.

Studart, R. (1995): Investment Finance in Economic Development, Routledge, London.

Summers, L. (2014a): *US economic prospects: secular stagnation, hysteresis, and the zero lower bound*, keynote address at the National Association for Business Economics Policy Conference, Arlington, VA, 24 February 2014.

Summers, L. (2014b): *Reflections on the 'new secular stagnation hypothesis'*, in R. Baldwin and C. Teulings (eds): Secular Stagnation: Facts, Causes and Cures, VoxEU ebook, CEPR Press.

Sweezy, P. (1942): The Theory of Capitalist Development, Oxford University Press, New York.

Taylor, A. and Taylor, M. (2004): *The purchasing power parity debate*, Journal of Economic Perspectives, Vol. 18 (4), pp. 135–158.

Tesfatsion, L. and Judd, K. (2006): Handbook of Computational Economics, Volume 2: Agent-Based Computational Economics, Elsevier, Amsterdam.

Thirlwall, A. (1979): *The balance of payments constraint as an explanation of international growth rate differences*, Banca Nacionale del Lavoro Quarterly Review, Vol. 32 (128), pp. 45–53.

Thirlwall, A. (2011): *Balance of payments constrained growth models: history and overview*, PSL Quarterly Review, Vol. 64 (259), pp. 307–351.

Timmer, M., de Vries, G. and de Vries, K. (2014): *Patterns of structural change in developing countries*, GGDC Research Memorandum No. 149, Groningen Growth and Development Center, University of Groningen.

Tobin, J. (1982): *Money and finance in the macroeconomic process*, Journal of Money, Credit and Banking, Vol. 14 (2), pp. 171–204.

Tobin, J. and Buiter, W. (1976): *Long run effects of fiscal and monetary policy on aggregate demand*, in J.L. Stein (ed.): Monetarism, North Holland, Amsterdam.

Tong, H. and Wei, S.J. (2011): *The composition matters: capital inflows and liquidity crunch during a global economic crisis*, Review of Financial Studies, Vol. 24 (6), pp. 2023–2052.

Toporowski, J. (2013): *Michal Kalecki: an Intellectual Biography*, Volume 1, Palgrave Macmillan, Basingstoke.

UNCTAD (2001): Trade and Development Report, UNCTAD, Geneva.

UNCTAD (2003): Management of Capital Flows: Comparative Experiences and Implications for Africa, UNCTAD, Geneva.

UNCTAD (2006): Trade and Development Report, UNCTAD, Geneva.

UNCTAD (2014): Trade and Development Report, UNCTAD, Geneva.

UNCTAD (2015): Trade and Development Report, UNCTAD, Geneva.

Valdecantos, S. (2012): *Macroeconomic dynamics in Argentina in the light of a Structuralist-Post Keynesian stock-flow consistent model*, mimeo.

Valdecantos, S. and Zezza, G. (2012): *Reforming the international monetary system: a stock-flow consistent approach*, in M. Marcuzzo (ed.): Speculation and Regulation in Commodity Markets: The Keynesian Approach in Theory and Practice, Rapporto Tecnico No. 21, Dipartimento di Scienze Statistiche, Universitá di Roma La Sapienza.

Van Treeck, T. (2009): *A synthetic, stock-flow consistent macroeconomic model of 'financialisation'*, Cambridge Journal of Economics, Vol. 33 (3), pp. 467–493.

Vergeer, R. and Kleinknecht, A. (2007): *Jobs versus productivity? The causal link from wages to labour productivity growth*, TU Delft Innovation Systems Discussion Papers, IS 2007-01, Delft.

Vergeer, R. and Kleinknecht, A. (2011): *The impact of labour market deregulation on productivity: a panel data analysis of 19 OECD countries (1960–2004)*, Journal of Post Keynesian Economics, Vol. 33 (2), pp. 369–404.

Vergeer, R. and Kleinknecht, A. (2012): *Do flexible labour markets indeed reduce unemployment? A robustness check*, Review of Social Economy, Vol. 70 (4), pp. 451–476.

Vianello, F. (1989): *Effective demand and the rate of profits: some thoughts on Marx, Kalecki and Sraffa*, in M. Sebastiani (ed.): Kalecki's Relevance Today, Macmillan, London.

Wicksell, K. (1935): Lectures on Political Economy, Routledge, London.

Wicksell, K. (2001): *A new theory of crises*, Structural Change and Economic Dynamics, Vol. 12 (3), pp. 335–342.

Wolff, E.N. and Zacharias, A. (2009): *Household wealth and the measurement of economic well-being in the United States*, Journal of Economic Inequality, Vol. 7 (2), pp. 83–115.

Wood, A. (1997): *Openness and wage inequality in developing countries: the Latin American challenge to East Asian conventional wisdom*, World Bank Economic Review, Vol. 11 (1), pp. 33–57.

World Bank (2013): *World Development Indicators Database.*

Wray, L.R. (1997): *Government as employer of last resort: full employment without inflation*, Working Paper No. 213, Levy Economics Institute of Bard College, Annandale-on-Hudson.

Wray, L.R. (2000): *The Employer of Last Resort approach to full employment*, Working Paper No. 9, Center for Full Employment and Price Stability, University of Missouri-Kansas City.

Wray, L.R. (2012): Modern Money Theory: A Primer on Macroeconomics for Sovereign Monetary Systems, Palgrave Macmillan, New York.

You, J.I. and Dutt, A.K. (1996): *Government debt, income distribution and growth*, Cambridge Journal of Economics, Vol. 20 (3), pp. 335–351.

Zak, G. and Dalle, D. (2014): *Elasticidades del comercio exterior de la Argentina: ¿una limitación para el crecimiento?*, Revista Argentina de Economía Internacional, No. 3, pp. 31–46.

Zezza, G. (2008): *U.S. growth, the housing market, and the distribution of income*, Journal of Post Keynesian Economics, Vol. 30 (3), pp. 379–405.

Name index

Subject index

Agent-based models 83

Balance of payments-constrained
 growth theory 72, 161
Balance of trade
 in a Kaleckian model 49, 51
 in Argentina 66
 response to inflation in SFC model
 113–116
Buffers
 bank accounts 97
 inventories 77

Cambridge growth model
 by Joan Robinson 27–29
 by Nicholas Kaldor 27–28, 30
Capital controls 129–130, 164–166
 IMF's 'institutional view' on capital
 controls 129
Capital flights 146, 162
Capital gains 95, 106, 108–109, 112
Classical economics 16
Conflicting claims approach to income
 distribution 94, 140–141
Consumption decisions 96
Credit conditions via government
 orientation 163, 174
Currency convertibility 109

Demand regimes 38–39, 144, 148–149,
 169
 in Argentina 59, 61–67
 in Mexico 155–157
 in South Korea 157–158
Development banks 162–163
Diminishing marginal returns
 in David Ricardo 17
 in neoclassical economics 21
Distribution of Income
 and global financial inflows 141, 162
 and human capital 23

and social discontent 22–23
and technical conditions 21
hypotheses about its evolution 7–9
in Argentina 56–58
interaction with economic growth 3,
 16, 54
trends 5–7

Emergent phenomena 78
Endogenous money 99–100
Error Correction Model 60–61
Exchange rate
 pass-through to prices 91–93,
 140–141
Exchange rate determination
 by monetary policy 49
 closures in SFC models 100–101
 expectations by heterogeneous
 agents 98–99, 106, 117, 145

'Financial Dutch disease' 162
Financialization 8–9, 48
 in SFC models 79–80
Foreign debt trends 11–12
Foreign private debt
 in Chile 135
 in East Asia 111
 in Kaleckian model 131
 in Mexico 149–152
 in South Korea 149–151
 in the Eurozone 131, 137, 159, 172
 recent global trends 132–134,
 165–166
Foreign public debt
 trends 132, 134
 currency risk 96–99, 159–160
Foreign reserves accumulation 164

Global capital flows
 after deregulation 64, 72, 136–137
 and income distribution 141